The Mystery of Mary

The Mystery of Mary

Paul Haffner

GRACEWING

HillenbrandBooks

First published in 2004
jointly by

Gracewing
2 Southern Avenue,
Leominster
Herefordshire
HR6 0QF

Liturgy Training Publications
Archdiocese of Chicago
1800 North Hermitage Avenue
Chicago
Illinois 60622–1101

Published in the USA and Canada by Liturgy Training Publications
under the imprint Hillenbrand Books. The imprint is focused on
contemporary and classical theological thought concerning the liturgy
of the Catholic Church. Further information available from the
University of St Mary of the Lake/Mundelein Seminary, 1000 East
Maple Avenue, Mundelein IL 60060. litinst@usml.edu

NIHIL OBSTAT   Monsignor Gerald Chidgey, Prot. Ap.,
                   J. C. D. Censor
IMPRIMATUR   Most Revd. Peter Smith, Ll.B., J. C. D.,
                   Archbishop of Cardiff
Date   16 June 2004

The *Nihil Obstat* and *Imprimatur* are offical declarations that a book or
pamphlet is free of doctrinal error. No implication is contained therein
that those who have granted the *Nihil Obstat* and *Imprimatur* neccessar-
ily recommend or endorse the book or pamphlet.

UK ISBN 0 85244 650 0
US ISBN 1–59525–008–5

Typeset by Action Publishing Technology Ltd,
Gloucester GL1 5SR

Printed in England by Antony Rowe Ltd,
Chippenham, Wiltshire SN14 6LH

CONTENTS

PREFACE

This book offers an overall view of the theology of Mary, known as Mariology. With several texts available, one may ask why another one should be offered. First, concerning Mary one can never say enough, *de Maria numquam satis*, as St Louis Grignon de Montfort wrote, quoting an earlier tradition, going back maybe as far as St Bernard of Clairvaux. Then it is a joy for every theologian to reflect and shed light upon Mary's being and action in the economy of salvation. Next, the present work offers a realist perspective, not reducing the concrete aspects of Mary's gifts and privileges to mere symbols on the one hand, and not confusing doctrine and devotionalism on the other. Above all, this book represents a little shrine of the mind and heart for Our Lady, to celebrate the one hundred and fiftieth anniversary of the definition of the dogma of her Immaculate Conception by Pope Blessed Pius IX.

This text is primarily concerned with giving a theological and doctrinal panorama concerning Mary, in a historical perspective. Therefore questions concerning spirituality, devotion and pastoral practice are not dealt with directly. Nevertheless, it is the author's conviction that the foundation for fruitful devotion to the Mother of God starts from sound doctrine based in Scripture and Tradition, and is nurtured by good theology. The book proceeds in thematic order. The first chapter outlines the basic scheme of what constitutes Mariology; not in isolation but in relation to other branches of theology. The second chapter deals with the Old Testament preparation for, and prefiguration of, the mystery of Mary. Next, the New Testament sources for a Marian theology are proposed in chapter three. Chapter four examines the doctrine of the Immaculate Conception, and other truths about Our Lady being full of grace. The fifth chapter looks at Mary as Mother of God, the central dogma of Mariology. Then the various dimensions of the perpetual Virginity of Mary are elaborated in the sixth chapter. Mary's discipleship, a relatively recent theological acquisition, is examined in the seventh chapter, and this forms the basis for a discussion of her special and active participation in the Redemption. Chapter eight illustrates the end of Mary's earthly life and her glorious Assumption body and soul into the glory of heaven. The ninth and final chapter traces Mary's continuing Motherhood in the Church, in which she is the Mediatrix of all graces.

This book owes much to many, and it is impossible here to offer individual thanks to all who helped me in some way with its preparation. My gratitude above all goes to HRH the Duke of Bragança who kindly wrote the Foreword for this text. Thanks are due to Fr Thomas Williams, LC, who gave me helpful encouragement when I discussed this book with him. Fr Ken Martin made some very valuable suggestions, for which I am grateful. Once again at the publishers, Tom Longford and Jo Ashworth deserve my gratitude for their constant help and encouragement in the various stages of production. In this work, I would like also to commemorate Fr Redemptus Valabek, o. carm., who died last year, and was a great inspiration as a lecturer in theology especially in this field of Mariology.

Rome, 25th March 2004
Solemnity of the Annunciation

FOREWORD

I warmly commend this book, *The Mystery of Mary*, written by Revd Dr Paul Haffner, on the auspicious occasion of the 150th anniversary of the definition of the Dogma of the Immaculate Conception. Portugal was the first place in the world to accept this Dogma.

During the reign of King Dom João IV (which began in 1640), in thanksgiving for the miracle of Portugal's reacquisition of its liberty after sixty years of Spanish occupation, the King consulted Parliament, the University of Coimbra and all of the Bishops concerning this question and all of these institutions approved the initiative of offering the Kingdom of Portugal to the Blessed Virgin Mary under the Title of the Immaculate Conception. Following this act, the successive Kings of Portugal never again wore a crown, since Our Lady had been proclaimed the Reigning Sovereign of Portugal.

This devotion has its headquarters in the Shrine of the Castle of Vila Viçosa, where King Dom João IV had lived and where the image he had crowned still exists. There also exists at Vila Viçosa a Confraternity of Our Lady of Conception and I have the honour of being the Grand Master of the Order of Our Lady of Conception. A stone plaque, proclaiming this act of consecration of Portugal to the Immaculate Conception, was placed in all castles in Portugal and at the gates of all Portuguese cities. This decision of the Portuguese nation which crowned Mary Immaculate as Queen of Portugal has never been revoked by any legislative act of Parliament, and thus continues to this day to be legally in force.

Curiously, the date which the republic proclaimed as the day of Portugal, 10 June, the birthday of the epic sixteenth-century poet Luís de Camões, is also the day which is dedicated to the Guardian Angel of Portugal. Certainly these two heavenly protectors, Our Lady Immaculate and the Guardian Angel, are the ones who have enabled our country to survive with its faith intact, despite political upheaval, frequent anti-Christian political views and less intelligent decisions taken by our leaders. The last great sign of Divine Protection consisted in the apparitions of the Blessed Virgin Mary and the Angel of Portugal at Fatima in 1917.

I hope we are all able to correspond to those very special Divine favours in order to continue to deserve the protection of Our Queen and Mother!

Dom Duarte, Duke of Bragança
1 July 2004

ABBREVIATIONS

ASS =   *Acta Sanctae Sedis.*
            Romae: 1865–1908. 41 vols.

AAS =   *Acta Apostolicae Sedis. Commentarium officiale.*
            Rome: Vatican Polyglot Press, 1909–.

CCC =   *Catechism of the Catholic Church*
            Dublin: Veritas, 1994.

CCL =   *Corpus Christianorum series latina*
            Tournai: Brepols, 1954– .

CSEL =   *Corpus Scriptorum Ecclesiasticorum Latinorum.*
            Wien: 1866–.

DS =   H. Denzinger. *Enchiridion Symbolorum, Definitionum et Declarationum de rebus fidei et morum.* Bilingual edition edited by P. Hünermann.
            Bologna: EDB, 1995.

EM =   *Enchiridion Marianum Biblicum Patristicum* (ed. D. Casagrande)
            Rome: «Cor Unum», 1974.

EV =   *Enchiridion Vaticanum.* Documenti ufficiali della Chiesa.
            Bologna: Edizioni Dehoniane.

IG =   *Insegnamenti di Giovanni Paolo II.*
            Vatican City: Vatican Polyglot Press, 1978– .

IP =   *Insegnamenti di Paolo VI*
            Vatican City: Vatican Polyglot Press, 1963–1978.

Mansi =   J. D. Mansi, *Sacrorum Conciliorum nova et amplis-sima collectio.*
            Graz: 1960–1962.

ND =   J. Neuner and J. Dupuis, *The Christian Faith in the Doctrinal Documents of the Catholic Church.* Sixth edition.
            New York: Alba House, 1996.

OR =   *L'Osservatore Romano*, daily Italian edition.

ORE =   *L'Osservatore Romano*, weekly English edition.

PG =   J. P. Migne. *Patrologiae cursus completus, series graeca.* 161 vols.
            Paris: 1857–1866.

PL =   J. P. Migne. *Patrologiae cursus completus, series latina.* 221 vols.
            Paris: 1844–1864.

SC =   *Sources Chrétiennes.*
            Paris: Cerf, 1942– .

TN =   N. P. Tanner (ed.), *Decrees of the Ecumenical Councils.* 2 vols.
            London: Sheed and Ward, 1990

The Scriptural quotations and abbreviations in this work are generally taken from the New Jerusalem Bible.

The psalms are from the Grail edition with Hebrew numbering.

CHAPTER 1

A THEOLOGY FOR MARY

Christ's mirror she of grace and love,
Of beauty and of life and death:
By hope and love and faith
Transfigured to His likeness, 'Dove,
Spouse, Sister, Mother,' Jesus saith.

Christina Rossetti,
'Herself a Rose Who bore the Rose'

The mystery of Mary lies at the very heart of Christian theology. This theme highlights God's relation with His creatures in clear relief, and reveals the human response to God at its most perfect. In the Incarnation of the Son of God, the enduring and definitive synthesis is forged, a synthesis which the human mind of itself could not even have imagined: the Eternal enters time, the Whole lies hidden in the part, God takes on a human face. The truth communicated in Christ's Revelation is offered to every man and woman who would welcome it as the word which is the absolutely valid source of meaning for human life. In Christ, all have access to the Father, since by His Death and Resurrection Christ has bestowed the divine life which the first Adam had refused.[1] God comes to us in the realities we know best and can verify most easily, the people and events of our everyday life, in which we understand ourselves. And so, God's coming into the world is inseparably bound with the reality of His Mother Mary. Thus, in Christ's coming, we see most particularly and clearly what God does for humanity, in the marvels He has worked in and for the Blessed Virgin Mary. Therefore a study of Mary, Mother of God is like a microcosm or synthesis of the whole of theology, because of her intimate link with Christ in His act of creation, His Incarnation, the Redemption wrought by Him, and eschatology, which is still to be completed. The words of Mary the Mother of God, 'the Almighty has done great things for me, Holy is His name' are echoed by the Church and humanity.

In arriving at an understanding of Mary, Mother of God, just as in other areas of theology, a realist perspective is required. Realism is the philosophical bridge which guarantees the true relation between the knower and reality and is thus the right currency in which to frame theological discourse, to link reason with Christian belief in God.[2] Interestingly, even theologians who write about Mariology from the perspective of liberation theology insist on the importance of realism: 'Realist anthropology provides Marian theology with a concrete support that can fit the changing reality of human existence ... It is today's life that gives life to Mary's life in the past.'[3] Thus the realist fabric of God's action in time and space guarantees the perennial value of a discourse on Mariology as well as about other theological topics. Pope Paul VI echoed this when he affirmed:

> We wish to point out that our own time, no less than former times, is called upon to verify its knowledge of reality with the word of God, and, keeping to the matter at present under consideration, to compare its anthropological ideas and the problems springing therefrom with the figure of the Virgin Mary as presented by the Gospel. The reading of the divine Scriptures, carried out under the guidance of the Holy Spirit, and with the discoveries of the human sciences and the different situations in the world today being taken into account, will help us to see how Mary can be considered a mirror of the expectations of the men and women of our time.[4]

Realism requires a serious grasp of the various events in Mary's existence, like her Immaculate Conception, her perpetual Virginity, her divine Motherhood and her bodily Assumption. These Marian mysteries have a bearing on the material world, and this physical aspect must be taken seriously as well. Thus realism defends Marian truths against a mythological perspective, or an excessively symbolic view of their nature, which often, in modernist and rationalist circles, tends to water them down. At the same time, a realist perspective defends Mariology from dissolving into pious sentimentalism, and instead grounds it solidly in the Word of God and right reason. Furthermore, Mariology guarantees a realist basis for the whole of theology, since Mary is the guarantee of the reality of the Incarnation, which is itself the base for all realism. The mystery of God the Son coming at a fixed point in time and assuming what He had created adds to a realist appreciation of time and matter. It is no longer possible to escape up the blind alleys of cyclic notions of time, of pantheistic notions of matter, of idealistic notions of reality. All time, all history, all matter, all space, radiate from the moment when God the Son took human flesh.

In Mariology, as in Christology, both the horizontal and vertical aspects need to be kept in view.[5] This means that the figure of Mary as the humble Virgin of Nazareth and the Glorious Mary filled with grace are one and the same person. Similarly, as with the mystery of Christ so with the Marian mystery, there is no dichotomy or tension between the kenotic and the theophanic aspects. By the kenotic aspect, we understand the self-abasement of the Second Person of the Blessed Trinity (Ph 2:5–11, 2 Co 8:9). This does not mean, and cannot signify in any way, the abandoning of the divine nature, but rather involves the acceptance by Christ of the limits of human existence, reaching a climax in the humiliation of the Cross. The theophanic aspect involves the visible manifestation of God, as prepared in the Old Testament and as realized in the New. While it was affirmed in the Old Testament that it was not possible to see God and live (Ex 19:21; 33, 20; Jg 13:22), Moses and others experienced theophanies (Ex 3:1–6; 33:17–23; 34:5–9; Is 6:1–5). The Gospels depict the theophanies of the Baptism of the Lord in the Jordan (Mt 4:16–17; Mk 1:9–11; Lk 3:21–22; Jn 1:29–34), the Wedding at Cana (Jn 2:1-12) and His Transfiguration on Mount Tabor (Mt 17:1–13; Mk 9:2–8; Lk 9:28–36), and above all in the appearances of Christ after His Resurrection from the dead.

A brief history of Mariology

In the history of Christianity, the periods in which Marian doctrine and devotion have flourished are also the periods when the worship and adoration of her Son were most prominent.[6] The first major period ranges from the second to the ninth centuries, essentially the Patristic era. During this time, the Church reflected on Mary's role as the New Eve and acclaimed her divine maternity and perpetual virginity in patristic writings and various Councils. This was also the period when the great Trinitarian and Christological dogmas were debated and defined. During these first few centuries of the Church, there arose three Christological heresies which bear on the issue of the divine maternity. Docetism, while acknowledging the divinity of Christ, rejected the reality of His human nature, reducing it to a mere appearance. Arianism, on the other hand, accepted Jesus' humanity but denied that He was the Son of God, the Second Person of the Trinity. Both of these heresies rejected the dual nature of Christ and the mystery of the Incarnation. If Docetism were correct, Mary could not be called the Mother of God, since she would not be the Mother of God the Son incarnate. If Arianism were true, Jesus was not divine, and Mary could not be considered the Mother of God. At the First Council of Nicaea (AD 325), the first ecumenical council convened by the Church, both of these positions were condemned, and the reality of Jesus as true God and true man was infallibly defined.

After Nicaea, a third Christological heresy arose, called Nestorianism, which proposed two persons in Christ, rather than two natures in one Person. Mary would then be the mother of the human person of Christ only, and therefore not the Mother of God. Nestorianism was condemned by the third ecumenical council, held in Ephesus (AD 431). After the council, the Formula of Union declared that Jesus was 'begotten of the Father before all ages, as to his divinity and the same in the latter days born of the Virgin Mary as to his humanity for us and for our salvation ... A union of the two natures has taken place ... In accordance with this union without confusion, we profess the Holy Virgin to be Mother of God (*Theotokos*), for God the Word became flesh and was made man and from the moment of conception united to Himself the temple He had taken from her.'[7]

The parallel between Eve and Mary was well developed in the writings of the Fathers of both East and West, for example in St Justin Martyr, St Irenaeus, St Ephraem and Tertullian.[8] From the New Testament Pauline and Johannine typology there developed the idea of Mary as type of the Church: 'symbol, central idea, and as it were, the summary of all that is meant by the Church in her nature and vocation.'[9] St Ambrose was the first to provide the classic formula that Mary is a type of the Church.[10] Augustine further developed this idea placing Mary before the Church as her ideal image and as perfect member of the body of Christ.[11] During the eight and ninth centuries when the Second Council of Nicaea (AD 787) defined the veneration of images, Christians pondered more closely Mary's relationship to her Son, her sharing in His resurrection, her freedom from sin and the importance of her intercession.

The second period comprised the Scholastic era, when, among others notably St Anselm, St Thomas Aquinas, St Bonaventure and Blessed John Duns Scotus provided a systematic framework for Christology and a clearer understanding of Mary's role in the mystery of salvation. In particular, Scotus paved the way for an understanding of the Immaculate Conception of Mary.

The third period stretched from 1400 to 1800, from the end of the Middle Ages through the Renaissance and Reformation until the Enlightenment. This was a period during which many of the great truths of Christianity increasingly came under attack. On the one hand, Luther maintained throughout his life the historic Christian affirmation that Mary was the Mother of God: 'She is rightly called not only the mother of the man, but also the Mother of God ... It is certain that Mary is the Mother of the real and true God.'[12] Again, all his life, Luther held that Mary's perpetual virginity was an article of faith for all Christians, and interpreted Galatians 4:4 in the sense that Christ was 'born of a woman' alone: 'It is an article of faith that Mary is Mother of the Lord and still a Virgin.'[13] However, on the other hand, Luther was very critical of the traditional doctrines of Marian mediation and intercession. He accepted however that Mary should be honoured: 'The veneration of Mary is inscribed in the very depths of the human heart.'[14] In his last sermon at Wittenberg in January 1546, Luther affirmed: 'Is Christ only to be adored? Or is the holy Mother of God rather not to be honoured? This is the woman who crushed the Serpent's head. Hear us. For your Son denies you nothing.'[15] Calvin and Zwingli, while not so faithful to Marian doctrine as Luther, still venerated the Mother of God. The question is then why the Marian affirmations of the Reformers did not survive in the teaching of their heirs. The real reason for the break with the past must be attributed to the iconoclastic frenzy of the followers of the Reformation and the consequences of some Reformation principles. Although the Protestant Reformers had initially tried to hold to some Christological and Mariological truths, many of their heirs gradually fell under the sceptical influence of the Enlightenment.

Even more influential therefore in the break with the traditional doctrine concerning Mary was the influence of the Enlightenment era which essentially questioned or denied all the mysteries of faith. The Enlightenment was partly stimulated by the obvious success of reason in the natural sciences and mathematics. The dominant concept of the cosmos as a mechanism governed by a few simple and discoverable laws led to a desire to establish a purely rational religion. The product of a search for a natural and purely rational religion was deism, the false notion according to which, having created the world, God leaves it to its own devices, or at best allows it not to be destroyed. Deism was related to the Masonic concept of the Supreme Being as the Architect of the cosmos. Beyond the natural religion of the deists lay the more radical products of enlightenment exaggeration of reason in the religious sphere: scepticism, atheism, and materialism.[16]

The lowest point was reached when atheism was on the ascendant and Christian doctrine was emptied of substance even within various Christian communities. Marian doctrines were lost by later Protestants because of 'the spirit of the Enlightenment with its lack of understanding of mystery, and especially of the mystery of the Incarnation, which in the eighteenth century began the work of destruction.'[17] The majority of Protestants have drifted away from the proper attitude towards Mary, which Martin Luther had indicated on the basis of Holy Scripture. This loss of devotion to Mary is partially due to the rise of Rationalism which discarded the sense of the sacred. In Rationalism man sought to understand everything, and that which he could not comprehend he rejected. Because Rationalism accepted only that which could be explained rationally, Church festivals in honour of Mary and everything else reminiscent of her were done away with in the Protestant Church. All biblical relationship to the Mother Mary was lost, and we are still suffering from this heritage.[18] Despite the clouds of darkness hanging over Christendom, this period nevertheless saw the production of a number of devotional Marian masterpieces. After a longstanding liturgical and doctrinal interest in the role of the Mother of God in relation to Christ and His economy of salvation, the first systematic treatises were written in the sixteenth century. F. Suárez (1548–1617) treated Mariological questions in a systematic way, and P. Nigido first coined the term Mariology when he wrote the systematic treatise *Summae sacrae mariologiae* in 1602.[19]

The fourth and final period ranges from AD 1800 to the present day. It may be said that God launched a Marian counter-attack on the Enlightenment and the French Revolution in its nerve centre, through a series of Marian apparitions in France. These were the great nineteenth-century apparitions of the Miraculous Medal, La Salette and Lourdes which continue to exert a tremendous influence as tangible manifestations of the supernatural world denied by the Enlightenment.[20] Such influential apparitions have continued into the twentieth century, the most notable example being Fatima in Portugal.[21] Accompanying these reminders of the Marian heritage, there has been a revival of interest in Marian doctrine and devotion that continues even today. However, many of the Christian communities who have rejected Marian doctrine and devotion have gradually departed from Christological doctrine as well.[22]

At the beginning of the twentieth century, many treatises were written, but then, later, Mariology fell into disfavour among those theologians who criticized it for being too isolated and autonomous, over-emphasizing Mary's close link with Christ and ignoring her condition as creature. The biblical, patristic, kerygmatic and liturgical movements called for a reintegration of Mariology within the framework of the history of salvation and with the rest of theology. The importance given to Mary by the Church is not simply based on her appearance in the Bible or upon her privileges but derives from her particular and unique role in the history of salvation. The foundation for this is the theological conception of the human person, who is called to play an active part in the work of salvation. Everyone has a particular role, but Mary's is unique because only she is Mother of the Saviour and Mother of the Church. Mariology studies her participation in the mystery of salvation, but it also studies her special privileges because these are related to her mission.

Classically, the Reformers rejected the possibility of a Mariology and Mary's unique participation in the history of salvation because of their anthropology. They reject the very possibility of an active collaboration of man in his salvation. In Reformed theology, traditionally the human person receives salvation, faith and grace passively. Some theologians suggest that ecumenical studies should start with the particular and concrete case of Mary and not the theory of justification. The question arises as to whether Mary responded actively or passively to her vocation. If we conclude that she participated actively, this clearly would also radically challenge the Protestant theory of man's incapacity to collaborate in his salvation.

Within Eastern Christendom, Mariology is not a separate theological discipline. Eastern Christians have never developed a separate Mariological 'theology', but always treat it as an inseparable part of Christology, Pneumatology and ecclesiology.[23] Indeed, 'there is no Christian theology without permanent relation to the person and role of the Holy Virgin in the history of salvation.'[24] Eastern Christendom lays the emphasis on the being of Mary, in the economy of salvation, while Western theology has often, since St Augustine, focused on Mary as an example and as a disciple. The Eastern tradition speaks about the relationship of the *Theotokos* and the Holy Trinity in the context of the history of salvation. According to St John Damascene, the 'name of the Mother of God contains all the history of the divine economy in this world.'[25] The work of salvation and renewal of the world is made by God the Father through the Son in the Holy Spirit. The *Theotokos* is at the centre of the history of salvation, as St Gregory Palamas teaches: 'She is the cause of what came before Her, the champion of what came after Her and the agent of things eternal. She is the substance of the prophets, the principles of the apostles, the firm foundation of the martyrs and the premise of the teachers of the Church. She is the glory of those upon earth, the joy of celestial beings, the adornment of all creation. She is the beginning and the source and the root of unutterable good things; she is the summit and the consummation of everything holy.'[26] This special role of the *Theotokos* flows from the fact that she alone is found between God and humanity.[27] She was placed in a unique and exceptional relationship to the Holy Trinity, even before the Incarnation, as the prospective Mother of the Incarnate Lord to carry out the final consummation of God's eternal plan. [28]

In recent years, Western theology has focused on two main emphases concerning Mary's role in the work of salvation, namely the Christological and the ecclesiological tendencies. The Christological tendency stressed Mary's relationship with her Son as Mother of God. Her privileges derive from this relationship and are parallel to Christ's because she is intimately associated with Him. For example, her virginity is a consequence of her divine Maternity. Her Immaculate Conception derives logically from her dignity as the Mother of God and is a preparation for the Incarnation. Her Assumption is also a consequence of her motherhood and places her in a category by herself. Because of her active role she is also the 'Mother of the Church', 'Coredemptrix' and 'Mediatrix'.[29]

The ecclesiological tendency emphasized Mary as figure or type of the Church. Due to this parallelism between Mary and the Church, her privileges must be understood in light of the properties of the Church. For example, her divine Motherhood is a prototype for the Church and constitutes the moment of the Church's formation. Mary is not above the Church but is a part of the Church. She is the Church's first and pre-eminent member, but like all members is redeemed by Christ. One of the problems with this tendency is that it undervalued Mary's active participation in the history of salvation. These two tendencies, the Christological and the ecclesiological, are not opposed to one another but rather are mutually complementary.

In recent years, it has also been necessary to counter feminist claims concerning Mariology. A small group of feminists maintains that 'the Church has failed to understand or promote women in general, while venerating Mary in particular.'[30] Feminists proposed that Mary must be freed from the projections of a male-dominated hierarchy, and at the same time women must be freed from those images of Our Lady which they claim dominate them. The picture of Mary must take account of women's experience. Feminists often take account only of a kenotic approach to Christ and Mary, a horizontal approach, without sufficient awareness of the other more divine and transcendental aspects.

The present work also rejects a type of Modernist approach to Mariology. The Modernists based their thought on Kantian subjectivism and upon an evolutionary concept of truth. With their liberal approach to biblical criticism, they attempted to undermine the doctrine of the divine inspiration of Scripture. They tended to deny the divine and supernatural aspects of the revelation and its transmission in the Church. Instead, since one of the fundamental principles of Modernism was historical development, they often regarded Christian doctrine as having developed from pagan ideas according to purely human and social factors. Thus a kind of neo-Modernist idea would propose that the figure of Mary is somehow connected with pagan as well as Christian roots, for example in ancient cults of pagan goddesses.[31] A further error which this work rejects is the mistaken idea, following the psychology of Jung, that Mary is simply an expression of a need for the feminine within theology, or even an attempt to project or recover the dimension of the divine femaleness.[32] Alongside this false notion lies also that of considering Mary simply as an expression of the eternal feminine principle within the cosmos, in the line of Teilhard de Chardin.[33]

Within the ecumenical sphere, it is clear that between the Orthodox and Catholic Churches there is a great deal of consensus on Marian doctrines. With the communities resulting from the Reformation, such agreement does not yet exist. However, many theologians from these communities support Marian doctrine. For example, the Anglican Eric Mascall affirmed:

> The relation of Mary to the Church is (as the modern logicians would say) the relative product of two more fundamental relations. The first of these is Mary's relation to her Son; he is still man and she is still his mother. The second is his relation to us and to the Church; we are his members and the Church is his body. Therefore Mary is our mother and we are her children by adoption into her Son. This is not an exuberance of devotion but a fact of theology.[34]

Charles Dickson, a Lutheran scholar, pointed out that

> Luther referred to Mary as 'God's workshop' and went on to say 'As the Mother of God, she is raised above the whole of humankind' and 'has no equal'. Contrast this with the modern Protestant attitude that criticizes Marian devotion in the belief that it detracts from the central and unique place Christ occupies in human salvation and you begin to get a picture of the current crisis of division. What Protestants have had difficulty understanding are the intentions of Catholic teachings about Mary. In the Immaculate Conception and the Assumption teachings it has not been the intention of the Catholic Church to elevate the Blessed Virgin Mary to deity status but rather to show her as the shining model of genuinely Christian hope. It is the hope for all humankind. Such a rereading and enlightened understanding on the part of the Protestant community will help to refocus the attention of the entire Christian world on Mary, not as a point of division, but as the real bridge to unity for us all.[35]

Recent ecumenical dialogue with Reformed Christians has

yielded a greater openness on the part of Protestants to accept that the dogmas of the Immaculate Conception and the Assumption do enjoy a place in the Gospel of salvation.[36]

Relation of Mariology to other theological themes

Mariology is a central theme within theology and is organically related to other areas of this sacred science. The Mother of God is involved in the central mysteries of salvation. She is intimately linked with the Incarnation of the Word (Lk 1:26–28; Mt 1: 18–25), with the manifestation of Jesus Christ to the shepherds (Lk 2:8–14) and His epiphany to the Magi (Mt 2:9–10), who represent respectively the Jews and the Gentiles. Mary is actively present in the Messianic revelation of Jesus in the temple to Simeon and Anna (Lk 2: 22–38), and at the beginning of the public life and ministry of the Lord (Gn 2:1–12). She accompanied her Son even to His death on the Cross (Gn 19:25–27), and participated in the coming of the Holy Spirit at Pentecost (Ac 1:12–14; 2:1–4).

Mariology and Protology

Protology is the theological study of beginnings, the beginning of the cosmos, of man and woman, human salvation, and Christian anthropology. Mary is the Mother of the Creator. In Mary, the Mother of God, who was preserved from the stain of Original Sin, it is revealed that the new creation is even more marvellous than the old:

> It is an error to think that the day of the redemption can be compared with the day of the creation. In the beginning the earth was created, today it has been renewed; at the beginning, its produce was cursed through Adam's sin, but today peace and security are restored to it. In the beginning, death passed to all men because of the sin of our first parents; but today, through Mary, we have passed from death to life.[37]

In Mary the Mother of the Creator the mystery of grace and nature reaches its apex. She is the flower of all creation, the thornless rose who bore her Creator. In her is focused all the goodness of creation, all the perfection of nature. At the same time, she is the one filled with grace and in her response to God, grace and nature find a perfect partnership, a true marriage. She is the Seat of Wisdom and held in her womb Him who the world cannot hold within its bounds. She gave birth to Him Who bestows truth, goodness, oneness and beauty to all created things. Christ was both 'the Creator of Mary and created from Mary.'[38] Mary is the new Eve, the Mother of the New Creation, and the hope of creation on its earthly pilgrimage. Through her glorious Assumption, she is also the hope of the new heavens and the new earth where Christ will 'be all in all' (Col 3:11). She helps all humanity to be constantly renewed in the image of Him Who is the Creator of man (cf. Col 3:10).

Mary was predestined from all eternity to be Mother of God, and this predestination was associated with the Incarnation of the Divine Word.[39] Theological tradition has seen the divine choice of Mary as somehow connected with the act of creation; liturgical tradition has illustrated this idea in its choice of the following passage from the Old Testament Wisdom literature for Masses in honour of Our Lady:

> The Lord created me when His purpose first unfolded,
> before the oldest of His works.
> From everlasting I was firmly set,
> from the beginning, before earth came into being.
> I was by His side, a master craftsman,
> delighting in day after day,
> ever at play in His presence,
> at play everywhere in His world,
> delighting to be with the sons of men. (Pr 8:22–23, 30–31)

The key to interpreting this passage is to realize that it refers both to the eternal predestination of Christ and of

Our Lady in such a way that the Our Lady's role is clearly subordinate to that of Christ. Thus, within the mystery of Christ, Mary is present even before the creation of the world, as the one whom the Father has chosen as Mother of His Son in the Incarnation.[40]

The bridegroom in the Song of Songs calls his bride an 'enclosed garden' and a 'sealed fountain' (Sg 4:12). Tradition has applied these expressions to Mary, the Mother of God. Our Lady is an 'enclosed garden' and 'sealed fountain' because of her perpetual virginity and at the same time her fruitful maternity. Mary welcomed into her womb the God who created her and thus, in a sense, she became a new garden of paradise, in which was planted Christ, the true Tree of Life: 'O blessed and more than blessed Virgin, through your blessing all creation is blessed … God Himself, who made all things, made Himself from Mary. In this way, He remade all that He had made.'[41] Not only is Our Lady truly the Model of the New Creation, but she also exercises an *active* and *dynamic* role in the restoration of creation. The Mother of God was associated in a special way with her Son's life and ministry, for example in the Wedding Feast at Cana (Jn 2:1–12), where Christ's miraculous powers over the Creation were expressed when He changed water into wine. This miracle prefigures the still greater wonder of the Holy Eucharist. The intimate link between Christ and His Mother persevered unto the moment of the Crucifixion and continued thereafter (Jn 19:26–27). Mary is, in a manner totally subordinate to Christ and completely dependent on Him, the Mediatrix of all graces.[42] Thus all graces which the Spirit bestows to restore and recreate the cosmos come to us through the hands of the Blessed Virgin Mary. This manifold work of Mary is well-expressed by the Acathist hymn of the Byzantine tradition:

Hail, O Tendril whose Bud shall not wilt;
hail, O Soil whose fruit shall not perish!

hail, O Gardener of the Gardener of Life!
Hail, O Earth who yielded abundant mercies;
hail, O Table full-laden with appeasement.
Hail, for you have greened anew the pastures of delight;
hail, for you have prepared a haven for souls.
Hail, acceptable Incense of prayer;
hail, expiation of the whole universe!
Hail, O you favour of God to mortal men;
hail, O you trust of mortals before God![43]

It is significant how this hymn uses images from created reality to illustrate Our Lady's part in the restoration of creation by her Son. The role of Mary in the creation is intimately linked with her role in the economy of salvation:

Mary is God's garden of Paradise, His own unspeakable world, into which His Son entered to do wonderful things, to tend it and to take his delight in it. He created a world for the wayfarer, that is, the one we are living in. He created a second world – Paradise – for the Blessed. He created a third for Himself, which He named Mary. She is a world unknown to most mortals here on earth. Even the angels and saints in heaven find her incomprehensible, and are lost in admiration of a God who is so exalted and so far above them, so distant from them, and so enclosed in Mary, His chosen world, that they exclaim: 'Holy, holy, holy' unceasingly.[44]

The Father's plan for mankind was carried out in an eminent manner in the Sacred Humanity of Christ, the New Man. Mary as the New Woman also enjoys a special place in the divine economy of salvation. Mary was filled with grace from the beginning of her existence at the Immaculate Conception, while at the end of her earthly existence she was completely transfigured to Christ in the glory of her Assumption. Therefore, in her first of all and most perfectly of all, was brought about the process of predestination, election, justification and glorification in Christ (Rm 8: 29–30), in Whom every man and woman is called (Ep 3:1–14). Mary is presented as the creature in whom full freedom and complete obedience to God are combined; the aspirations of the soul are perfectly harmonized with the values of the body, human action was completely married with divine grace.

Mariology and Christology

Jesus Christ, the Son of God made man was born of Mary, is flesh of her flesh, because she conceived Him by the power of the Holy Spirit, gave birth to Him, suckled Him at her virginal breast, and along with St Joseph, brought Him up and educated Him. Mary is therefore truly the Mother of Jesus, and therefore between her and the incarnate Word there exists an indissoluble bond. The Person and the mission of the Son cast a clear light upon the profile of His Mother. Thus Christology exercises an impact upon Mariology; however, at the same time, Mariology contributes to Christology because knowledge of the true Catholic doctrine regarding Mary furnishes a key for the true understanding of the Mystery of Christ and of His Church. An example of this is how the expression Mother of God (*Theotokos*) is a guarantee of Christian orthodoxy.[45] Through Mary who is the unique witness of the mystery of Christ, the Church has more fully understood what the *kenosis* of the Son of God has involved, the Son who became in her a 'Son of Adam'. The Church has thus become aware of the historical roots of the 'Son of David' and His belonging to the Jewish people.

Mariology and Soteriology

Mary was redeemed in a more sublime manner than all other men and women, in view of the merits of her Son, and therefore she is the first fruits and the greatest fruit of the Redemption. She is the icon and model of redeemed humanity. As Mother of the Redeemer and as His generous Disciple, she cooperated in a most special manner in His work of salvation. As a result of her personal consent to the redemptive Incarnation of her Son, and her loving service to the Person and the work of her Son, as well as with her constant heavenly intercession, and her maternal presence in the life of the Church, the Blessed Virgin Mary has cooperated and continues to cooperate, according to God's good pleasure, in the salvation of humankind.

Mariology and Pneumatology

Mary the All-Holy (*Panaghia*) is the first creature completely formed by the Holy Spirit, and at the same time is the first bearer of the same Holy Spirit. Her life was motivated and guided by the Holy Spirit, so that she can truly be regarded as the icon of the Spirit. According to the contemplative tradition of the Church, the Holy Spirit enabled Mary to utter her 'Yes' or salvific '*fiat*' (Lk 1:38) and to proclaim her song of thanksgiving, the *Magnificat* (Lk 1: 46–55). The same Spirit suggested to Christ's Mother a cultic attitude which transformed the rite of redemption for the firstborn into a prefiguration of and a prelude to the offering of the Sacrificial Lamb of God (Lc 2:22–24). The Spirit inspired the maternal request to her Son to help the bridal pair at Cana in Galilee (Jn 2:3) and the exhortation to the servants to carry out His commands (Jn 2:5). The Consoler sustained the Blessed Virgin Mary under the immense weight of suffering which she underwent at the foot of Christ's Cross, and expanded her immaculate heart so as to accept the testament of her dying Son, who made her Mother of His disciples (Jn 19:26). The Paraclete kept alive in Mary the faith in the Risen Christ, and aroused in her the prayer of the Upper Room in preparation for Pentecost (Ac 1:12–14).

Mariology and Ecclesiology

Mary is present in a key and active manner during the essential steps in the formation of the Church. First, at Nazareth and Bethlehem in the Conception and Birth of

Christ, because these moments involve the members as well as the Head of the Mystical Body. Already at the Wedding Feast of Cana His disciples believed in Him and with His Mother formed a communion of faith with their Lord and Master (Jn 2:11). In Jerusalem, the sacrament of the whole Church was born in Blood and water from the wounded side of Christ as He hung upon the Cross in the presence of Mary. Then finally, the community of all the followers of Jesus was formed at Pentecost, the birthday of the Church, open to her universal mission (Ac 1: 1–40). The relationship between Mary and the Church is highlighted by the fact that she is the privileged member of the Church, the most loving Mother of the Church, the fulfilled Image of the Church, the prophetic Type and Figure of the Church, and also the eschatological Icon of the same. The Church possesses an intrinsic 'Marian dimension' in her ontological makeup; her features are anticipated in the face of the Blessed Virgin of Nazareth.[46]

Mariology and Eschatology

The Byzantine liturgy in the Kontakion for the solemnity of the Dormition, greets Mary as 'our steady hope and protection.'[47] Just as the Mother of Jesus, glorified in body and soul in heaven, 'is the image and beginning of the Church as it is to be perfected is the world to come, so too does she shine forth on earth, until the day of the Lord shall come, as a sign of sure hope and solace to the people of God during its sojourn on earth.'[48] Therefore the Church contemplates in Mary the image of that purity which she desires to attain and to be. In Mary, time past present and future condense and mutually enlighten each other. The *yesterday* of Israel and of the Church becomes present through liturgical memorial; *today* is marked by constant and active presence of Our Lady in the pilgrimage of the Church towards its goal; *tomorrow* is a reality which is already imperfectly anticipated, and this offers confidence and hope. In Mary assumed into the glory of heaven, the fear of the future has been overcome, the enigma of death has been defeated, and the true destiny of man and woman has been unveiled in the Risen Christ.

Mariology offers a theological synthesis

The examples we have offered above are only a selection which clearly illustrate that Mariology is very closely tied in with the other areas of theology, and is therefore not an isolated topic, but supremely a part of theology. Fundamental Theology which examines the bases of the faith in relation to reason and the relation between Scripture, Tradition and the Magisterium as well as the development of dogmas cannot fail to take account of the many and varied instances of Mariological discourse. In Dogmatic Theology, Mariology represents a *meeting point* for the other theological disciplines as well as being an *area of synthesis*. Mariology is a point of encounter, since in Mary all is oriented to God the Father for Whom she is the servant and beloved daughter, to God the Son for Whom she is true Mother, generous and devoted disciple, and finally to the Holy Spirit who filled her with grace from the moment of her conception and evershadowed her that she might bear the Saviour, and accompanied her until she was assumed into heaven. Mary is related to her own people of Israel for which she is the personification, the apex and the most pure expression, and also to the Church of which she is the first fruits and the eschatological fulfilment. Humanity of all times and in all places is to be seen in her light as she is the finest and most perfect realization of all peoples. She is also to be seen as the peak and most beautiful ornament of the cosmos.

Mariology thus presents a rich opportunity for theological synthesis. The economy and history of salvation, from the eternal predestination of the Incarnate Word, to the Second Coming of the Lord, from Genesis to the Apocalypse, is summarized in the Mother of God. Mary is in a sense the Crossroads of theology, where all the various strands meet, she is the microcosm of the economy of creation and salvation. Mary, 'since her entry into salvation history unites in herself and re-echoes the greatest teachings of the faith as she is proclaimed and venerated, calls the faithful to her Son and His sacrifice and to the love of the Father.'[49]

From this, it can be concluded that the study of the Blessed Virgin Mary is central to the faith and to theology. It is a road which leads directly to the heart of the Christian mystery and herein lies the sign of its fruitfulness.[50] Thus the position of those who wish to relegate this study to the fringe of theology is not acceptable. It is not possible for the Christian to consider marginal the Incarnation of the Word, which changed human history, to which Mary consented and in which she actively collaborated, neither are the words of Christ addressed to His Mother at the foot of the Cross to be considered peripheral, nor yet is the event of Pentecost, in which Our Lady was actively involved, to be put on the sidelines of Christian faith. It is thus necessary that all theological reflection take due account of the presence of Mary, and of the relationship of the whole of theology with the Marian mystery. Conversely, it will also be seen as each chapter of this book unfolds that the various aspects of Mariology are linked with and rooted in the Christian mystery as a whole.

Notes

1   See Pope John Paul II, Encyclical Letter *Fides et Ratio*, 12. See also Rm 5:12–15.
2   See P. Haffner, *The Mystery of Reason* (Leominster: Gracewing, 2001), pp. 12–19.
3   I. Gebara and M. C. Bingemer, *Mary, Mother of God, Mother of the Poor*, Liberation and Theology 7 (Tunbridge Wells: Burns and Oates, 1989), p. 9.
4   Pope Paul VI, Apostolic Exhortation *Marialis Cultus* (1974), 37.
5   Sometimes, the horizontal aspect is referred to as Christology or Mariology 'from below' and the vertical aspect is called 'from above'.

6   See C. O'Donnell, 'Growth and Decline in Mariology' in J. Hyland (ed.), *Mary in the Church*, (Dublin: Veritas Press, 1989), pp. 32–41.

7   *The Formula of Union between Cyril of Alexandria and the Bishops of Antioch* in ND 607.

8   For Patristic references to the Mary-Eve-parallel, see for example, St Justin Martyr, *Dialogue with Trypho*, 100 in *PG* 6, 710–711; St Irenaeus, *Adversus haereses*, Book 3, chapter 22, n. 4 in *PG* 7, 959; *ibid.*, Book 5, chapter 19, n. 1 in *PG* 7, 1175–1176; St Ephraem, *Sermo in Genesi III, 6* in *EM* 309–310; *Sermo I de Nativitate Domini* in *EM* 311; *Hymnus de Beata Maria*, 10 in *EM* 364; Tertullian, *The Flesh of Christ* 17, 4 in *PL* 2, 782.

9   H. Rahner, *Our Lady and the Church*, trans. S. Bullough (London: Darton, Longman & Todd, 1961), p. 5. See chapter 9, pp. 240–243 below where this is treated.

10   St Ambrose's classical formula *Maria est typos ecclesiae* is from *Expositio evangelii secundum Lucam II, 7*, in *CSEL XXXII, 4, 45*.

11   See St Augustine, *De sancta virginitate 6*, in *PL* 40, 399; and Idem, *Sermo XXV, 7*, in *PL* 46, 938.

12   M. Luther, *Martin Luther's Works*, English translation edited by J. Pelikan (St Louis: Concordia, 1959–1986), *Sermon on the Mount and the Magnificat*, volume 24, p. 107.

13   M. Luther, *Martin Luther's Works*, *Selected Commentaries on the Psalms*, Volume 11, pp. 319–320.

14   M. Luther, *Martin Luther's Works*, *Selected Commentaries on the Psalms*, 10, III, p. 313.

15   M. Luther, *Martin Luther's Works*, *Sermons*, Volume 51, pp. 128–129.

16   See P. Haffner, *The Mystery of Reason*, p. 121–122.

17   F. Heiler, 'Die Gottesmutter im Glauben und Beten der Jahrhunderte', *Hochkirche* 13 (1931), p. 200.

18   Cf. B. Schlink, *Mary, the Mother of Jesus* (London: Marshall Pickering, 1986), pp. 114–115.

19   See F. Suárez, *De Mysteriis vitae Christi* (Paris: Vivès, 1877), Volume 19, d. 1–23. P. Nigido, *Summae sacrae mariologiae* (Panormi: apud Io. Antonium De Franciscis, 1602).

20   See D. A. Foley, *Marian Apparitions, the Bible, and the Modern World* (Leominster: Gracewing, 2002), pp. 113–186.

21   *Ibid.*, pp. 231–252.

22   This phenomenon can be seen in the denial of the essential truths concerning Christ within the Anglican Communion in the series of essays edited by J. Hick, *The Myth of God Incarnate* (London: SCM, 1977). Other Anglicans replied with the work edited by M. Green, *The Truth of God Incarnate* (London: Hodder and Stoughton, 1977).

23   Cf. V. Lossky, 'Panagia', in: *In the Image and Likeness of God*, ed. J. H. Erickson and T. E. Bird (Crestwood, NY 1985), p. 195.

[24] N. Nissiotis, 'Marie dans la théologie orthodoxe' in *Concilium* 19 (1983), cah. 188, p. 60.

[25] St John Damascene, *On the Orthodox Faith*, Book III, chapter 12 in *PG* 94, 1029–1030.

[26] St Gregory Palamas, *A Homily on the Dormition of Our Supremely Pure Lady Theotokos and Ever-Virgin Mary* (Homily 37), in *PG* 151, 472.

[27] Cf. P. Sherwood, 'Byzantine Mariology' in *The Eastern Churches Quarterly* 14/8 (Winter 1962) p. 396.

[28] Cf. G. Florovsky, 'The Ever-Virgin of God', in: *Creation and Redemption*. Volume Three of the *Collected Works of Georges Florovsky* (Belmond, Mass. 1976), p. 176.

[29] For more on the theme of Mary Mother of the Church, see chapter 9 below. For further elaboration (including Scriptural, Patristic and Magisterial references) of the doctrines of Mary as Coredemptrix and Mediatrix see chapter 8, pp. 187–201, and chapter 9, pp. 254–266 below respectively.

[30] J. Robinson, *The Inner Goddess* (Leominster: Gracewing, 1998), p. 61.

[31] See S. Benko, *The Virgin Goddess. Studies in the pagan and Christian roots of Mariology* (Leiden: Brill, 1993).

[32] See V. White, *Soul and Psyche* (London: 1960).

[33] See H. de Lubac, *L'Eternel Féminin. Etude sur un texte du Père Teilhard de Chardin* (Paris: Aubier-Montaigne, 1968).

[34] E. L. Mascall, 'The Dogmatic Theology of the Mother of God' in E. L. Mascall (ed.) *The Mother of God*, (London: Dacre Press, 1949), p. 43.

[35] C. Dickson, *A Protestant Pastor Looks at Mary* (Huntington, Indiana: Our Sunday Visitor, 1996), pp.109–110.

[36] See J. Wicks, The Virgin Mary in Recent Ecumenical Dialogues' in *Gregorianum* 81 (2000), pp. 25–57.

[37] St Ephraem the Syrian, deacon, *Sermo III de diversis* in *EM* 325.

[38] St Augustine, *In Ioannis Evangelium Tractatus*, 8, 9 in *PL* 35, 1456: 'ipse creator Mariae, ipse creatus ex Maria.'

[39] See Vatican II, *Lumen Gentium*, 61.

[40] See Pope John Paul II, Encyclical Letter *Redemptoris Mater*, 8.5.

[41] St Anselm, *Oration 52* in *PL* 158, 955–956.

[42] For further elaboration of the doctrine of Mary, Mediatrix of all graces, including Scriptural, Patristic and Magisterial references, see chapter 9, pp. 254–266 below.

[43] The Acathist Hymn, Fifth Chant.

[44] St Louis Grignon de Montfort, *The Secret of Mary*, 19.

[45] St Gregory Nazianzen in his *Epistle 101* made the title *Theotokos* the touchstone of orthodoxy. His argument runs as follows: If there were two persons in Christ, Mary would be the Mother of only the human person. If there were only one nature in Christ, and that

human, she would not be the Mother of God. If there were only one nature in Christ, divine nature, she would not be the Mother of Christ. Hence the doctrine of *Theotokos* implies one person, a divine person, and two natures, divine and human. Similarly, St Cyril of Alexandria, in his *Homily 15 on the Incarnation*, also makes Theotokos the test of orthodoxy. Cyril's writings give clear and unequivocal statements about the Real Presence of Christ in the Eucharist and the position of Mary, the Theotokos, within the doctrine of her Son's Incarnation. See also chapter 5, pp. 110–116 below.

[46]   See B. Leahy, *The Marian Principle in the Church according to Hans Urs von Balthasar* (Frankfurt am Main: Peter Lang, 1996).

[47]   J. Raya and J. de Vinck, *Byzantine Daily Worship* (Allendale, NJ: Alleluia Press, 1969), p. 756.

[48]   Vatican II, *Lumen Gentium*, 68. The Preface for the Mass of the Assumption also refers to Our Lady as a 'sign of hope and comfort.'

[49]   Vatican II, *Lumen Gentium*, 65.

[50]   See H. de Lubac, 'Preface' in *Maria: Etudes sur la Sainte Vierge* (Paris: Beauchesne, 1961), Volume 6, p. 11.

CHAPTER 2

DAUGHTER OF SION

Her presence in the midst of Israel – a presence so discreet as to pass almost unnoticed by the eyes of her contemporaries – shone very clearly before the Eternal One, who had associated this hidden 'daughter of Sion' with the plan of salvation embracing the whole history of humanity.

Pope John Paul II, *Redemptoris Mater* 2

In the Old Testament, God's economy of salvation gradually unfolds towards the coming of Christ the Saviour, born of the Virgin Mary. Inasmuch as the Old Covenant is a preparation, prefiguration, and prophetic foretelling of the coming of Christ it also fulfils the same function with regard to His Mother. The Mother of God is both prefigured and prophetically foretold in the Old Testament. Prefiguration involves the foreshadowing of the New Testament in the Old Testament through persons, events and things: 'The New is in the Old concealed, the Old is in the New revealed.'[1] This idea is related to the *typical sense* of Bible texts which is the deeper meaning that some elements (persons, places, things and events) of the Bible have, because God, the divine author of the Bible, intended that these elements foreshadow or prefigure further things. Originally a type (*tupos*) meant a 'model' or 'pattern' or 'mould' into which clay or wax was pressed, that it might take the figure or exact shape of the mould. In our case, a type means an Old Testament person, place, thing, or event that prefigures a person, place, thing, or event in the New Testament called the antitype.[2] The typical sense is an indication of the divine inspiration of texts. On the other hand biblical prophecy involves the use of words rather than deeds. This prophecy is a teaching relating to the Covenant relationship between God and His people going back to the beginning of their history as a nation. The prophets of the Old Testament communicated God's love for His people. The prophets often indicated future events that God would bring about, sometimes in their lifetime and sometimes in the far distant future. Above all, these future events were connected with the coming of Jesus the Messiah.

In approaching the Scriptures, it is important to realize that faith is based on a realist understanding of history.[3] The tendency, begun in liberalism and modernism which reduces faith to a mere idea, culminated in R. Bultmann's approach. The continuing influence of M. Dibelius and R. Bultmann, the principal founders of the form-critical phase of historical-critical interpretation, continues to have a massive impact on modern exegesis. Bultmann's conclusions are not the scientific result of historical findings but emerge from a framework of systematic presuppositions, involving the use of an evolutionist model of natural science within biblical theology, as well as an existentialist philosophy.[4] The liberal or modernist approach to Scriptural interpretation exaggerates the role of human techniques in the formation of the Bible and in its exegesis. In a rationalist way, it seeks to reduce to merely symbolic or mythological meanings that which in fact Scripture teaches as true at the deepest level. Both Catholic and Protestant theologies have at various times suffered the ravages of modernist reductionism.

Prefiguration

The Old Testament as a whole prefigures the New Testament. In particular, typology in an Old Testament story serves as a prelude for an event in the New Testament. An obvious example of typology is how the crossing of the waters of the Red Sea from slavery in Egypt to the Promised Land prefigures the waters of Baptism, whereby a person is transformed from the captivity of original sin to new life in Christ. The life of Jesus Christ was foreshadowed in the Old Testament, as also were His apostles, His Church, His sacraments and above all His Mother. Mary is prefigured in some of the prominent women of the Old Testament, in a similar way that Adam, Moses and David prefigure Christ. As Ronald Knox remarked:

> But through this tangled skein runs a single golden thread; between these soiled pages lies now and again, a pressed flower that has lost neither its colour nor its sweetness. That thread, that flower, is the mention, by type and analogue, of her whom all generations of Christendom have called blessed, the Virgin of Virgins, the Queen of Heaven, the Holy Mother of God ... For Our Lady is, after all, the culmination of that long process of selection, of choosing here and rejecting there a human instrument suited to His purpose, which is so characteristic of God's dealings with His ancient people.[5]

One of the most poignant Marian images in Scripture is that of the Daughter of Sion. This linguistic expression had its origin in the Northern Kingdom (Israel) and was usually applied to a little town or colony which depended upon a larger and more important city (cf. Nb 21:25; 32:42; Jos 15:45–47) Its use extended to the South after the exile in Babylonia (Ne 11:25) and is also found in the Chronicles (1 Ch 5:16; 2 Ch 13:19). The prophet Micah was the first to apply the precise expression daughter of Sion to a colony dependent on Jerusalem (Mi 1:13; 4:10,13). Studies show that the Daughter of Sion is the new quarter of Jerusalem, north of the City of David, where the refugees from the North came, the 'little remnant of Israel'. Around the year 640 BC, Jerusalem had a government which was favourable

to the Assyrians. The prophet Zephaniah proclaimed the
hope that the liberation of the people would begin from
the remnant of Israel, a humble and lowly people, the
daughter of Sion renewed by the love of the Lord (Zp 3:12,
14, 17).[6] In the Old Testament, Sion or Jerusalem is
depicted as Spouse and Daughter, Virgin and Mother as is
Mary in the New. Daughter Sion is the Spouse of Yahweh,
Mother of the People of God (Mother Sion), the Virgin
Israel. The Daughter of Sion representation of Mary is
evident in the parallelism between a great number of texts
in the Old and the New Testaments. Mary 'stands out
among the poor and humble of the Lord, who confidently
hope for and receive salvation from Him. After a long
period of waiting the times are fulfilled in her, the exalted
Daughter of Sion, and the new plan of salvation is established.'[7] Many of the Old Testament texts describing the
Daughter of Sion are easily applied to Mary in the New
Testament. The woman Mary, the Mother of God, is the
historical realization of the symbolic figure denoted by the
expression Daughter of Sion. Israel's expectation of salvation was projected upon this symbolic figure. The
Messianic Daughter of Zion, described by the prophets,
becomes concrete in one daughter of Israel, Mary, who
thus becomes the personification of the messianic people
in eschatological times.[8]

In Mary the exalted Daughter of Sion, 'after a long
expectation of the promise, the times were at length
fulfilled and the new dispensation established. All this
occurred when the Son of God took a human nature from
her, that He might in the mysteries of His flesh free man
from sin.'[9] The structure and style of the following passage
from the book of Zechariah is a case in point: 'Sing, rejoice,
daughter of Sion, for now I am coming to live among you
– Yahweh declares!' (Zc 2:14).[10] It is mirrored in the
account which the evangelist St Luke renders of the
Annunciation: 'Rejoice, you who enjoy God's favour! The
Lord is with you. Mary, do not be afraid; you have won
God's favour. Look! You are to conceive in your womb

and bear a Son, and you must name Him Jesus' (Lc 1:28, 30, 31).

At three decisive moments in salvation history, the Garden of Eden, the Exodus from Egypt, and the establishment of the Davidic kingdom, God disclosed a coming fulfilment that was Christ-centred, but was marked with a definite and discernible Marian dimension. The three decisive moments involve a prefiguration of Our Lady as the New Eve, as the Ark of the Covenant, and as the Queen Mother. These titles correspond to three Old Testament realities, of course, but at the same time point to a glorious fulfilment expressed in three major Marian doctrines: Mary's Immaculate Conception, her Assumption and her Queenship.

When God speaks to the serpent after the Fall of Adam and Eve, we learn in Genesis of the promise of a Redeemer from the *woman*, 'I shall put enmity between you and the woman, and between your offspring and hers; it will bruise your head and you will strike its heel' (Gn 3:15). This is strictly speaking a prophecy of Mary which will be discussed below. However, Eve herself, the mother of all the living (Gn 3:20) prefigures Mary who is the Mother of all the living in the order of grace.[11]

Mary is the bridge between the Old and the New Testaments, and this is most clearly illustrated in the consideration of the Mother of God as the Ark of the Covenant. Luke's initial characterization of Mary as the Daughter of Zion leads to his magnificent vision of Mary as the Ark of the Covenant (Lk 1:26–28), a vision that is continued in both the Gospel of John and the book of Revelation. Studies of Luke's Gospel have pointed out that his way of introducing Old Testament themes or prophecies comes through allusions rather than direct assertions of 'prophetic fulfilment.' In introducing Mary as the Ark, Luke draws on Old Testament texts that any Jewish reader would understand and identify with the Ark. A striking example is the similarity between the presence of God in the tent of dwelling in the Old Testament and its fulfilment in the New Testament episode of the Annunciation. The divine overshadowing, designated by the characteristic word *episkiasei*, evoked the cloud which was the sign of God's presence. The cloud covered the Ark of the Covenant with its shadow, while the glory of God filled it from within: 'The cloud covered the Tent of meeting and the glory of Yahweh filled the tabernacle' (Ex 40:34). In her turn, Mary was the object of this double theophany: a presence from above that signifies transcendence, and a presence of the Lord from within: 'The power of the Most High will cover you with its shadow. And so the child will be holy and will be called Son of God' (Lk 1:35).[12]

Significant and profound parallels also exist between Mary's visit to Elizabeth and the transportation of the Ark of the Covenant from the house of Abinadab to that of Obed-Edom and to Jerusalem. The two 'journeys' take place in Judea. In both cases, surprise is expressed. In the Old Testament, there is wonder that the Ark of God should come to Obed-Edom: 'How can the Ark of Yahweh come to be with me?' (2 S 6:9). In Mary's visit, a similar question is voiced by Elizabeth: 'Why should I be honoured with a visit from the mother of My Lord?' (Lk 1:43). The Ark was accompanied by rejoicing when it came up to Jerusalem: 'And David danced before the Lord with all his might ... Thus with war cries and blasts on the horn, David and the entire House of Israel brought up the ark of Yahweh' (2 S 6:14–15). This prefigured the arrival of the New Ark, and the joy of John the Baptist in his mother's womb: 'Look, the moment your greeting reached my ears, the child in my womb leapt for joy.' (Lk 1:44). There are shouts of jubilation from the people and from Elizabeth and both David and John the Baptist 'exult for joy'. Blessings were poured on the people who received the Ark into their home: 'And Yahweh blessed Obed-Edom and his whole family' (2 S 6:11). In Old Testament times, fertility was associated with God's blessing. Elizabeth in the New Testament was blessed with the birth of John the Baptist: 'The time came for Elizabeth to have her child, and she gave birth to a son' (Lk 1:57). The time that the Ark remained in the house of Obed-Edom was three months: 'The ark of Yahweh remained in the house of Obed-Edom of Gath for three months' (2 S 6:11). This is also clearly a prefiguration of Mary's time with Elizabeth: 'Mary stayed with her some three months' (Lk 1:56).[13]

The theme of the Ark is taken up a final time, at the end of the infancy gospel, in the event of the Lord's Presentation in the Temple:

> As Jesus enters the Temple Simeon greets him as 'the glory of Israel' (Luke 2:32). This is a divine title. The glory of Yahweh that had deserted the Temple once it was bereft of the Ark of the Covenant now reenters the Temple as Mary comes there carrying Jesus. Thus it is that Simeon can die happy (Luke 2:26, 29): he now can 'see death' since he has 'seen the glory of the Lord.' The time has been fulfilled. Here Mary, eschatalogical Daughter of Zion and new Ark of the Covenant, accomplishes her mission in a way in bringing to the Temple the one whose place it properly is. This is what Jesus himself will affirm in the very last episode of the infancy gospel, that of his being found in the Temple: 'I must be in my Father's house' (Luke 2:49).[14]

Parallels can also be seen between the Infancy narrative in Luke and the Prologue of the Gospel of John. There is reason to believe that in his Prologue John refers both to the Virgin Birth and to the Ark symbolism. The Ark symbolism and its relationship to Mary continue in the Book of Revelation in chapters 11 and 12 where the home of God or 'Ark' is also a 'Woman': 'Then the sanctuary of God in heaven opened, and the ark of the covenant could be seen inside it ... Now a great sign appeared in heaven: a woman, robed with the sun, standing on the moon, and on her head a crown of twelve stars. She was pregnant' (Rv 11:19–12:2). In a later significant verse, closely linked with this passage, the relation between the Ark and the Woman is also clearly indicated: 'I saw the holy city, the new Jerusalem, coming down out of heaven from God, prepared as a bride dressed for her husband. Then I heard a loud voice call from the throne, "Look, here God lives among human beings. He will make His home among them; they will be His people, and He will be their God, God-with-them"' (Rv 21:2–3). The identification of the Ark of the Covenant with Mary, so clear to Jewish readers of Luke and John, was grasped by the early Christian community as confirmed by references in ancient liturgies, litanies, hymns such as the *Akathistos* and the writings of the Fathers (for instance, Athanasius). Thus the affirmation of Mary as the Ark of the Covenant, deriving from Scripture, became a part of the Apostolic Faith. The Ark lies at the centre of the Old Covenant and its continuation into the New Covenant in the person of Mary is an invitation to awe-filled meditation on the role of Our Lady in the economy of salvation.

Mary's role at the side of her royal Son is prefigured in the Old Testament depictions of the Queen Mother. The title of Queen Mother or *Gebirah* in Hebrew was well-known in Old Testament times and she played a very influential part in national affairs and acted as regent when the king was absent or dead. Since the importance of the Queen Mother was recognized by the ancient Hebrews, the first Christians honoured the Mother of their King in this way. Queen Mothers held an important position in the royal courts of the ancient Near East and especially in Israel. Their names have been faithfully recorded in the Books of the Kings (1 K 14:21; 15:2; 22:42; 2 K 9:6; 12;2: 14:2; 15:2, 33; 18:2; 22:1; 23:31, 36; 24:18). They were closely associated in the honour and position of the monarch (Jr 13:18; 22:6). Sometimes it was evident that the position of the king's mother was more important than that of his wife, as can be seen in the comparison between 1 Kings 1:16,31 and 2:19, where Bathsheba prostrates herself before King David, her husband, whereas Solomon, her son, after he has become king, prostrates himself before her and makes her sit at his right hand. The prefigurative prophetic texts noted above therefore glimpse Mary essentially as the Queen Mother of the eschatological king, involved as such in the honour paid to his reign.[15]

The Old Testament figure of the Queen Mother also furnishes an authentic foreshadowing of the role of the Mother of Jesus as Queen and Advocate for the People of God.[16] The office and authority of the Queen Mother in her close relationship to the king made her the strongest advocate to the king for the people of the kingdom. The Old Testament understanding of an advocate is a person who is called in to intercede for another in need and particularly at court, and no one had more intercessory power with the king than the Queen Mother, who at times sat enthroned at his right side (1 K 2:19–20). The Queen Mother also enjoyed the function of counsellor to the king in regards to matters of the kingdom (cf. Pr 31:8–9; 2 Ch 22:2–4). The recognized role of advocate of the Queen Mother with the king for members of the kingdom is manifested in the immediate response of King Solomon to his mother, Bathsheba, in this Queen Mother's petition for a member of the kingdom: 'So Bathsheba went to King Solomon to speak to him about Adonijah; the king got up to meet her and bowed before her; he then sat down on his throne; a seat was brought for the king's mother, and she sat down on his right. She said, "I have one small request to make you; do not refuse me." "Mother," the king replied, "make your request, for I shall not refuse you."' (1 K 2: 19–20).[17]

Throughout the Old Covenant, many holy women prepared for and prefigured Mary. At the very beginning there was Eve; despite her disobedience, she received the promise of a posterity that will be victorious over the evil one, as well as the promise that she will be the mother of all the living (Gn 3:15, 20). By virtue of this promise, Sarah conceived a son in spite of her old age (Gn 18:10–14; 21:1–2). Miraculous births prefigured the Birth of Christ. Against all human expectation, God chose those who were considered powerless and weak to show forth His faithfulness to His promises: Hannah, the mother of Samuel; Deborah; Ruth; Judith and Esther; and many other women.[18] In particular, Judith is regarded as a figure of the Blessed Virgin Mary: 'On coming to her house, they blessed her (Judith) with one accord, saying: You are the glory of Jerusalem! You are the great pride of Israel! You are the highest honour of our race! By doing all this with your own hand you have deserved well of Israel, and God has approved what you have done. May you be blessed by the Lord Almighty in all the days to come! And the people all said, "Amen!"'(Jdt 15:9–10).

The Matriarchs of the Old Testament also foreshadow Mary and Elizabeth *taken together* in the New Testament, as in the examples of Sarah and Hagar, Rachel and Leah, and Hannah and Peninnah. Hagar the Egyptian maid had Ishmael (Gn 16:15) by Abram, and Sarah had Isaac (Gn 21:2) by Abraham, after God established His Covenant with him, making him a father of a host of nations. Rachel and Leah were the daughters of Laban, and Leah had six of Jacob's twelve sons, but it was Rachel who bore his eleventh son Joseph (Gn 30:24). Peninnah had many children for Elkanah, but it was the barren Hannah who bore Samuel (1 S 1:20). The hymn of Hannah in the First Book of Samuel 2:1–10 is clearly a source for the Magnificat of Mary. The books of Esther and Judith portray two heroines of Israel. Each of these women, with their spirit of resilience and indestructible spiritual strength, personify Israel itself. In fact, woman and Israel become interchangeable in the Book of Hosea, where the marriage of Hosea to his unfaithful wife is symbolic of God's Covenant of love with the unfaithful people of Israel (Ho 11:1–9).

The theme of Divine Wisdom woven through the Old Testament yields yet another basis for the theological prefiguration of Mary. Wisdom is not just the result of mere human experience after human reflection. The wise King Solomon realized that true Wisdom can only come from God through prayer, understanding His Divine plan.

A passage from the Book of Proverbs (Pr 8:22–31) shows that Wisdom is not just the eternal plan of God, but is a person, God's companion from the beginning. The rich background in the Old Testament predisposes one to understand how the whole history of Israel looks to its fulfilment in the Messiah. Mary, the young Jewish virgin, becomes a symbol for Israel herself, the one that bore Jesus, the Messiah. The passages in Proverbs 8 and Ecclesiasticus 24 which speak of Wisdom have also been applied to Mary as she is the *seat of wisdom*:

> Wisdom speaks her own praises, in the midst of her people she glories in herself. She opens her mouth in the assembly of the Most High, she glories in herself in the presence of the Mighty One. In the holy tent I ministered before him and thus became established in Sion. In the beloved city he has given me rest, and in Jerusalem I wield my authority. I have taken root in a privileged people, in the Lord's property, in his inheritance (Si 24: 1–2; 10–12).

In addition to the prefigurations already discussed, the principle 'the law of prayer grounds the law of belief'[19] provides many other allusions in the prayers and liturgies of the Church. In this sense, many of the titles bestowed on Our Blessed Lady in her litany and in the 'Ave maris stella' have prefigurative value. The Antiphons and Responses found in the Offices recited on the various feasts of Our Blessed Lady suggest a number of types of Mary. For example, the liturgy for the Solemnity of Mary Mother of God sees in the bush burning without being consumed (Ex 3:2), a figure of Mary conceiving her Son without the loss of her virginity. Also, in Gideon's fleece which was wet with dew while all the ground beside had remained dry (Jg 6:37–38), the Church Fathers see a type of Mary receiving in her womb the Word Incarnate.[20]

The figure from psalm 45, the royal wedding song, has also been viewed as a prefiguration of Mary, Mother of God. After the introduction it is divided into two parts. The first sings the praises of the king, the second his bride.

Although this passage refers to an historical king, he is the figure of the Messiah in the fullest sense of Scripture. Some have said that the queen is a figure of Mary, but this proposal has to be carefully qualified.

> The daughters of kings are among your loved ones.
> On your right stands the queen in gold of Ophir.
>
> Listen, O daughter, give ear to my words:
> forget your own people and your father's house.
> So will the king desire your beauty:
> He is your lord, pay homage to him.
>
> And the people of Tyre shall come with gifts,
> the richest of the people shall seek your favour.
> The daughter of the king is clothed with splendour,
> her robes embroidered with pearls set in gold.
>
> (Ps 45:10–14)

The psalm seems to refer to the wedding between the Messiah and Israel, after she has broken her links with paganism (forget your own people and your father's house). This presupposes an infidelity in the past which cannot be applied to Mary. Nevertheless the psalm is adopted in the liturgy for the Assumption of Our Lady.

Prophecy

In Old Testament prophecy also, Mary represents a bridge between the Old and New Covenants. St Andrew of Crete once wrote that our Lady is 'the seal of the Old and of the New Testament; she is clearly the fulfilment of every prophecy.'[21] The Old Testament refers indirectly to Mary in all those prophecies which predict the incarnation of the Word of God. In particular, there are at least three clear direct prophecies of Mary in the Old Testament, namely Genesis 3:15, Isaiah 7:14 and Micah 5:1–3, which all in varying degrees bring into striking relief a 'maiden', a 'queen', 'one who was to give birth' in eschatological times to a 'son of David' who would be Son of God (2 S 7:14; Ps 2 and 110).[22]

The first prophecy referring to Mary is found in the very opening chapters of the Book of Genesis: 'I shall put enmity between you and the woman, and between your offspring and hers; it will bruise your head and you will strike its heel' (Gn 3:15). This rendering, based on the Vulgate, appears to differ in two respects from the original Hebrew text. First, the Hebrew text employs the same verb for the two expressions 'it will bruise or crush' and 'you will strike' while the Greek Septuagint renders the verb both times by the expression 'to strike'. Some translators like St Jerome interpret the Hebrew verb by expressions which mean to crush or to bruise rather than to strike or to lie in wait.[23] Nevertheless, in his Latin Vulgate translation, he employed the verb 'to crush' (*conterere*) in the first place, and 'to lie in wait' (*insidiari*) in the second. Hence the punishment inflicted on the serpent and the serpent's retaliation are expressed by the same Hebrew verb: but in the Vulgate the wound of the serpent is mortal, since it affects his head, while the wound inflicted by the serpent is not mortal, being inflicted on the heel.

The second point of difference between the Hebrew text and the Greek and Latin versions concerns the agent who is to inflict the mortal wound on the serpent. The Hebrew text reads *hu'* (*autos, ipse*) which indicates the seed of the woman. 'It' refers to the offspring which is masculine in Hebrew, and Christian tradition has referred this to Christ.[24] The human race is thus opposed to the devil and his 'seed', and a hint is given of humanity's ultimate victory, in a first glimpse of salvation; hence the passage is referred to as the *proto-evangelium*. The Greek version has a masculine pronoun, which ascribes the victory to one of the woman's descendants in particular, rather than just the offspring in general. This allusion to Christ is consonant with the Messianic interpretation of many Fathers of the Church. The Vulgate reads 'she' (*ipsa*) which refers to a woman. Thus, according to the Vulgate reading, the woman herself will win the victory; according to the Hebrew text, she will be victorious through her offspring, rendered by 'it'. The reading 'she' (*ipsa*) is neither an intentional corruption of the original text, nor is it an accidental error; it is rather an explanatory version expressing explicitly the fact of Our Lady's part in the victory over the serpent, which is contained implicitly in the Hebrew original.

As is quite commonly admitted, the Divine judgement is directed not only against the serpent as the originator of sin, but also against the seed of the serpent denoting its followers, the 'brood of vipers', the 'generation of vipers', those whose father is the devil, the children of evil.[25] One may understand the offspring or seed of the woman in a similar collective sense, embracing all who are born of God. However, seed often denotes a particular person in biblical theology, if the context allows it. St Paul gives this explanation of the word offspring or 'progeny' as it occurs in the patriarchal promises: 'Now the promises were addressed to Abraham *and to his descendants* – notice, in passing, that scripture does not use a plural word as if there were several descendants, it uses the singular: to his posterity, which is Christ.' (Ga 3:16). Finally the expression 'the woman' in the clause 'I will put enmity between you and the woman' is a literal version of the Hebrew text. Peculiar to the Hebrew language is the use of the article in order to indicate a person or thing, which is not yet known and possibly later to be more clearly described, either as present or as to be taken into account within the context.[26] Since our indefinite article serves this purpose, we may translate: 'I will put enmity between you and a woman.' Hence the prophecy promises a woman, Our Blessed Lady, who will be the enemy of the serpent to a marked degree; besides, the same woman will be victorious over the devil, at least through her offspring. The completeness of the victory is emphasized by the contextual phrase 'on dust you will feed as long as you live' (Gn 3:14), which is a common old near-Eastern expression denoting the deepest humiliation.[27]

The second prophecy referring to Mary is found in Isaiah 7:1–17. Scholars have asserted that this passage is part of a series of occurrences and sayings from the life of the prophet, known as his memoirs, possibly put together by Isaiah himself.[28] According to 2 Kings 16:1–4 and 2 Chronicles 28:1–5, Ahaz, who began his reign in 736 BC, openly professed idolatry, so that God gave him into the hands of the kings of Syria and Israel. It appears that an alliance had been concluded between Pekah, King of Israel, and Razon, King of Aram, for the purpose of opposing the Assyrian aggressions. Ahaz, against the urgings of Isaiah, submitted to the Assyrians, whose king Tiglath-Pileser III moved against Syria and Israel (2 K 16:7–9).[29] The allies invaded his territory, intending to substitute for Ahaz a more subservient ruler. Immediate preparations needed to be made for a protracted siege, and Ahaz was busily engaged near the upper pool from which the city received the greater part of its water supply. Hence the Lord says to Isaiah 'Go out with your son Shear-Jashub, and meet Ahaz at the end of the conduit of the upper pool, on the road to the Fuller's Field' (Is 7:3). The prophet's commission was of an extremely consoling nature: 'Pay attention and keep calm. Do not be frightened or demoralised by these two smouldering sticks of firewood, by the fierce anger of Razon, Aram and the son of Remaliah' (Is 7:4). The scheme of the enemies shall not succeed: 'This will not happen, it will never occur, for the head of Aram is Damascus, and the head of Damascus is Razon; another sixty-five years, and Ephraim will cease to be a people' (Is 7:7–8). Ahaz had abandoned the Lord for Molech, and put his trust in an alliance with Assyria; hence the conditional prophecy concerning Juda, 'If you will not take your stand on me you will not stand firm' (Is 7:9). The test of belief follows immediately: 'Ask the Lord your God for a sign, either in the depths of Sheol or in the heights above' (Is 7:11). Ahaz hypocritically answers: 'I will not ask. I will not put the Lord to the test' (Is 7:12), thus refusing to express his belief in God, and preferring his Assyrian policy. The king prefers Assyria to God, and Assyria will come: 'Yahweh will bring times for you, your people and your ancestral House, such as have not been seen since Ephraim broke away from Judah' (Is 7:17). The house of David has sinned not only against men, but above all against God, by its unbelief; hence it shall not stand firm and, by an irony of Divine punishment, it will be destroyed by those very men whom it trusted instead of God.

Nevertheless, in this context, the general Messianic promises made to the house of David cannot be frustrated:

> The Lord will give you a sign in any case: It is this: the young woman is with child and will give birth to a son whom she will call Immanuel. On curds and honey will he feed until he knows how to refuse the bad and choose the good. Before the child knows how to refuse the bad and choose the good, the lands whose two kings are frightening you will be deserted (Is 7:14–16).

Despite the fact that some scholars regard the young woman as a wife of Ahaz,[30] Christian tradition has always accepted that the young woman mentioned by the prophet is a virgin, Mary the Mother of Christ. The argument is based on the premises that the prophet's virgin is the mother of Immanuel, and that Immanuel is Christ. The relation of the virgin to Immanuel is clearly expressed in the inspired words; the same indicate also the identity of Immanuel with the Christ. The connection of Immanuel with the extraordinary Divine sign which was to be given to Ahaz predisposes one to see in the child more than a common boy. In Isaiah 8:8, the prophet ascribes to him the ownership of the land of Juda: 'and the spreading of its wings will cover the whole extent of your country, Immanuel!' Later, the government of the house of David is said to be upon his shoulders, and he is described as being endowed with more than human qualities: 'For a son has been born for us, a son has been given to us, and dominion has been laid on his shoulders; and this is the name he has been given, "Wonder-Counsellor, Mighty-God, Eternal-Father, Prince-of-Peace"' (Is 9:5). Finally, the prophet calls Immanuel 'a shoot sprung from the stock of Jesse' endowed with 'the spirit of the Lord, the spirit of wisdom and insight, the spirit of counsel and power, the spirit of knowledge and fear of the Lord'; his advent shall be followed by the general signs of the Messianic era, and the remnant of the chosen people shall be again the people of God (Is 11:1–16).

One possible objection could raised: 'How can Ahaz verify the "sign" which the prophet offers, if the sign will come to pass only eight centuries later?' The difficulty can be resolved in this way. Isaiah's prophecy addresses not only Ahaz, but the whole 'house of David' (Is 7:13), because it was intended to serve a far broader and weightier end, namely, to state that the Lord would keep his promise to preserve the line of David, and to make David's throne stand fast forever through the coming of Christ, the Immanuel. Whatever obscurity or ambiguity there may be in the prophetic text itself is removed by St Matthew. After narrating the doubt of St Joseph and the angel's assurance, 'she has conceived what is in her by the Holy Spirit', the Evangelist proceeds: 'Now all this took place to fulfil what the Lord had spoken through the prophet: Look! the virgin is with child and will give birth to a son whom they will call Immanuel, a name which means "God-is-with-us"' (Mt 1:20–22). It can be deduced from all this that Mary is mentioned in the prophecy of Isaiah as Mother of Jesus Christ; in the light of St Matthew's reference to the prophecy, we may add that the prophecy predicted also Mary's virginal conception of the Immanuel. Catholic tradition maintains that the prophecy is Messianic, and that it would be emptied of its meaning, even in purely historical terms, unless it foretells the virginal conception of the Messiah.[31] Moreover, traditional exegesis would point out that in this prophecy lies at least the probability that Isaiah indicated also the virgin Birth of Christ, namely not only that the virgin would conceive but would also bring forth Immanuel.

A third prophecy referring to Our Blessed Lady is contained in Micah 5:1–3:

> But you Ephrathah, the least of the clans of Judah, from you will come for me a future ruler of Israel whose origins go back to the distant past, to the days of old. Hence the Lord will abandon them only until she who is in labour gives birth, and then those who survive of his race will be reunited to the Israelites. He will take his stand and he will shepherd them with the power of Yahweh, with the majesty of the name of his God, and they will be secure, for his greatness will extend henceforth to the most distant parts of the country.

The Hebrew text identifies the city of Ephrathah as Bethlehem, the city of Jesse and of his son David.[32]

Though the prophet Micah (about 750–660 BC) was a contemporary of Isaiah, his prophetic activity began a little later and ended a little earlier than that of Isaiah. There can be no doubt that the Jews regarded the foregoing prediction as referring to the Messiah. The Gospel of St Matthew shows how this text was interpreted. According to St Matthew (Mt 2:6) the chief priests and scribes, when asked where the Messiah was to be born, answered Herod in the words of the prophecy, 'And you, Bethlehem, in the land of Judah ...' According to St John, the Jewish populace gathered at Jerusalem for the celebration of the feast asked the rhetorical question: 'Does not scripture say that the Christ must be descended from David and come from Bethlehem, the village where David was?' (Jn 7:42).

The question is then how the prophecy refers to the Virgin Mary. Our Blessed Lady is denoted by the phrase, 'until she who is in labour gives birth'. It is true that 'she who is in labour' has been referred variously to the Church, or to the Gentiles united with Christ, or again to

Babylon. However, on the one hand, there is hardly a sufficient connection between any of these events and the promised Redeemer, and on the other hand, the passage ought to read 'till the time wherein she that is *barren* shall bring forth' if any of these events were referred to by the prophet. Nor can 'she who is in labour' be referred to Sion: Sion is spoken of, but not in figurative terms, before and after the present passage so that we cannot expect the prophet to lapse suddenly into figurative language. Moreover, the prophecy thus explained would not give a satisfactory sense. The contextual phrases 'the ruler of Israel', 'will come for me', which in Hebrew implies birth, and 'those who survive of his race' denote an individual, not a nation; hence we infer that these phrases must refer to the same person. Furthermore, there is a link between the use of the verb 'come forth' applied to the law in Micah 4:2 ('the Law issues from Sion and Yahweh's word from Jerusalem') and to the birth of the Messianic King.[33] The person of the ruler is thus the Messiah; hence 'she who is in labour' must denote the mother of Christ, or Our Blessed Lady. Thus explained the whole passage becomes clear: the Messiah must be born in Bethlehem, an insignificant village in Judah: His family must be reduced to poverty and obscurity before the time of His birth; as this cannot happen if the theocracy remains intact, if David's house continues to flourish, hence the Lord will abandon them only until she who is in labour gives birth to the Christ.

The prophecies of Micah 5:1–3, and those of Genesis 3:15 and Isaiah 7:14 are all related. In all three cases, the figure of the mother is presented alone with her son. No earthly father of the Messiah-Saviour is mentioned in any of these three great Old Testament prophecies. If we look at these prophecies from the standpoint of their fulfilment, the mother appears always as virgin mother. The virginity of the mother is the ever-present, luminous backdrop for the event of the Annunciation and that of the birth of the Messiah. This virginity is an evident sign that the Messiah is truly a new creation, the new humanity, the beginning of the salvific era: the Redemption.[34]

A fourth prophecy referring to Mary is found in Jeremiah 31:22: 'For Yahweh is creating something new on earth: the Woman sets out to find her Husband again.' The text of the prophet Jeremiah offers substantial difficulties for the biblical scholar. Several conservative Protestant interpreters have claimed that the passage means 'a woman shall protect a man'; but such a motive would hardly induce the men of Israel to return to God. The explanation 'a woman shall seek a man' hardly agrees with the text; besides, such an inversion of the natural order is presented in Isaiah 4:1, as a sign of the greatest calamity. Another rendering, 'a woman shall change into a man', is hardly faithful to the original text. Other commentators see in the woman a type of the community of Israel or of the Church, in man the type of God, so that they explain the prophecy as meaning, 'God will dwell again in the midst of the people of Israel' or 'the Church will protect the earth with its valiant men.' However, the Hebrew text hardly suggests such a meaning; moreover, this explanation renders the passage tautological: 'Israel shall return to its God, for Israel will love its God'. Some recent writers render the Hebrew original: 'God creates a new thing upon the earth: the woman (wife) returns to the man (her husband)'. According to the old law (Deuteronomy 24:1–4; Jeremiah 3:1) the husband could not take back the wife once repudiated by him; but the Lord will do something new by allowing the faithless wife, namely the guilty nation, to return to the friendship of God. This explanation rests upon a conjectural correction of the text; besides, it does not necessarily bear the Messianic meaning which is expected from the passage.

The Greek Fathers generally follow the Septuagint version: 'The Lord has created salvation in a new plantation, men shall go about in safety.' In particular, St Athanasius maintains that the new plantation is Jesus Christ, and that the new thing created in woman is the body of the Lord, conceived within the virgin without the co-operation of man.[35] St Jerome also understands the prophetic text as referring to the Virgin conceiving the Messiah.[36] This meaning of the passage satisfies the text and the context. The Hebrew text literally means 'a female shall encompass a man.'[37] As the Word Incarnate possessed from the first moment of His conception all His perfections excepting those connected with His bodily development, His mother is rightly said to 'encompass a man.' The condition of a newly-conceived child is rightly called 'a new thing upon earth.' The context of the prophecy describes after a short general introduction (Jr 30:1–3), Israel's future freedom and restoration in four stanzas: 30:4–11, 12–22; 30:23; 31:14, 15–26; the first three stanzas end with the hope of the Messianic time. The fourth stanza, too, must be expected to have a similar ending. Moreover, the prophecy of Jeremiah, uttered about 589 BC and understood in the sense just explained, agrees with the contemporary Messianic expectations based on Isaiah 7:14; 9:6 and Micah 5:3. According to Jeremiah, the mother of Christ is to differ from other mothers in that her child, even while He is within her womb, shall possess all those properties which constitute real manhood.

A fifth prophecy which is said to have Mariological links is Ezekiel 44:2: 'This gate will be kept shut. No one may open it or go through it, since the Lord God of Israel, has been through it. And so it must be kept shut.' Given the analogy between the Temple of the Old Law and the Blessed Virgin Mary, provided by prefiguration, this passage can be interpreted as a prophetic allusion to the womb of the Blessed Virgin Mary. Her womb remained shut after Jesus Christ, true God and true Man passed through. This passage forges a link between prefiguration and prophecy in regard to the Blessed Virgin Mary, which will be made clearer by a consideration of the New Testament in the next chapter.

Notes

[1]   See St Augustine, *Quaestionum in Heptateuchum* cap. 2, 73, in *PL* 34, 623: 'Novum Testamentum in Vetere latet, Vetus in Novo patet'. The adage can also be formulated: 'The New is in the Old contained; the Old is in the New explained,' or 'The New is in the Old enfolded; the Old is in the New unfolded.' See also Vatican II, *Dei Verbum*, 16.

[2]   See 1 Co 10:6 for the Scriptural basis for the idea of type: 'Now these happenings were examples (τύποι), for our benefit, so that we should never set our hearts, as they did, on evil things.'

[3]   See Pontifical Biblical Commission, *Instructio de historica Evangeliorum veritate* in *AAS* 56 (1964), pp. 712–718.

[4]   See J. Ratzinger, 'L'interpretazione della Bibbia in conflitto' in I. de la Potterie (ed.), *L'esegesi cristiana oggi* (Casale Monferrato: Piemme, 1991), pp. 104–111.

[5]   R. Knox, 'Esther as a Type of Our Lady' in F. J. Sheed, *The Mary Book* (London and New York: Sheed and Ward, 1950), pp. 15–16.

[6]   See H. Cazelles, 'Fille de Sion et théologie mariale dans le Bible' in *Bulletin de la Societé Française d'Études Mariales* 21 (1964), pp. 51–71.

[7]   Vatican II, *Lumen Gentium*, 55.

[8]   See I. de la Potterie, *Mary in the Mystery of the Covenant* (New York: Alba House, 1992), p. 203.

[9]   Vatican II, *Lumen Gentium*, 55.

[10]   Several other passages from the Old Testament are similar in style and structure, for example: 'Shout for joy, daughter of Sion, Israel, shout aloud! Rejoice, exult with all your heart, daughter of Jerusalem! Sion, have no fear. Yahweh your God is there with you, the warrior-Saviour' (Zp 3:14, 16, 17). 'Rejoice heart and soul, daughter of Zion! Shout for joy, daughter of Jerusalem! Look, your king is approaching' (Zc 9:9).

[11]   See the Patristic texts cited in chapter 1, footnote 8 on p. 22 above. See also J. H. Newman, *Certain Difficulties felt by Anglicans in Catholic Teaching*, Volume II (London: Longmans, Green and Co., 1910), p. 36.

[12]   See R. Laurentin, *A Short Treatise on the Virgin Mary* (Washington, New Jersey: AMI Press, 1991), pp. 27–30.

[13]   See S. Manelli, *All Generations Shall Call Me Blessed* (New Bedford, Mass.: Academy of the Immaculate, 1995), p. 152.

[14]   R. Laurentin, *A Short Treatise on the Virgin Mary*, pp. 29–30.

[15]   See R. Laurentin, *A Short Treatise on the Virgin Mary*, pp. 278–279.

[16]   Further development on these topics will be given in chapter 8, pp. 229–232 below, and chapter 9, pp. 254–266 below.

[17]   See M. I. Miravalle, *Mary: Coredemptrix, Mediatrix, Advocate* (Santa Barbara, CA: Queenship Publishing, 1993), pp. 58–59.

[18] See *CCC* 489.

[19] The Latin expression is *lex orandi, lex credendi*. See Prosper of Aquitaine, *Indiculus*, c. 8 in *PL* 51, 209.

[20] See St Ambrose, *De Spiritu Sancto*, I, 8–9, in *PL* 16, 705; St Jerome, *Epistula*, 108, 10 in *PL* 32, 886.

[21] St Andrew of Crete, *Oratio IV for the Birth of the Most Holy Mother of God* in *PG* 97, 865–866: 'Salve, legis ac gratiae mediatrix, veteris novique testamenti obsignatio, totius prophetiae perspicua plenitudo.'

[22] See R. Laurentin, *A Short Treatise on the Virgin Mary*, p. 281.

[23] See St Jerome, *Hebraicae quaestiones in Genesim* in *PL* 23, 943.

[24] See R. J. Clifford and R. E. Murphy, 'Genesis' in R. E. Brown, J. A. Fitzmeyer, R. E. Murphy, *The New Jerome Biblical Commentary* (Englewood Cliffs, NJ: Prentice-Hall, 2000), p. 12.

[25] Cf. Ws 2:25; Mt 3:7; 23:33; Jn 8:44; 1 Jn 3:8–12.

[26] See F. H. W. Gesenius and E. Kautzsch, *Hebräische Grammatik* (Leipzig: F. C. W. Vogel, 1909), p. 402.

[27] Cf. A. Jeremias, *Das Alte Testament im Lichte des alten Orients* (Leipzig: J. C. Hinrichs, 1916), p. 216. See also St Justin, *Dialogue with Trypho*, 100 in *PG* 6, 712; St Irenaeus, *Adversus haereses*, III, 23 in *PG* 7, 964; St Epiphanius, *Haereses*, III, ii, 18 in *PG* 42, 729.

[28] See J. Jensen and W. H. Irwin, 'Isaiah 1–39' in R. E. Brown, J. A. Fitzmeyer, R. E. Murphy, *The New Jerome Biblical Commentary* (Englewood Cliffs, NJ: Prentice-Hall, 2000), p. 234.

[29] *Ibid.*, p. 235.

[30] *Ibid.*, p. 235. The authors maintain that the expression *hā'almâ* is not the technical Hebrew term for a virgin, *bĕtûlâ*. For a general panorama of the interpretation of Isaiah 7:14, see R. Brown, *The Birth of the Messiah* (New York: Doubleday, 1977), pp. 147ff.

[31] See E. May, 'Mary in the Old Testament' in J. B. Carol, *Mariology*, Volume 1 (Milwaukee: The Bruce Publishing Company, 1955), pp. 50–56, 62–65. See also J. Coppens, 'La Prophétie de la 'Almah' in *Ephemerides Theologicae Lovaniensis* 28 (1952), pp. 649–682.

[32] See L. Laberge, 'Micah' in R. E. Brown, J. A. Fitzmeyer, R. E. Murphy, *The New Jerome Biblical Commentary* (Englewood Cliffs, NJ: Prentice-Hall, 2000), p. 253.

[33] *Ibid.*

[34] See S. Manelli, *All Generations Shall Call Me Blessed*, pp. 46–48.

[35] See St Athanasius, *Expositio Fidei*, 3 in *PG* 25, 205–206; Idem, *Sermo maior de Fidei*, 22 in *PG* 26, 1275–1276.

[36] See St Jerome, *Commentariorum in Jeremiam Prophetam*, Liber 6, cap. 31 in *PL* 24, 880–881.

[37] See G. P. Couturier, 'Jeremiah' in R. E. Brown, J. A. Fitzmeyer, R. E. Murphy, *The New Jerome Biblical Commentary* (Englewood Cliffs, NJ: Prentice-Hall, 2000), p. 289. The Hebrew is *nĕqēbâ tesôbēb gāber*.

CHAPTER 3

HANDMAID OF THE LORD

The Gospels are the first fruits of all Scripture and the Gospel of John is the first of the Gospels: no one can grasp its meaning without having leaned his head on Jesus' breast and having received Mary as Mother from Jesus.
Origen, *Commentary on St John's Gospel*

Mary fulfils the Old Testament

At first sight, Holy Scripture seems to offer relatively little detail about Mary. One reason for this may be the focus on Jesus Christ, the Son of God. However, a deeper look at the Scriptures reveals that beneath the surface, beyond the purely literal sense of the Bible, a wealth of indications are to be found concerning the Mother of God. Mary serves as a link between the two Covenants not just through parallel or prophetic verses but by embodying common themes. She is a bridge between the Old and the New Testaments because Scripture shows her representing both the people of Israel and the Church begun by her Son:

A very important insight of modern exegesis has brought to light that the mystery of Mary forms in some way the synthesis of all the former revelation about the people of God, and of all that God by his salvific action wishes to realise for his people. In Mary are accomplished all the important aspects of the promises of the Old Testament to the Daughter of Zion, and in her real person there is an anticipation which will be realised for the new people of God, the Church. The history of revelation on the subject of the theme of the Woman Zion, realised in the person of Mary, and continued in the Church, constitutes a doctrinal bastion, an unshakeable structured ensemble for the comprehension of the history of salvation, from its origin up to its eschatology. A vision of the mystery of Mary, biblically founded, ecclesiologically integrated and structurally developed, gives then a complete image of the concrete realisation of the total mystery of the Covenant.[1]

Various different schemes from biblical theology, which attempt to organize the data contained in Scripture, can be applied to Mary as the fulfilment of the Old Testament. Negative (or *apophatic*) theology considers that, despite having revealed Himself to man, God remains a mystery. According to this approach, characteristic in some ways of Eastern Christendom, God is better understood in silence than in a discourse about Him. Within this perspective, Mary appears at the climax of the time of promise, as the convergence of the fulfilment of God's ways. Because God remains hidden despite His revelation, also the way of Mary is shrouded in mystery; it reveals and yet veils God's revelation. Biblical theology can also be organized according to positive (or *kataphatic*) theology. One example of this direction is the thematic approach, characteristic of Western Christendom, where specific topics such as Covenant, the Kingdom of God, the Name of Yahweh, election, and redemption are considered. Our Lady is the woman of the Covenant who is the realization of the prophecies concerning the Daughter of Sion, in view of the indissoluble union between God and man.

A further approach involves the narrative method. Here, the Old Testament describes an economy of salvation which is brought to fulfilment in the New. The

Scriptures trace God's mode of action and discover the principles that guide this. The Christ-event is the fundamental principle of the Bible. According to the scheme promise-fulfilment, the Old Testament is intrinsically open to the future and Christ is the final cause of the whole of the Old Covenant. Here, the principle of election-substitution consists in the election of a minority for the redemption of the totality. The history of salvation consists in two movements. One proceeds from plurality to unity: Israel is elected for the salvation of the world; the faithful remnant replaces the people as a whole; this remnant is reduced to one Man, the servant of Yahweh or the Son of Man; Jesus fulfils this mission becoming the Centre of history. Mary stands alongside her Son as this faithful remnant. The second movement starts with Christ and proceeds from unity to plurality in the Church, applying the salvation which He has won. Here also, Mary collaborates in the distribution of the effects of Christ's salvation within the Church.[2]

A further scheme of biblical theology concerns the event of a dialogue. Biblical revelation is based not only upon concepts such as election, salvation, covenant, but above all upon actions. The theology of the Old Testament as fulfilled in the New, is based on the actions and words of God and man's response. The encounter with God takes the form of an experience of salvation (danger, invocation, God's listening, salvation, answer). The concepts of election and covenant are dependent on this relationship of dialogue, which is not however between two equal partners. The person who partakes of a dialogue with God in an eminent manner is Mary, the woman who experiences God's blessing and salvation. She is in a way, a 'microhistory of salvation', since God's ways converge in her, and again in her the exemplary response to God's economy of salvation can be found. This is seen, for example in her response to the Annunciation: 'You see before you the Lord's servant, let it happen to me as you have said' (Lk 1:38). The various Old Testament categories which we have discussed are thus brought to fulfilment in the New, in Mary.

Mary in the Synoptic Gospels

THE GOSPEL OF MARK

There are three passages in St Mark's Gospel which reveal certain questions for Mariology. These passages are Mark 3:20–21, Mark 3:31–35 and Mark 6:1–6 respectively.[3] The issues are first Jesus' relation with His family; second, the unusual title *Son of Mary*; and third the question of the brothers of Jesus. As regards this first question, Mark never says explicitly that Mary opposed Jesus, but rather just His fellow citizens, relatives, and family. The passage poses a distinction between the biological family of Jesus and His eschatological family, the Church. This would also imply that Mary always had a growing knowledge of Jesus' salvific mission, even if earlier on that knowledge was partial. Next, the title *Son of Mary* can be partially explained by St Joseph's death. Nevertheless, its meaning is above all that Mark knew about the virginal conception and wanted to avoid any confusion which would arise by calling Him the son of Joseph. Thus, Mark's expression draws specific attention to the virginal conception and birth of Christ.[4] Third, as regards the question of the brothers of Jesus, these brothers are never called sons of Mary. Also, two of the four sons (James and Joset) are sons of another Mary as can be seen from a later passage of Mark's Gospel: 'There were some women watching from a distance. Among them were Mary of Magdala, Mary who was the mother of James the younger and Joset, and Salome' (Mk 15:40, see 15:47). Further, in Semitic languages, brother is the title used to refer to more distant relations like nephews or cousins.[5] Thus, these passages present no problem for the doctrine concerning Mary's virginity. Rather, they witness to her maternal care and her growth in faith, but not from incredulity to faith but rather from a Judaic faith to a faith in Christ.

Even through the first two chapters of St Matthew's Gospel are written in a popular form of the time and not according to the criteria of modern history, their testimony belongs to a mature Christian faith and they transmit historical events. The text reveals a theological development in Judaeo-Christian circles. According to Matthew, Mary forms part of the salvific plan announced in the Old Covenant and fully realized in the New.

Matthew begins his Gospel with the genealogy of Jesus. He does this for three reasons. First, to focus on the identity of Jesus by showing that He belongs to the people of Israel as *Son of David* and *Son of Abraham*. Second, he wishes to stress the special status of Jesus as the awaited Davidic Messiah. Third, Matthew desires to present Jesus as the summit and synthesis of history. This genealogy shows how God works in the history or economy of salvation. Matthew presents the virginal conception and Birth under the scheme of prophecy-fulfilment:

> 'Joseph son of David, do not be afraid to take Mary home as your wife, because she has conceived what is in her by the Holy Spirit. She will give birth to a Son and you must name Him Jesus, because He is the one who is to save His people from their sins.' Now all this took place to fulfil what the Lord had spoken through the prophet: Look! the virgin is with child and will give birth to a son whom they will call Immanuel, a name which means 'God-is-with-us' (Mt 1:20–23).

In Matthew 1:25, it is stated that Joseph had not had marital relations with Mary when she gave birth to a Son, and named Him Jesus. Some English translations are closer to the Greek, saying that Joseph 'knew her not until she had borne a son; and he called His name Jesus.' The word 'until', in biblical language, negates an action in the past, but does not imply that it will occur in the future.[6] This indicates that Matthew is concerned to emphasize that St Joseph had no part in the conception of Jesus.

In the episodes of the Magi and of the flight into Egypt, St Matthew repeatedly asserts that Christ is the Child of Mary and not of Joseph, and represents Joseph as simply the guardian and protector of them both. In the example of the adoration of the Magi, we read: 'and going into the house they saw the Child with His mother Mary, and falling to their knees they did Him homage. Then, opening their treasures, they offered Him gifts of gold and frankincense and myrrh' (Mt 2:11). Later, we find that an angel appeared to St Joseph: 'After they had left, suddenly the angel of the Lord appeared to Joseph in a dream and said, "Get up, take the Child and His mother with you, and escape into Egypt, and stay there until I tell you, because Herod intends to search for the Child and do away with Him."' (Mt 2:13). St Joseph's response was that he 'got up and, taking the Child and His mother with him, left that night for Egypt' (Mt 2:14). Later again, an angel encourages St Joseph to return from Egypt: 'Get up, take the Child and His mother with you and go back to the land of Israel, for those who wanted to kill the Child are dead' (Mt 2:20). It is noteworthy that in all these passages the angel who addresses Joseph concerning Our Lord, never refers to Him as 'your child.' According to Matthew, Mary is not only the 'Mother of God' but also 'the Virgin' who conceives in an extraordinary manner. While the legal adoptive paternity of St Joseph ensures Jesus' Davidic descent, the virginity of Mary guarantees His divine origin. Her virginity, therefore, has a Christological function as it reveals Christ's true identity.

In St Matthew's Gospel, several passages deal with Jesus' relationship with His family, and by that token also with His Mother. However, these texts stress above all the intimate relationship with His new and larger family constituted by His disciples, with ecclesiological connotations. These passages adopt a specific Semitic structure which appears to deny one reality in order to emphasize another one:

> He was still speaking to the crowds when suddenly His mother and His brothers were standing outside and were anxious to have a word with him. But to the man who told Him this Jesus replied, 'Who is my mother? Who are my brothers?' And stretching out His hand towards His disciples He said, 'Here are my mother and my brothers. Anyone who does the will of my Father in heaven is my brother and sister and mother' (Mt 12: 46–50).

This passage does not therefore deny in any way that Jesus Christ is the only Son of Mary the Virgin, but rather seeks to extend His human family in an ecclesiological and eschatological sense, as is seen fulfilled when Jesus entrusts His Mother to John at the Crucifixion.

In the following chapter of St Matthew's Gospel, there is a passage which has often been discussed in relation to Mary's virginity:

> When Jesus had finished these parables He left the district; and, coming to His home town, He taught the people in the synagogue in such a way that they were astonished and said, 'Where did the man get this wisdom and these miraculous powers? This is the carpenter's son, surely? Is not His mother the woman called Mary, and His brothers James and Joseph and Simon and Jude? His sisters, too, are they not all here with us? So where did the man get it all?' And they would not accept Him. But Jesus said to them, 'A prophet is despised only in his own country and in his own house,' and He did not work many miracles there because of their lack of faith (Mt 13:53–58).

The text names the following as 'brothers' of Jesus: James, Joseph, Simon and Jude.[7] However, Matthew 27:56 indicates that Mary, the mother of James and Joseph, was at the foot of the Cross. On the other hand, Mark 15:40 states that Mary the mother of James the younger and Joset was there. So, although the proof is not conclusive, it seems that (unless we propose these were others with the same names), the first two, James and Joseph (Joset) had a mother other than the Mother of Jesus. Therefore, the term 'brother' was employed for those who were not sons of Mary the Mother of Jesus. So the same use of language could easily have been applied with the other two, Simon and Jude. Further, if Mary had given birth to other natural sons and daughters too by the time of the Cross, it would be strange for Jesus to ask John to take care of her, rather than one of His hypothetical blood brothers. In particular, according to St Paul's Letter to the Galatians (Ga 1:19), James the 'brother of the Lord' was alive in AD 49. He should have taken care of Mary, if he were her son. This usage of the expression 'brother' or 'sister' to denote a close relative, who is not a brother or sister according to modern terminology, is common in ancient Semitic culture, as can be seen in the Old Testament. One example is Lot, who although the nephew of Abraham (cf. Gn 11:27–31) is called his brother (Gn 13:8 and 14:14–16). The Hebrew and Aramaic expression 'ah' was adopted for various types of relations.[8] Hebrew had no word for cousin. The people of Israel could say 'ben-dod' which means son of a paternal uncle, but for other kinds of cousins they would need a complex phrase, such as 'the son of the brother of his mother' or, 'the son of the sister of his mother.'[9]

THE GOSPEL ACCORDING TO LUKE AND ACTS

Luke adopts the scheme 'promise-fulfilment' in his Gospel and presents Mary as part of the culmination of the economy of salvation. For Luke, John the Baptist fulfils the time of preparation and Jesus inaugurates the eschatological era.

The Annunciation in Luke 1:26–38 is one of the key Mariological high points of the New Testament, and has been much represented in art and literature.[10] Four different schemes of interpretation can be proposed for the wonder of the Annunciation. First, the consideration of a miraculous birth scheme. The Annunciation shares the same structure as the other miraculous birth scenes in the Old and New Testaments (Gn 18:1–15; Jg 13:3–22; Lk 1:5–25). The scheme runs in this fashion: apparition – perturbation – message – obedience – sign. The miraculous birth is brought about by the creative action of the Holy Spirit. The second scheme is that of vocation or calling. There are similarities between Mary's calling and that of Gideon (Jg 6:11–24). The structure of this scheme runs as follows: angel's greeting – doubt or perturbation – first message – difficulty – second message – sign – consent. Mary answers a divine call. A third possible scheme is that of apocalyptic whereby everything starts from God above, leading to a new beginning. Finally, the Covenant scheme is also helpful in illustrating the Annunciation. This scheme consists of a discourse concerning a mediator and an answer from the people. By proclaiming herself as the Lord's servant, Mary enters into the work of salvation with total availability. Her 'fiat' is a positive and immediate cooperation in the redemptive Incarnation. Without this, the Incarnation would not have taken place.

The salutation of the angel to Mary ('Rejoice, you who enjoy God's favour! The Lord is with you' Lk 1:28), recalls the expressions used of the Daughter of Sion in the Old Testament, who rejoices because the time of the Messiah is near. The angel Gabriel, addressing the Virgin of Nazareth uses the greeting *chaire* (Rejoice in Greek) and then calls her *kecharitomene* (full of grace). The words of the Greek text, *chaire* and *kecharitomene*, are essentially interconnected: Mary is invited to rejoice primarily because God loves her and has filled her with grace in view of her divine Motherhood.[11] This fullness of grace indicates a condition or state of being, a gift signifying divine favour. It implies a divine choice or election in relation to the Covenant. The expressions 'Full of grace' and 'you who enjoy God's favour' are renderings of the Greek word *kecharitomene*, which is a passive participle. The verb utilized here by Luke (*charitoun*) is very rare in Greek. It is present only twice in the New Testament: in the text of Luke on the Annunciation (Lk 1:28) 'kecharitomene', and in the Epistle to the Ephesians (Ep 1:6) 'echaritosen.' These verbs convey the idea of a change of something in the person or the thing affected. Thus, since the root of the verb 'charitoo' is 'charis' or grace, the idea which is expressed is that of a change brought about by grace. In addition the verb used by Luke is in the past participial form. 'Kecharitomene' signifies then, in the person to whom the verb relates, that is, Mary, that the action of the grace of God has already brought about a change. It does not tell us how that came about. What is essential here is the affirmation that Mary has been transformed by the grace of God. The perfect passive participle is used by Luke to indicate that the transformation by grace has already taken place in Mary, well before the moment of the Annunciation.

In what then would this transformation of grace consist? According to the text of the Letter to the Ephesians, Christians have been transformed by grace in the sense that according to the richness of His grace, they find redemption by His blood, the remission of sins (cf. Ep 1:7). This grace, in reality, takes away sin. This sheds light on the case of Mary, who has been sanctified by the grace of God. Mary has been transformed by the grace of God in view of the task which she awaits, that of becoming the Mother of the Son of God, while remaining a virgin. There is a double announcement from the angel: Mary as Mother brings to the world the Son of the Most High (v. 33), but that will take place by the 'power of the Most High' (v. 35), that is virginally. God had prepared Mary for this by inspiring in her the desire for virginity.[12]

Therefore to convey even more exactly the nuance of the Greek word, one should not say merely 'full of grace', but 'made full of grace', or even 'filled with grace', which would clearly indicate that this was a gift given by God to the Blessed Virgin. This term, in the form of a perfect participle, enhances the image of a perfect and lasting grace which implies fullness. The same verb, in the sense of 'to bestow grace', is used in St Paul's Letter to the Ephesians to indicate the abundance of grace granted to us by the Father in His beloved Son (Ep 1:6), and which Mary receives as the first fruits of the Redemption.[13] The greeting 'the Lord is with you' used by the angel is customary in the context of accounts of callings in the Bible, and highlights Mary's special vocation in God's new Covenant. The angel's invitation 'Mary, do not be afraid; you have won God's favour', provides reassurance that God is acting. It stresses that Mary is the recipient of a unique favour and privilege in the history of salvation, namely to give birth to the Son of God. The Annunciation shows that God chooses the humble. The words of the angel, 'You are to conceive in your womb and bear a son, and you must name Him Jesus' reflect the structure of the words of the promise in the book of Isaiah: 'the young woman is with child and will give birth to a son whom she will call Immanuel' (Is 7:14). Thus the prophetic promise and its fulfilment are intimately linked. Moreover, the expression of the angel to Mary, 'He will be great and will be called Son of the Most High' re-echo the prophecy of Nathan to David regarding the Davidic dynastic, and thus the phrase emphasizes the fulfilment of the Messianic prophecy. Mary's words of concern, 'But how can this come about, since I have no knowledge of man?' bear various possible interpretations. The most probable opinion is that she had made a vow of virginity, because when she received the angel's greeting she was already betrothed to Joseph, and therefore, in the ordinary course of events, would be expecting to conceive with him, unless she had already made a vow.[14]

The Annunciation parallels certain biblical accounts that relate the communication of an extraordinary birth to a childless woman. Those cases concerned married women who were naturally sterile, to whom God gave the gift of a child through their typical conjugal life (1 S 1:19–20), in response to their anguished prayers (cf. Gn 15:2, 30:22–23, 1 S 1:10; Lk 1:13). Mary receives the angel's message in a different situation. She is not a married woman with problems of sterility; by a voluntary choice she intends to remain a virgin. Therefore her intention of virginity, the fruit of her love for the Lord, appears to be an obstacle to the motherhood announced to her. At first sight, Mary's words would seem merely to express only her present state of virginity: Mary would affirm that she does not 'know' man, that is, that she is a virgin. Nevertheless, the context in which the question is asked: 'How can this come about?', and the affirmation that follows: 'since I have no knowledge of man', emphasize both Mary's present virginity and her intention to remain a virgin. The expression she uses, with the verb in the present tense, reveals the permanence and continuity of her state.[15]

The angel answered: 'The Holy Spirit will come upon you, and the power of the Most High will cover you with its shadow. And so the child will be holy and will be called Son of God' (Lk 1:35). The expression which the angel used is characteristic of a consecration of the temple. Mary's response is one of totally free adherence as consecration to God's will: 'Behold the handmaid of the Lord; be it done to me according to your word' (Lk 1:38).

The Magnificat

The Visitation is rich in both Christological and Mariological perspectives. It follows the same structure as the narration of the transportation of the ark to Jerusalem (2 S 6:2–15). Both take place in the region of Judah and involve expressions of joy and acclamation. Blessings are received, religious fear is present and a period of three months is significant.[16] Through these parallelisms, Luke expressed the truth that Mary, the Mother of the Lord is

God's dwelling place and the Ark of the New Covenant, bringing the old one to fulfilment and perfection. Also, Elizabeth's exclamation 'Most blessed are you among women, and blessed is the fruit of your womb' can be compared with two other significant passages, both from the Old Testament. The first is the blessing of Abram by Melchizedek: 'Blessed be Abram by God Most High, Creator of heaven and earth. And blessed be God Most High for putting your enemies into your clutches.' (Gn 14:19). The second passage reports the blessing imparted by Uzziah upon Judith: 'May you be blessed, my daughter, by God Most High, beyond all women on earth; and blessed be the Lord God, Creator of heaven and earth, who guided you to cut off the head of the leader of our enemies!' (Jdt 13:18). These parallels highlight the fact that the blessings imparted by God to Abram, to Judith and to Mary form part of an economy of salvation, in which the person who is blessed is to be a mediator of God's loving kindness. However, in the case of Mary, there is something greater: Mary and her Son Jesus are together united in being blessed, which joins them in the culmination of God's economy.

Mary's greeting to Elizabeth causes John, filled with the Holy Spirit, to leap with joy. Elizabeth recognizes who Mary is and greets her with three titles: Most blessed among women, the mother of my Lord, and 'blessed is she who believed'. Mary responds with a special song of thanksgiving. This Canticle, known as the *Magnificat* (Latin) or *Megalynei* (Byzantine), is the song both of the Mother of God and of the Church; the song of the Daughter of Sion and of the new People of God; the song of thanksgiving for the fullness of graces poured out in the economy of salvation and the song of the 'poor' or 'little ones' (*anawim*) whose hope is met by the fulfilment of the promises made to our ancestors, to Abraham and to his posterity for ever.[17]

Mary's Song of thanksgiving closely parallels the Song of Hannah, Samuel's mother, in 1 Samuel 2: 1–10, with some very specific similarity in detail. For example, Hannah proclaims: 'My heart exults in Yahweh, in my God is my strength lifted up' (1 S 2:1). This is very similar to Mary's formulation: 'my spirit rejoices in God my Saviour ... He has routed the arrogant of heart' (Lk 1: 47, 51). Hannah portrays herself three times as the Lord's 'servant' (1 S 1:11, 16), which Mary does twice (Lk 1:38, 48). The mother of Samuel proclaims: 'Yahweh makes poor and rich, He humbles and also exalts. He raises the poor from the dust, He lifts the needy from the dunghill to give them a place with princes, to assign them a seat of honour' (1 S 2: 7–8). Mary exclaims: 'He has used the power of His arm, He has routed the arrogant of heart. He has pulled down princes from their thrones and raised high the lowly. He has filled the starving with good things, sent the rich away empty' (Lk 1: 51–53). Furthermore, the relation between Mary and Hannah continues from the Magnificat into Luke's second chapter. Hannah took her child, Samuel, into the temple of the Lord at Shiloh (1 S 1: 24). Similarly, Mary presents her Child, Jesus, to the Lord in the temple in Jerusalem (Lk 2: 22, 27).

The Magnificat contains, in a sense, the most ancient Mariology. The first part refers to God's action in Mary and the second to God's action in human history. She praises God for having looked upon the lowliness of His servant. This refers to the spiritual attitude of the poor of Yahweh. The praise of Mary is based on both her humility and the great things the Almighty has done for her. The proclamation, 'The Mighty One has done great things for me, and holy is His name' contains the expression 'great things' (*megala* in Greek) which is a technical term signifying all the magnificent actions the Lord has carried out for His people throughout the history of His chosen people, culminating in the coming of Christ through Mary. However, these great things can also include the wonders worked by God in His Church, right from the early moments of its life.

The Presentation of the Lord

When Our Lady fulfilled the demands of the Mosaic Law and presented Jesus in the Temple, Simeon proclaimed: 'Now, Master, You are letting your servant go in peace as You promised; for my eyes have seen the salvation which You have made ready in the sight of the nations; a light of revelation for the gentiles and glory for your people Israel' (Lk 2:29–32). Simeon also said to Mary His mother, 'Look, He is destined for the fall and for the rise of many in Israel, destined to be a sign that is opposed – and a sword will pierce your soul too – so that the secret thoughts of many may be laid bare' (Lk 2:34–35). Simeon's hymn reveals the universality of the redemption. Simeon also announces a prophecy with regard to Mary which complements the angel's message. The 'sword' has been interpreted variously the challenge to Mary's faith when faced with the scandal of the cross; the word of God which penetrates the soul; Jesus' passion which will have its impact upon Mary's soul and make her an intimate sharer in it, to the point of earning the palms of martyrdom at the foot of the Cross; the opposition against Jesus which Mary shares.[18]

The Finding in the Temple

In a sense, the 'sword' is already present, as a stimulus to a growth in faith for Our Lady, when Jesus goes to Jerusalem for the feast of the Passover, when He was twelve years old. Jesus stayed behind in Jerusalem without His parents knowing it. Three days later, they found Him in the Temple, sitting among the teachers, listening to them, and asking them questions; and all those who heard Him were astounded at His intelligence and His replies. It is certainly no accident that Mary and Joseph found Him three days later, because this episode foreshadows the Death of Christ and His Resurrection on the third day. When Jesus is lost to Mary and Joseph, this prefigures His death, and when He is found, it foreshadows His Resurrection. 'They were overcome when they saw Him, and His mother said to Him, "My child, why have you done this to us? See how worried your father and I have been, looking for you." He replied, "Why were you looking for me? Did you not know that I must be in my Father's house?" But they did not understand what He meant' (Lk 2:48–50). This moment marks a growth in faith for Mary and maybe also a sense of the sorrow, as well as the joy, which lie in the future.

During the ministry of Jesus, He makes an affirmation which does not undermine the importance of Mary's blood relationship to Him, but rather extends it. 'It happened that as He was speaking, a woman in the crowd raised her voice and said, "Blessed the womb that bore you and the breasts that fed you!" But He replied, "More blessed still are those who hear the word of God and keep it!"' (Lk 11:27–28). This passage highlights the fact that Mary is the first hearer and keeper of the Word of God, she has carried the eternal Word in her womb and kept Him, and she is also Christ's first and foremost disciple.[19]

Mary and the early Christian Community

St Luke also recounts, in his Acts of the Apostles, that with one heart all the Apostles 'joined constantly in prayer, together with some women, including Mary the mother of Jesus, and with his brothers' (Ac 1:14). This passage shows that Mary enjoyed a special place in the Jewish-Christian community of Palestine due to her union with Christ as Mother. Moreover, she is part of the community and prays, believes and practices the faith with the others. She forms part of the new people of God which receives the Spirit and proclaims the risen Christ. Mary is called to enter into the divine plan with a special mission of her own. She responds to God's calling with exemplary faith, which is a most important aspect of her spiritual life.

Mary in the writings of St John

There is a well-known passage of Origen on the presence of Mary and John on Calvary: 'The Gospels are the first fruits of all Scripture and the Gospel of John is the first of the Gospels: no one can grasp its meaning without having leaned his head on Jesus' breast and having received Mary as Mother from Jesus.'[20] It is most probable that in the years which Mary spent with St John in the house traditionally held to be at Ephesus, Our Lady would have shared with the beloved disciple many of her most profound insights regarding Jesus Christ her Son. In the quiet and humble way that characterized Mary's life on earth, therefore, John's Gospel should be regarded also as a profoundly Marian Gospel. One of the keys to understand St John's Gospel is the use of the expression 'woman', by which Jesus addresses His Mother. Far from being a way of distancing Himself from His blessed Mother, the expression is a term of intimacy, great respect and love all at the same time. 'Here,' writes de la Potterie, 'the Old Testament texts of the "Daughter of Zion" are applied to a definite woman ... This is precisely the reason why, in the Fourth Gospel, both at Cana and at the Cross, Jesus addresses Mary calling her Woman.'[21] In this context, the relation between the Wedding Feast at Cana, Mary at the foot of the Cross and the Woman of the Apocalypse is of capital importance.

As regards, the wedding at Cana in Galilee, it is highly significant that it takes place on the third day, like the Resurrection. There are links between this passage and the texts dealing with the establishment of the Covenant at Sinai (Ex 19:3–8; 24:3.7). Using the scheme of the Covenant, John shows that Cana is the new Sinai. Jesus takes Yahweh's place and Mary that of Moses. In the Old

Testament, the chosen people were often represented by the figure of a woman. The wedding is thus inscribed in a series of theophanic mysteries, which reveal the divinity of Christ and His economy of salvation, of whom the key player next to Christ is His blessed Mother (Jn 2:1–11). The key figures are therefore Christ and His Mother, rather than the couple who had just married. The enormous quantity of wine which Jesus offered, changed from the water in the six stone water jars, each holding twenty or thirty gallons, indicates the divine generosity. The fact that the best wine was kept till last indicates the fulfilment of God's economy in the New Covenant, in which Mary plays a singular part. It is curious also that the servants are not referred to as *douloi*, but *diakonoi*, indicating a liturgical role, rather than a merely functional one. This is all the more interesting given the fact that this miracle also prefigures the far greater wonder in which wine will be changed into His Precious Blood. The miracle of the multiplication of the loaves (Jn 6:1–13) is also a New Testament prefiguration of the Eucharist.[22] At the wedding feast at Cana, water is changed into wine; at the Last Supper, in which wine is changed into Christ's Blood, we have a kind of wedding feast in which the marriage of Christ to His Church is celebrated. This is supported by Christ's own words at the Last Supper 'From now on, I tell you, I shall not drink wine until the day I drink the new wine with you in the kingdom of my Father' (Mt 26:29). Jesus' words indicate that the Eucharist is a participation in the definitive Wedding Feast of the Lamb.

Closely linked with the miracle of Cana is the scene of Mary standing at the foot of Christ's Cross. 'Near the cross of Jesus stood His mother and His mother's sister, Mary the wife of Clopas, and Mary of Magdala. Seeing His mother and the disciple whom He loved standing near her, Jesus said to His mother, "Woman, this is your son." Then to the disciple He said, "This is your mother." And from that hour the disciple took her into his home' (Jn 19:25–27). This scene is linked to Cana. Both use the term 'woman' and talk about Jesus' 'hour'. Mary becomes the mother of the beloved disciple. She has a role to fulfil in the history of salvation as mother of Jesus' disciples. Mary is the Daughter of Sion, who generates a messianic people. The standing at the foot of the Cross is not merely physical, but also in the context of St John's Gospel refers to the co-operation of Mary in Christ's work of Redemption.[23] The parallelism 'this is your son' and 'this is your mother' highlights the fact that here we are witnessing not only an historical fact, but a spiritual motherhood of Mary within the Church.[24]

Finally, the two passages just considered are linked with a third Mariological passage in St John's Apocalypse. The expression *woman*[25] as found in the Wedding at Cana and as addressed by Jesus to Mary at the Foot of the Cross, is also employed in chapter twelve of the book of Revelation, and sheds light on the Mariological import of that chapter. The book of Revelation never mentions Mary by name, and does not speak explicitly of her. The perspective offered is essentially ecclesiological; however the figure of the *Woman* in chapter twelve, although a personification of the new people of God, cannot be adequately explained unless full account be taken of the historical role of the Mother of Jesus.[26] 'Now a great sign appeared in heaven: a woman, robed with the sun, standing on the moon, and on her head a crown of twelve stars. She was pregnant, and in labour, crying aloud in the pangs of childbirth' (Rv 12:1–2). The Woman represents first of all the messianic people who become the Church. However, she also represents Mary, the mother of Jesus and figure of the Church. In Mary, the maternal function of the New Testament community is inaugurated. The figure of the woman is symbolic, but in a polyvalent sense, referring to both Mariological and ecclesiological realities. It would therefore be incorrect to detach this symbol from its concrete historical point of reference, namely Mary. Therefore it is completely one-sided and incomplete to stress solely the ecclesiological interpretation of this passage from the Book of the Apocalypse at the expense of the Mariological one. In St John's writings, Mary is progressively Mother of Jesus, the woman at the service of the faith of the Apostles, and finally mother of the beloved disciple, and Mother in turn of all those 'who obey God's commandments and have in themselves the witness of Jesus' (Rv 12:17). It is most likely that St John would have therefore based his ecclesiological symbolism on a Mariological foundation.

One difficulty which could be raised is how the Woman in Revelation could refer to Mary if she suffered the pains of childbirth. This difficulty can be eliminated by the following consideration. In Revelation 5:6, Christ appears in heaven in the form of an *immolated* lamb (cf. Jn 19:36). The sufferings of the woman who also appears in heaven (Rv 12:2), stands in relation to the *immolation* of the celestial Lamb (Rv 12:11). Thus, in the twelfth chapter of Apocalypse, the reference is not to the childbirth at Bethlehem, but to the birth pangs of the Redemption, echoed in the words of Christ upon the Cross: 'Son, behold your Mother' (Jn 19:27). Thus, here John is speaking about a different type of suffering, which is also found in other parts of the New Testament. For example, addressing the Galatians, Paul went through the pain of giving birth until Christ was formed within his readers (see Ga 4:19). Also, the Letter to the Romans states: 'We are well aware that the whole creation, until this time, has been groaning in labour pains' (Rm 8:22). What is being described is the spiritual motherhood of Mary and the compassion with which the Mother of Jesus shares in the sufferings of the immolated Lamb. The woman of the Crucifixion and the woman of the Apocalypse are closely tied together. In each passage, Mary's motherhood *in relation to the disciples* entails a context of suffering.[27]

The writings of St Paul

Paul's writings present God's great economy of salvation, in which He offers to all, Jews and Gentiles alike, the gift of eternal life, in Jesus who has died and is risen from the dead. The Christian participates in this gift of salvation, by being united to Christ by faith, dying in Him to sin, and sharing in the power of His Resurrection. This salvation is still being completed in His Body the Church, until He comes again in glory (see Col 1:24). Paul presents Christ's death and resurrection as a expiatory sacrifice, bringing the Jewish sacrifices to fulfilment (Rm 3:24–25; 1 Co 15:3; 2 Co 5:21). Christians participate in this mystery through baptism and the Eucharist. In this context, one finds the only reference to Mary given by Paul but it is very important because of its antiquity and its relation to the history of salvation. Even if the person of Mary remains anonymous, her function is indispensable for the kenotic and salvific Incarnation of the Son of God: 'When the completion of the time came, God sent His Son, born of a woman, born a subject of the Law, to redeem the subjects of the Law, so that we could receive adoption as sons' (Ga 4:4–5). In this only direct reference to Mary, Paul refers to her as 'woman'. Thus, Mary is again referred to as 'woman', even outside a Johannine context. This phraseology of 'a woman' being tied to Mary has evidently been passed on to Paul, who hands it on to his readers. Here he indicates implicitly the fact of the virginal conception of Jesus. This is highlighted by the expression 'born of a woman' in a Semitic society where the usual expression would be 'born of Jesse' or whoever the father was. Pointing to Jesus as born of a 'woman' instead of a man indicates the uniqueness of the Virginal Conception and therefore of the Incarnation.

Conclusions

Although the citations in Scripture referring to Mary may seem be few in number, they are nevertheless of great importance. Passages which at first seem rather terse convey a rich tradition. What is important is not the quantity but the quality and depth of the texts. This richness may not be apparent upon a cursory and superficial reading, but becomes clear through a profound analysis which reveals that Mary is present and plays an important part in all the decisive moments of the history of salvation.

Scripture presents a series of harmonic images of Mary. There is perhaps a development in the portrayal of Mary in the New Testament. First, an historical presentation of Mary features in Matthew and Luke, which speak of her fullness of grace, her virginal maternity and her relationship with Jesus as a disciple. John proposes a mature theological reflection on Mary in which she recognizes the messianic transcendence of her Son and receives from Him her maternal mission. Scripture always presents Mary in union to the mystery of Christ. The history of salvation is the context of this presentation in all its stages. Mary appears in the prophecies and prefigurations in the Old Testament, and is then united with Christ in the mysteries of His infancy. She is present at the beginning of the public ministry of her Son. She participates in the Paschal mystery and is attendant at the beginning of the Church. Mary cannot be separated from this economy of salvation and this economy cannot be understood apart from Mary. It will now be our task to begin examining Mary's role in the economy of salvation, beginning with her fullness of grace.

Notes

[1]   I. de la Potterie, *Mary in the Mystery of the Covenant* (New York: Alba House, 1992), p. 262.

2   These ideas are taken up again later. The collaboration of Mary with Christ's act of Redemption and then with the distribution of the effects of this act is dealt with in chapter 7, pp. 187–201 and chapter 9, pp. 254–266 below respectively.

3   For the convenience of the reader we set out the three passages here.
1) 'He went home again, and once more such a crowd collected that they could not even have a meal. When his relations heard of this, they set out to take charge of Him; they said, "He is out of his mind"' (Mk 3:20–21).
2) 'Now His mother and his brothers arrived and, standing outside, sent in a message asking for Him. A crowd was sitting round him at the time the message was passed to Him, "Look, your mother and brothers and sisters are outside asking for you." He replied, "Who are my mother and my brothers?" And looking at those sitting in a circle round Him, He said, "Here are my mother and my brothers. Anyone who does the will of God, that person is my brother and sister and mother"' (Mk 3:31–35).
3) 'Leaving that district, He went to his home town, and His disciples accompanied Him. With the coming of the Sabbath He began teaching in the synagogue, and most of them were astonished when they heard Him. They said, "Where did the man get all of this? What is this wisdom that has been granted Him, and these miracles that are worked through Him? This is the carpenter, surely, the son of Mary, the brother of James and Joset and Jude and Simon? His sisters, too, are they not here with us?" And they would not accept Him. And Jesus said to them, "A prophet is despised only in his own country, among his own relations and in his own house"; and He could work no miracle there, except that He cured a few sick people by laying His hands on them. He was amazed at their lack of faith' (Mk 6:1–6).

4   See R. Laurentin, *La Vergine Maria* (Rome: Edizioni Paoline, [3]1983), p. 22, note 4.

5   We will discuss this question in greater detail in the context of the Virginity of Mary. See pp. 159–166 below.

6   The Greek expression is ἕως. To confirm this usage see Ps 110:1 and 2 S 6:23.

7   The manuscripts vary on the spelling of at least one of these, namely Joseph, who in Mark 6:3 is put as Joset: '"This is the carpenter, surely, the son of Mary, the brother of James and Joset and Jude and Simon? His sisters, too, are they not here with us?" And they would not accept him.'

8   Cf. M. Sokoloff, *A Dictionary of Jewish Palestinian Aramaic of the Byzantine period* (Ramat-Gan, Israel: Bar Ilan University Press, 1990), p. 45.

9   See *ibid.*, pp. 111 and 139.

[10]   Among the famous artists who have painted the Annunciation are Leonardo da Vinci, Carolo Crivelli, Fra Angelico and Sandro Botticelli. Paul Claudel wrote *L'annonce faite a Marie* (Paris: Gallimard, 1950). The passage in question runs: 'In the sixth month the angel Gabriel was sent by God to a town in Galilee called Nazareth, to a virgin betrothed to a man named Joseph, of the House of David; and the virgin's name was Mary. He went in and said to her, "Rejoice, you who enjoy God's favour! The Lord is with you." She was deeply disturbed by these words and asked herself what this greeting could mean, but the angel said to her, "Mary, do not be afraid; you have won God's favour. Look! You are to conceive in your womb and bear a son, and you must name Him Jesus. He will be great and will be called Son of the Most High. The Lord God will give Him the throne of his ancestor David; He will rule over the House of Jacob for ever and His reign will have no end." Mary said to the angel, "But how can this come about, since I have no knowledge of man?" The angel answered, "The Holy Spirit will come upon you, and the power of the Most High will cover you with its shadow. And so the child will be holy and will be called the Son of God. And I tell you this too: your cousin Elizabeth also, in her old age, has conceived a son, and she whom people called barren is now in her sixth month, for nothing is impossible to God." Mary said, "You see before you the Lord's servant, let it happen to me as you have said." And the angel left her' (Lk 1:38).

[11]   See Pope John Paul II, *Discourse at General Audience* (8 January 1986), 1. See chapter 4, pp. 73–74 and chapter 5, pp. 107, 123–125 below.

[12]   See I. de la Potterie, *Mary in the Mystery of the Covenant* (New York: Alba House, 1992), pp. 17–20.

[13]   See Pope John Paul II, *Discourse at General Audience* (8 January 1986), 2.

[14]   See St Augustine, *De sancta virginitate*, I, 4, in *PL* 40, 398: 'Her virginity also itself was on this account more pleasing and accepted, since it was not that Christ by being conceived in her, rescued it beforehand from a husband who would violate it, preserving it Himself; but, before He was conceived, chose it, already dedicated to God, as that from which to be born. This is shown by the words which Mary spoke in answer to the Angel announcing her conception. She said: "But how can this come about, since I have no knowledge of man?" Which assuredly she would not say, unless she had before vowed herself unto God as a virgin. But, because the habits of the Israelites as yet refused this, she was espoused to a just man, who would not take from her by violence, but rather guard against violent persons, what she had already vowed.' See also p. 145 below.

[15] See Pope John Paul II, *Discourse at General Audience* (24 July 1996), 1.

[16] See chapter 2, pp. 30–31 above, where these parallels were dealt with in detail.

[17] See *CCC* 2619.

[18] See P. Benoit, 'Et toi-même, un glaive te transpercera l'âme' in *Catholic Biblical Quarterly* 25 (1963), pp. 251–261.

[19] The various aspects of Mary's discipleship will be developed in chapter 7 below.

[20] Origen, *Commentary on St John's Gospel* I, 6 in *PG* 14, 31. See St Ambrose, *Exposition on the Gospel according to St Luke*, X, 129–131 in *CSEL* 32/4, 504f.

[21] I. de la Potterie, *Mary in the Mystery of the Covenant* (New York: Alba House, 1992), p. 48.

[22] See P. Haffner, *The Sacramental Mystery* (Leominster: Gracewing, 1999), p. 77.

[23] This theme will be treated in more detail in chapter 7, pp. 187–201 below.

[24] The theme of the spiritual motherhood of Mary within the Church will be dealt with in chapter 9 below.

[25] In Greek the expression used is γυνή.

[26] A. Valentini, 'Il grande segno di Apocalisse 12. Una Chiesa ad immagine della Madre di Gesù' in *Marianum* 59 (1997), p. 62.

[27] See Jn 19:25 and Rv 12:2 and also S. Manelli, *All Generations Shall Call Me Blessed* (New Bedford, Mass. Academy of the Immaculate, 1995), pp. 359–360.

CHAPTER 4

FULL OF GRACE

Mother! whose virgin bosom was uncrost
With the least shade of thought to sin allied.
Woman! above all women glorified,
Our tainted nature's solitary boast;
Purer than foam on central ocean tost;
Brighter than eastern skies at daybreak strewn
With fancied roses, than the unblemished moon
Before her wane begins on heaven's blue coast;
Thy image falls to earth. Yet some, I ween,
Not unforgiven the suppliant knee might bend,
As to a visible Power, in which did blend
All that was mixed and reconciled in thee
Of mother's love with maiden purity,
Of high with low, celestial with terrene!
William Wordsworth, 'The Virgin'

The early centuries

The angel Gabriel greeted Mary with the words 'Rejoice, you who enjoy God's favour!' (Lk 1:28), in Greek *'chaire kecharitomene'*. Just as Mary pondered the meaning of this greeting (Lk 1:29), so also the Church has deepened her understanding of Mary's fullness of grace. It has already been seen that Luke presents this greeting with an alliterative play on words. The same basic root (*charis* or 'grace') is present in both the expression for 'Rejoice' and also 'you who enjoy God's favour', in order to highlight the special nature of God's gift of grace to Mary.[1] Moreover, the past perfect participial form of the verb, *'charitoo'* present in *kecharitomene*, is causative, indicating a change or transformation in the recipient, prior to the grace of maternity. Thus, foreseen from all eternity, God had prepared Mary to be the mother of Jesus Christ in the plenitude of grace, a 'grace upon grace' (Jn 1:16). In St Paul's Letter to the Ephesians 1:3–8, we find the second and only other occurrence in the New Testament of the transformative meaning of the verb *charitoo* (Ep 1:6), as the grace which makes us 'holy and faultless.' The idea that God 'chose us in Christ before the world was made to be holy and faultless before him in love, marking us out for himself beforehand, to be adopted sons, through Jesus Christ' (Ep 1:4–5) can be applied to the mystery of the preparation of Mary to be the Mother of God. In the angel's greeting the expression 'full of grace' serves almost as a name: it is Mary's name in the eyes of God. In Semitic usage, a name expresses the reality of the persons to which it refers. As a result, the title 'full of grace' expresses the deepest dimension of the personality of the young woman of Nazareth as fashioned by grace and as the object of divine favour.[2]

During the early centuries, there was an increasing awareness and understanding of Mary's holiness. Many reflected on the meaning of the biblical expression 'full of grace.'[3] The Fathers of the Church first focused on the Christological faith of the Church and, in relation to this, they went on to deal with the holiness of Christ's Mother. The theological concerns of this early Patristic period were different from those of later development, but nevertheless, the doctrine concerning Mary's holiness was already present in a form which required further elaboration. In Eastern Christendom, the awareness that Mary was the first to fully participate in the grace of Christ's Paschal Mystery was expressed in the Greek word *Panagía*, meaning 'the All-Holy One'. It seems that the first Father to use this expression was the Alexandrian thinker Origen, as he commented on the angel's greeting to Mary: 'This greeting is reserved only to Mary. Because, if she had known that such a greeting had been addressed to others (she was well-versed in the Law, and was All-Holy, and had meditated on the prophecies), it would not have startled her as a special greeting.'[4]

Early Christian belief always associated Mary with Jesus in the divine plan. The Patristic writers of East and West referred to Mary as the 'new Eve,' who co-operated with Christ, the 'new Adam'. The Fathers expressed the holiness of Mary by seeing her as the New Eve. Mary, the New Eve, like the New Adam, was conceived immaculate, just as the first Adam and Eve were created immaculate. The Fathers contrasted the disobedience of the first Eve with the obedience offered by Mary, the second Eve. Because she is the New Eve, she shares the fate of the New Adam. Whereas the first Adam and Eve died and returned to dust, the New Adam and Eve were lifted up physically into heaven.

In the writings of Justin the Martyr (AD 165), we find the earliest illustration of Mary as the new Eve:

> [Jesus] became man by the Virgin so that the disobedience caused by the serpent might be destroyed in the same way it had begun. Eve, a virgin and undefiled, conceived the word of the serpent and bore disobedience and death. But the Virgin Mary received faith and joy when the angel Gabriel announced to her the glad tidings that the Spirit of the Lord would come upon her and the power of the Most High would overshadow her, for which reason the Holy One being born of her is the Son of God. And she replied 'Be it done unto me according to your word.'[5]

Tertullian developed this theme also slightly later, around the year 200:

> And again, lest I depart from my argumentation on the name of Adam: Why is Christ called Adam by the apostle [Paul], if as man he was not of that earthly origin? But even reason defends this conclusion, that God recovered his

image and likeness by a procedure similar to that in which he had been robbed of it by the devil. It was while Eve was still a virgin that the word of the devil crept in to erect an edifice of death. Likewise through a virgin the Word of God was introduced to set up a structure of life. Thus what had been laid waste in ruin by this sex was by the same sex re-established in salvation. Eve had believed the serpent; Mary believed Gabriel. That which the one destroyed by believing, the other, by believing, set straight.[6]

Again around the year 200, in St Irenaeus, Mary is portrayed as bringing into the world Christ who is Life, whereas Eve brought death, and Mary's humility and obedience is contrasted with Eve's pride and disobedience:

Consequently, then, Mary the Virgin is found to be obedient, saying, 'Behold, O Lord, your handmaid; be it done to me according to your word.' Eve, however, was disobedient, and, while still a virgin, she did not obey. Just as she, who was then still a virgin although she had Adam for a husband ... having become disobedient, was made the cause of death for herself and for the whole human race; so also Mary, betrothed to a man but nevertheless still a virgin, being obedient, was made the cause of salvation for herself and for the whole human race ... Thus, the knot of Eve's disobedience was loosed by the obedience of Mary. What the virgin Eve had bound in unbelief, the Virgin Mary loosed through faith.[7]

Mary's sinlessness was expressed in terms of the privilege accorded to her of being exempted from the pains in childbirth. This privilege was recorded early, before AD 100 in some Apocryphal writers. For example, the author of *The Ascension of Isaiah* writes that 'the report concerning the child was noised abroad in Bethlehem. Some said, "The Virgin Mary has given birth before she was married two months." And many said, "She has not given birth; the midwife has not gone up to her, and we heard no cries of pain."'[8] Furthermore, the writer of *The Odes of Solomon*, a collection of ancient Christian hymnody, remarks: 'So the Virgin became a mother with great mercies. And she laboured and bore the Son, but without pain, because it did not occur without purpose. And she did not seek a midwife, because He caused her to give life.'[9] Various other early Christian writers strongly suggested Mary's sinlessness in general terms. Even before the expressions 'original sin' and 'Immaculate Conception' had been defined, early Patristic passages implied these doctrines. Before the year 250, Hippolytus alluded in beautiful terms to the holiness of Mary: 'The Lord was without sin, made of imperishable wood, as regards His humanity; that is, of the virgin and the Holy Spirit inwardly, and outwardly of the word of God, like an ark overlaid with purest gold.'[10]

Around the year 390, St Ambrose remarked: 'Come, then, and search out your sheep, not through your servants or hired men, but do it yourself. Lift me up bodily and in the flesh, which is fallen in Adam. Lift me up not from Sarah but from Mary, a virgin not only undefiled, but a virgin whom grace had made inviolate, free of every stain of sin.'[11] Around the year 400, St Augustine was also noted for his belief in the sinlessness of Our Lady: 'We must except the Holy Virgin Mary, concerning whom I wish to raise no question on the subject of sins, out of honour to the Lord; for how can we know what abundance of grace for overcoming sin in every way was conferred upon her who had the merit to conceive and bear Him who undoubtedly had no sin?'[12] While having no doubts about the holiness of Mary in terms of the absence of personal sin, St Augustine is so not clear as to an affirmation of her freedom from original sin. In part, this is due to the fact that he strenuously opposed the Pelagians who also maintained Mary's holiness, which was for them a result of her own efforts. St Augustine proposed that Mary was holy in as much as she was redeemed by her Son, so that she was 'freed by grace in virtue of her rebirth.'[13]

Some Eastern Fathers had acknowledged a purification brought about by grace in Mary before the Incarnation, but many writers were not altogether clear when this took place. St Cyril of Jerusalem linked our Lady's deliverance from sin with the event of the Annunciation, when 'the Holy Spirit coming upon her sanctified her, so as to enable her to receive Him through whom all things were made.'[14] St Gregory Nazianzen seems to place the sanctification of Mary at some point before the Incarnation of her Son: 'Conceived by the Virgin, who first in body and soul was purified by the Holy Spirit, for it was needful both that Childbearing should be honoured, and that Virginity should receive a higher honour.'[15] Other Eastern Fathers, like St Ephraem the Syrian (around 350) seem to have indicated a prior purification of Mary through the agency of the Holy Spirit: 'Most holy Lady, Mother of God, alone most pure in soul and body, alone exceeding all perfection of purity ..., alone made in your entirety the home of all the graces of the Most Holy Spirit, and hence exceeding beyond all compare even the angelic virtues in purity and sanctity of soul and body ... Therefore you are altogether immaculate.'[16] St Ephraem often refers to Mary as immaculate: 'My Lady most holy, all-pure, all-immaculate, all-stainless, all-undefiled, all-incorrupt, all-inviolate immaculate robe of Him Who clothes Himself with light as with a garment ... sweet-smelling rose, flower unfading, shining white lily, alone most immaculate.'[17] However, elsewhere, Ephraem seems to have proposed that Christ regenerated His Mother through baptism.[18] However, the sanctification and purification of Our Lady of which these Fathers speak need have no connection with sin, whether original or actual. Theologically these descriptions could be classified as an increase of grace given to Mary in view of her Motherhood. This sanctification would therefore have as its object not forgiveness, but rather more intimate union with God.[19]

Then, in the East, it became clearer that the sinlessness of the Mother of God went back further than just before the Incarnation. This increasing clarity is connected with the Council of Ephesus in the year 431, which, as shall be seen, is a moment of capital importance for the under-standing of the Divine Motherhood.[20] For example, around the year 450, Theodotus of Ancyra declared that Mary was 'a virgin, innocent, spotless, free of all defect, untainted, undefiled, holy in soul and in body, like a lily sprouting among thorns, uninstructed in the vices of Eve.'[21] Furthermore, in the middle of the fifth century, St Proclus of Constantinople wrote: 'As He formed her without any stain of her own, so He proceeded from her contracting no stain.'[22] Proclus also beautifully described Mary as the heavenly orb of a new creation, 'in whom the ever-shining Sun of justice has put to flight from her entire soul all the night of sin.'[23]

Doctrinal reflection on the perfect holiness of Mary in relation to her Son considered that this perfection had to go back to the beginning of her existence. The turning point came when Bishop Theoteknos of Livias in Palestine, who lived between 550 and 650, moved in the direction of this original purity. In presenting Mary as 'holy and all-fair', 'pure and stainless', he referred to her birth in these words: 'She is born like the cherubim, she who is of a pure, immaculate clay.'[24] This last expression, recalling the creation of the first man, fashioned of a clay not stained by sin, attributes the same characteristics to Mary's birth: the Virgin's origin was also 'pure and immaculate', that is, without any sin. The comparison with the cherubim also emphasises the outstanding holi-ness that characterized Mary's life from the very beginning of her existence.

In the eighth century, St Andrew of Crete was the first theologian to relate the new creation to Mary's birth: 'Today humanity, in all the radiance of her immaculate nobility, receives its ancient beauty. The shame of sin had darkened the splendour and attraction of human nature; but when the Mother of the Fair One *par excellence* is born, this nature regains in her person its ancient privileges and is fashioned according to a perfect model truly worthy of God ... The reform of our nature begins today and the aged world, subjected to a wholly divine transformation, receives the first fruits of the second creation.'[25] His image of the new creation is further reinforced in another place: 'The Virgin's body is ground which God has tilled, the first fruits of Adam's soil divinized by Christ, the image truly like the former beauty, the clay kneaded by the divine Artist.'[26] St John Damascene, also in the eighth century, expressed a belief in Mary's freedom from original sin in a way which approaches the doctrine of the Immaculate Conception: 'O most holy daughter of Joachim and Anne, hidden from the principalities and powers, and from the fiery arrows of the Evil One. You set your dwelling place in the wedding chamber of the Holy Spirit and were conserved without stain as the bride of God, because with this nature of yours you became the Mother of God.'[27] St John Damascene also stressed the supernatural influence of God upon the generation of Mary by her parents St Joachim and St Anne. He proposes that, during the generation, they were filled and purified by the Holy Spirit, and freed from concupiscence: 'O most blessed loins of Joachim from which came forth a spotless seed! O glorious womb of Anne in which a most holy offspring grew.'[28] Consequently according to John Damascene, even the human element of her origin, the material of which she was formed, was pure and holy.

In the West, after the Council of Ephesus, there was also increasing clarity concerning the original sinlessess of Mary. St Maximus of Turin, writing around the middle of the fifth century affirmed: 'In her there sprouts no thorn of sin; because she was the shoot born not of the thorn, but from the stock, as the prophet affirms: "A shoot will spring from the stock of Jesse, a new shoot will grow from his roots" (Is 11:1): and this stock was Mary, pure, fine and virginal, who brought forth Christ as a flower from the integrity of her body.'[29] Later, about a century after the Council of Ephesus, St Fulgentius of Ruspe (468–533) centred Mary's sinlessness in a Christological key: 'Man disregarded God and abandoned Him; God, loving men, came towards men ... A woman with a corrupt soul, deceived the first man; an untouched Virgin conceived the Second. Through the wife of the first man, the devil's malice depraved his soul after seducing it; in the Mother of the Second Man, the grace of God conserved the integrity of her body and soul: it bestowed a firm faith to her soul and completely eradicated concupiscence from her body.'[30] During the Patristic period, the Eastern Fathers tended to see Mary as the beginning of a new race, while the Western Fathers saw her as an enclave protected from the contamination of sin.

The Immaculate Conception

Following St Augustine in the West, many Fathers and doctors believed in Mary's perfect holiness and the absence of any personal sin in her because of her dignity as Mother of the Lord. Nonetheless, they could not understand how the affirmation of an immaculate conception could be squared with the doctrine of the universality of original sin and the need of redemption for all of Adam's descendants. A feast of the Conception of Mary (or Conception by St Anne), which started in the monasteries of Palestine at least as early as the seventh century, was not based on the full understanding of Our Lady's freedom from sin expressed in the later feast of the Immaculate Conception. This feast in the course of centuries became the Feast of the Immaculate Conception, as theological refinement brought about clear ideas regarding the preservation of Mary from all stain of original sin. The earlier feast also appeared during the sixth and seventh centuries in the Greek Church as a celebration in honour of the conception of Our Lady by St Joachim and St Anne on 9 December, and by the tenth and eleventh centuries it had become firmly established as a holy day.[31] Probably the feast passed to Naples, which lay on an important trade route from Greece. A marble calendar dating from the ninth century testifies that the feast was celebrated at Naples.

The feast passed by way of Naples to the West, where it first took root in Ireland. Around the year 800, there is a record of a Feast of Our Lady's Conception being celebrated in Ireland. The first definite knowledge of the feast in the West comes from England from a calendar of Old Minster, Winchester, dating from about 1030, and in another calendar of New Minster, Winchester, composed between 1035 and 1056. The feast was also kept at Worcester, Exeter, Canterbury, and in the surrounding localities. This celebration was endorsed by episcopal authority and was observed by the Saxon monks with considerable solemnity. The establishment of the feast in England took place before the Norman Conquest in 1066. The Normans on their arrival in England tended to oppose and change English customs, and so the feast of Our Lady's Conception, which appeared to the invaders a peculiar Saxon devotion, was abolished in several places. However, it lived on in the hearts and minds of the faithful, and at the first favourable opportunity the feast was restored in a monastic setting.

St Anselm, Archbishop of Canterbury (1033–1109), was said to have written a specific treatise *De Conceptu virginali et originali peccato*,[32] which set down theological principles leading to a greater understanding of the doctrine of the Immaculate Conception. St Anselm first pointed out that the seed could not 'contain' sin, but only the will could cause sin.[33] He then drew the parallel between the creation of Eve from Adam and the Incarnation of Christ from Mary.[34] Hence, it is clear that the stain of sin could not at all have been present in that which the Son of God took to Himself from the Virgin Mary.[35] St Anselm was acquainted with the feast through the Saxon monks of Canterbury, and the Greeks with whom he came in contact during exile in Campania and Apulia (1098–99). However, St Anselm probably had no hand in introducing the feast into England. After the Norman Conquest, it was another

Anselm, the nephew of St Anselm, who re-introduced the feast.

An important theological development came about around 1120, when Eadmer, a monk of Canterbury, wrote the first treatise on the Immaculate Conception, and protested against the suppression of its liturgical celebration. Wishing to promote the restoration of this feast, the devout monk rejected the Augustinian objections to the privilege of the Immaculate Conception, based on the doctrine of the transmission of original sin in human generation. Eadmer countered the Augustianian objection by writing that the Holy Spirit could not be absent from the special beginnings of Mary: 'Where the Spirit is, there is freedom from sin.'[36] Eadmer proposed that God chose Mary from all eternity to be His dwelling place. Based on the idea of the house built by Wisdom for itself (Pr 9:1–16), Eadmer pointed out that God could not have allowed Mary to be stained by sin. 'The foundations' of His palace 'would be weak if the conception of Mary were in any way corrupted by the stain of sin.'[37] Instead, Mary became a tabernacle of the Holy Spirit. Eadmer also fittingly employed the image of a chestnut 'which is conceived, nourished and formed beneath its bur and yet is protected from being pricked by it.' Even beneath the bur of an act of generation which in itself must transmit original sin, Eadmer argued, Mary was preserved from every stain by the explicit will of God who 'was obviously able to do this and wanted to do so. Thus if he willed it, he did it.'[38]

Despite the reflections of Eadmer, the great theologians of the thirteenth century followed St Augustine according to the following argument: the Redemption accomplished by Christ would not be universal if the condition of sin were not common to all human beings. If Mary had not contracted original sin, she could not have been redeemed. Redemption in fact consists in freeing those who are in the state of sin. In particular, St Bernard opposed the doctrine of the Immaculate Conception and the celebration of the Feast in France in a forceful letter.[39] St Bernard held, following Augustine and Jerome, that in marital union there was always some taint of sin, which made it difficult for him to envisage how Mary could have been conceived immaculate: 'Could sanctity have been associated with conception in the embrace of marriage, so that she was conceived and sanctified at the same time? That is not reasonable. How could there have been sanctity without the sanctifying Spirit? How could the Holy Spirit be associated in any way with sin? How could sin not have been present where concupiscence was not absent?'[40]

Richard of St Victor wrote a treatise answering St Bernard, pointing out that the flesh of Mary needed no purification as it was sanctified before conception. However, St Albert the Great followed St Bernard in rejecting the doctrine of the Immaculate Conception. He observed: 'We say that the Blessed Virgin was not sanctified before animation, and the affirmative contrary to this is the heresy condemned by St Bernard in his epistle to the canons of Lyons.'[41] St Thomas Aquinas also followed this line. However, both St Albert and St Thomas were not opposed to a purification of Mary after animation.

In reality, St Thomas progressed in his view of the question. At the time of his *Commentary on the Sentences of Peter Lombard*, St Thomas inclined to favour this privilege for Mary.[42] However, in the *Summa Theologiae*, he found no way of reconciling it with the doctrine of universal redemption: 'If the soul of the Blessed Virgin had never incurred the stain of original sin, this would be derogatory to the dignity of Christ, by reason of His being the universal Saviour of all ... But the Blessed Virgin did indeed contract original sin, but was cleansed therefrom before her birth from the womb.'[43] St Thomas found a solution in having Mary purified as soon as possible in the womb of St Anne, a view which fitted in with his Aristotelian concept of animation: 'The sanctification of the Blessed Virgin cannot be understood as having taken place before animation ... because the sanctification of which we are speaking, is nothing but the cleansing from original sin ...

Now sin cannot be taken away except by grace, the subject of which is the rational creature alone. Therefore before the infusion of the rational soul, the Blessed Virgin was not sanctified.'[44] Thus, he taught the purification of Our Lady in the womb:

> Nothing is handed down in the canonical Scriptures concerning the sanctification of the Blessed Mary as to her being sanctified in the womb; indeed, they do not even mention her birth. But as Augustine, in his treatise on the Assumption of the Virgin, argues with reason, since her body was assumed into heaven, and yet Scripture does not relate this; so it may be reasonably argued that she was sanctified in the womb. For it is reasonable to believe that she, who brought forth 'the Only-Begotten of the Father full of grace and truth,' received greater privileges of grace than all others: hence we read (Lk 1:28) that the angel addressed her in the words: 'Hail full of grace!'[45]

At the end of his life he returned to his first position, which involved stronger adherence to a doctrine of the freedom from original sin of Mary, but without specifying *when* she was freed from this.[46] The problem of St Thomas and other medieval authors in grasping a doctrine of Immaculate Conception is also connected with their (now outdated) Aristotelian view of ensoulment, namely the idea that the human embryo receives the rational soul some weeks after conception.

Even in the Franciscan school before Blessed John Duns Scotus, great doctors like St Bonaventure did not hold Mary's freedom from original sin. Nevertheless his treatment of the question represented an advance towards that of Scotus. He proposed that the flesh of Our Lady was sanctified after the process of animation had taken place.[47]

The great breakthrough bringing greater understanding of the Immaculate Conception came with William of Ware and his pupil, Blessed John Duns Scotus. They were able to distinguish between a prevenient grace and a restorative grace, both of which were fruits of the Redemption. In particular, Scotus made the decisive step forward. Thus he introduced into theology the concept of Redemption by preservation, according to which Mary was redeemed in an even more wonderful way: not by being freed from sin, but by being preserved from sin. Scotus indicated that 'it is a more excellent benefit to preserve from evil, than to permit someone to fall into evil, even if one is freed from it afterwards. Therefore, if Christ merited grace and glory for many souls, and Christ is the Mediator for all of these, why could not someone be in debt to Him for her innocence?'[48] He proposed that the freeing of Mary from the stain of sin required, as a precondition, the creation and infusion of her soul, but that in terms of time, the sanctification and the animation were simultaneous.[49] Scotus also resolved the problem of how to square the Immaculate Conception of Mary with the issue of the universality of original sin. Christ is the perfect Mediator and perfect Redeemer, and thus it would be most fitting for Him, not only to preserve His Mother from all stain of actual sin, but also from original sin.[50] Thus Scotus held that Christ, the perfect Mediator, exercised the highest act of mediation precisely in Mary, by preserving her from original sin. Scotus proposed the famous formulation concerning God's power to preserve Mary from all stain of original sin, made popular by his disciple Francis de Mayronis: 'it was possible, it was fitting, therefore it was accomplished.'[51]

The controversy regarding the Immaculate Conception of Our Lady continued, with the opponents of this doctrine being mainly Dominicans. In 1439, the dispute was discussed at the Council of Basel which in its thirty-sixth session decreed the Immaculate Conception to be a doctrine which was pious, consonant with Catholic worship, Catholic faith, right reason, and Holy Scripture; nor was it henceforth allowable to preach or declare to the contrary.[52] This session was however held at a time when the Council was no longer in communion with the Pope, so that its decrees are not binding. Sixtus IV decreed on 28

February 1476 that the feast be adopted in the entire Latin Church and granted an indulgence to all who would assist at Mass and the Divine Offices of the solemnity.[53] As dissent still rumbled on after this decree, in 1483 Pope Sixtus IV published a constitution in which he punished with excommunication all those of either opinion who charged the opposite opinion with heresy.[54] In 1546, the Council of Trent discussed the question of original sin, but made it clear that 'it was not its intention to include in this decree dealing with original sin the Blessed and Immaculate Virgin Mary, Mother of God.'[55] However, this decree did not define the doctrine, and so the theological opponents of the mystery, although much reduced in numbers, did not yield. In particular, the Jansenists opposed the theology of the Immaculate Conception. In 1567, Pope St Pius V condemned a position of a Jansenist author, Michel de Bay, that 'no one but Christ is without original sin; hence the Blessed Virgin died on account of the sin inherited from Adam, and all her afflictions in this life were, like those of the rest of the just, punishment for actual or original sin.'[56] Nevertheless, in the fifteenth and sixteenth centuries, many European universities only admitted students who would swear an oath to do their utmost to defend and assert the Immaculate Conception of Mary.

In 1617, Pope Paul V decreed that no one should dare to teach publicly that Mary was conceived in original sin, and five years later, Gregory XV imposed silence, both in the written and the spoken word, even in private, upon the adversaries of the doctrine until the Holy See should define the question. At the request of King Philip IV of Spain, Alexander VII promulgated on 8 December 1661, the famous Brief *Sollicitudo omnium Ecclesiarum*.[57] He formulated the doctrine that belief that Mary's soul, 'in the first instant of its creation and in the first instant of the soul's infusion into the body, was, by a special grace and privilege of God, in view of the merits of Jesus Christ, her Son and the Redeemer of the human race, preserved free from all stain of original sin.'[58] He forbade all further discussion against the common and pious sentiment of the Church regarding this doctrine.

Finally, in 1849, Pope Blessed Pius IX consulted the bishops regarding the faith of the Church concerning the doctrine of the Immaculate Conception, and also whether a dogmatic definition in this regard would be opportune. The response was affirmative on both counts, and so, on 8 December 1854, Blessed Pius IX solemnly defined the doctrine of the Immaculate Conception in these words:

> We declare, pronounce, and define: the doctrine which holds that the most Blessed Virgin Mary was, from the first moment of her conception, by a singular grace and privilege granted by Almighty God and in view of the merits of Jesus Christ, the Saviour of the human race, preserved immune from all stain of original sin, is a doctrine revealed by God and therefore to be believed firmly and constantly by all the faithful.[59]

More recent theological reflection sees the Immaculate Conception in a Trinitarian key, as a pure gift of salvific love from the Holy Trinity. From a Christological point of view, the doctrine highlights the fact that the Word of God, the All-Holy, could not have assumed human nature from a creature who was, even for a brief instant, subject to the dominion of evil. In this sense, the Immaculate Conception is a prerequisite for the Incarnation:

> Had Mary not been preserved from Original Sin from the very moment she existed, she would have been literally torn apart on having in her womb the incarnate, infinite holiness. Not only sin, but also mere inclination to sin, are utterly incompatible with the most holy God. This is the reason, God's infinite incarnate holiness, why Mary had to be utterly free from Original Sin ... There God, the most holy God, has to be in a total symbiosis not only with the human nature it assumes but also forces that nature to be in a total symbiosis with a woman's womb as the very matrix

of its coming about, of its gradual growth and of its eventual birth. Such a womb must be absolutely immaculate.[60]

The doctrine is soteriological since it brings to light the universality of Christ's Redemption, revealing that Mary was its most special fruit, since she is Holy and Immaculate before God, in virtue of the Blood of her Son (Ep 1:4–7). The Immaculate Conception is Paschal, because the expression 'in view of the merits of Jesus Christ' refers above all to Easter, and in this sense the Immaculate Conception is an anticipation of the first fruits of Easter salvation. The ecclesiological perspective of the dogma indicates the realization of God's economy in His Mystical Bride the Church, whose prototype is Mary. From a pneumatological standpoint, the Immaculate Conception highlights the sanctifying presence of the Holy Spirit in Our Lady's conception. In this context, Pope Blessed Pius IX also mentioned a most important truth concerning Mary, that to her more grace was given than was necessary to conquer sin completely.[61] It is her freedom from actual sin which will now be illustrated.

Mary was free from actual sin

The expression of the angel Gabriel in the event of Annunciation 'Of all women you are the most blessed' (Lk 1:42) lies at the basis of any consideration of the lasting holiness of the Lord's Virgin Mother, both in her being and in her action. The being of Mary is the basis for her action, and her being is defined as blessed among women and full of grace. Mary's action as perfect disciple is based on this, according to the axiom *agere sequitur esse*.[62] The truth of Our Lady's initial holiness which spilled over into her whole life, leading to a freedom from actual sin, belongs to the common awareness of the Christian people.[63] While Western theology has often tended to emphasise the moral aspect to Mary's perfection and her example, Eastern thought has stressed Our Lady's holiness as being and gift.

While most of the Fathers, like St Augustine, St Ambrose and St Ephraem the Syrian, taught that Mary was sinless, some doubted in this matter. This was their personal opinion; it was never the official teaching of the Church. A very few Patristic writers who were not yet convinced of her perfect holiness, attributed imperfections or moral defects to Our Blessed Lady. For example, Origen, although he was the first to attribute to Mary the expression *Panagía* and to ascribe to her high spiritual privileges, thought that, at the time of Christ's passion, the sword of disbelief pierced Mary's soul; that she was struck by the dagger of doubt; and that for her sins also Christ died.[64] St Basil, interpreting the words of Simeon, seemingly under Origen's influence, suggests that Mary yielded to the sword of doubt on witnessing the crucifixion.[65] St John Chrysostom accuses her of ambition, and of putting herself forward unduly when she sought to speak to Jesus at Caparnaum.[66] It is clear that St John Chrysostom did not wish to imply that Our Lady committed any sin, but rather that she was taught by her Son, and that she underwent a development in faith. This theme is presented by Chrysostom in the context of the wedding at Cana, where alongside normal human sentiments, he proposes that Mary desired to collaborate in the spread of the glory of her Son in the world.[67] In any case, St Thomas Aquinas regarded St John Chrysostom's comments as limited by the circumstances of his time and out of place.[68] St Cyril of Alexandria also speaks of Mary's doubt and discouragement at the foot of the cross.[69] However, these Greek writers cannot be said to express an Apostolic tradition, when they express their private and singular opinions.

Certain particular Gospel texts cited by Fathers or more recent authors to justify these opinions provide no basis at all for attributing a sin or even a moral imperfection to the Mother of the Redeemer. The boy Jesus' reply to His mother: 'Why were you looking for me? Did you not know that I must be in my Father's house?' (Lk 2:49), has sometimes been interpreted as a veiled rebuke. A careful reading of the episode, however, shows that Jesus did not rebuke His mother and Joseph for seeking Him, since they were responsible for looking after Him. Finding Jesus after an anxious search, Mary asked Him only the 'why' of His behaviour: 'My child, why have you done this to us? See how worried your father and I have been, looking for you.' (Lk 2:48). This is only to Mary's credit, since it reveals her love for Jesus who answers with another 'why', refraining from any rebuke and referring to the mystery of His divine Sonship. This episode is therefore a revelation of the divine nature and mission of Christ.

The words spoken by Jesus at Cana: 'Woman, what do you want from me? My hour has not come yet.' (Jn 2:4), cannot be interpreted as a rebuff to His Blessed Mother. Seeing the likely inconvenience which the lack of wine would have caused the bride and groom, Mary speaks to Jesus with simplicity, entrusting the problem to Him. Though aware that as the Messiah He is bound only to obey the Father's will, He answers His Mother's implicit request. He responds above all to the Virgin's faith and thus performs the first of His miracles, thereby manifesting His glory. Some authors also gave a negative interpretation to the statement Jesus made when, at the beginning of His public life, Mary and His relatives asked to see him. Relating Jesus' reply to the one who said to Him 'Your mother and brothers are standing outside and want to see you' (Lk 8:20), the Evangelist Luke offers the interpretative key to the account, which must be understood on the basis of Mary's inner inclinations, which were quite different from those of His 'brothers' who 'had no faith in Him' (cf. Jn 7:5). Jesus replied: 'My mother and my brothers are those who hear the word of God and put it into practice' (Lk 8:21). In the Annunciation account, Luke actually showed how Mary was the model of listening to the word of God and of generous docility. Interpreted in this perspective, the episode offers great praise of Mary, who perfectly fulfilled the divine plan in her own life. Although Jesus' words can be interpreted as criticism of His 'brothers', they exalt Mary's fidelity to the will of God and the greatness of her motherhood, which she lived not only physically but also spiritually. With the expression 'My mother and my brothers are those who hear the word of God and put it into practice', Jesus stresses the nobility of Mary's conduct, and shows more clearly the Virgin's solidarity with and closeness to humanity on the difficult way of holiness. Lastly, the words: 'More blessed still are those who hear the word of God and keep it!' (Lk 11:28), spoken by Jesus in reply to the woman who had called His Mother blessed, far from putting into doubt Mary's personal perfection, bring out her faithful fulfilment of the word of God. The Gospel text actually suggests that He made this statement to reveal that the highest reason for His Mother's blessedness lies precisely in her intimate union with God and her perfect submission to the divine word.

Scripture and Tradition agree in ascribing to Mary the greatest personal sanctity; she is conceived without the stain of original sin; she shows the greatest humility and patience in her daily life (Lk 1:38, 48); she manifests an heroic patience under the most trying circumstances (Lk 2:7, 35, 48; Jn 19:25–27). The constant Tradition of the Church has regarded Mary as holy and free from all sin or moral imperfection. The Council of Trent expresses this conviction, affirming that no one 'can avoid all sins, even venial ones, throughout one's life, unless it be by a special privilege of God, as the Church holds of the Blessed Virgin.'[70] Even the Christian transformed and renewed by grace is not spared the possibility of sinning. Grace does not preserve him from all sin throughout his whole life, unless, as the Council of Trent asserts, a special privilege guarantees this immunity from sin. This special gift was bestowed upon Mary. The Council of Trent did not wish to define this privilege but stated that the Church vigorously affirms it and firmly holds it.[71] This teaching cannot simply be reduced to a pious devotional opinion, but is a solid doctrine, rooted in the deposit of faith as held by the People of God. Moreover, this conviction is based on the grace attributed to Mary by the angel at the time of the Annunciation. Calling her 'full of grace', *kecharitoméne*, the angel acknowledged her as the woman endowed with a lasting perfection and a fullness of sanctity, without shadow of sin or of moral or spiritual imperfection.[72]

Not only was Our Lady free from original and actual sin, but also from concupiscence. Concupiscence consists of three aspects, slavery to the pleasure of the senses, inordinate desire of earthly goods and the disordered affirmation of self against the dictates of reason (1 Jn 2:16).[73] Mary was preserved from this consequence of original sin. St Thomas Aquinas applied the passage from the Song of Songs 'You are wholly beautiful, my beloved, and without a blemish' (Sg 4:7) as an indication that concupiscence, the seed of sin (*fomes peccati*), which implies a blemish at least in the flesh, was not present in the Blessed Virgin Mary. The Angelic Doctor examined various opinions concerning the absence of concupiscence in Mary. Some authors held that concupiscence was entirely taken away when the Blessed Virgin was sanctified in the womb. Others said that it remained as far as it caused a difficulty in doing good, but was taken away as far as it causes a proneness to evil. Others again, that it was taken away as to the personal corruption, by which it makes us quick to do evil and slow to do good: but that it remained as to the corruption of nature, inasmuch as it is the cause of transmitting original sin to the offspring. Lastly, others said that, in her first sanctification, concupiscence remained essentially, but was fettered; and that, when she conceived the Son of God, it was entirely taken away. St Thomas pointed out that sensual concupiscence is said to be inordinate, in so far as it rebels against reason, and this it does by inclining to evil, or hindering from good. Consequently it necessarily inclines to evil, or hinders from good. Thus to say that concupiscence was in the Blessed Virgin Mary without an inclination to evil, is to combine two contradictory statements. Similarly, it is contradictory to say that it remained as to the corruption of nature, but not as to the personal corruption, for if it were entirely taken away as to personal corruption, it could not remain as to the corruption of nature. The only possibilities remaining are either that concupiscence was entirely taken away from her by her first sanctification or that it was fettered. St Thomas maintains that the Holy Spirit effected a twofold purification in the Blessed Virgin Mary. The first was preparatory to Christ's conception, which did not cleanse her from concupiscence. The second purification was effected in her by the Holy Spirit, when He purified her entirely from concupiscence. The Angelic Doctor held that, just as before the Resurrection of Christ in His immortal Flesh, nobody obtained immortality of the flesh, so it seems unfitting to say that before Christ appeared in sinless flesh, His Virgin Mother's or anyone else's flesh should be without concupiscence. Therefore it seems better to say that by the sanctification in the womb of her mother, the Virgin was not freed from concupiscence in its essence, but that it remained fettered. Afterwards, however, at the conception of Christ's flesh, in which for the first time immunity from sin was to be conspicuous, it is to be believed that entire freedom from concupiscence redounded from the Child to the Mother.[74] Nowadays, given the insight of Blessed John Duns Scotus into the prevenient and preventative aspects of the Redemption, it seems more reasonable to suppose that Mary enjoyed complete freedom from concupiscence from the first moment of her conception.

We can also say that Our Lady enjoyed the gift of a certain impeccability, by which is understood indefectibility in the moral order, or the inability to sin. One type of impeccability is that of Christ as man, owing to the hypostatic union. In Christ there is only one Person, that of the Word, to whom all actions, both divine and human, are attributed. Secondary causes of Christ's impeccability are also the fullness of habitual grace and the beatific vision. Hence Christ possesses *metaphysical* impeccability. On the other hand, the angels and saints enjoy *physical* impeccability, because they cannot turn away from the beatific vision of God in His essence. Our Lady, in her life on earth enjoyed *moral* impeccability, because given her personal dignity as Mother of God she could not incur the stain of sin.

The holiness of Mary

God willed to complement Mary's Immaculate Conception and freedom from concupiscence and actual sin with another gift: the fullness of grace, thereby joining to her freedom from sin a positive sanctity. This sanctity can be seen in a pneumatological perspective. Mary is 'the unwed Virgin espoused to the Spirit.'[75] She is the 'Temple of the Holy Spirit,' an expression that emphasizes the sacred character of the Virgin, now the permanent dwelling of the Spirit of God.[76] From the Paraclete, as from a spring, there flowed forth the fullness of grace and the abundance of gifts that adorned Mary. The Holy Spirit infused the faith, hope and charity that animated the Virgin's heart, imparted the strength that sustained her acceptance of the will of God, and the vigour that upheld her in her suffering at the foot of the Cross. The positive holiness, which was the work of the Paraclete, included also the infusion of the four cardinal virtues of Prudence, Justice, Fortitude, and Temperance, along with the seven gifts of the Holy Spirit: Our Lady was to enjoy all the grace that her dignity as the Mother of God demanded. However, this fullness would be able to enjoy increase, so that every time Mary freely and consciously cooperated with the will of God, her merit, grace and sanctity were augmented:

Only Christ Himself was full of grace in the absolute sense, incapable of receiving further increase, because of the hypostatic union. Our Lady was full of grace in another way: she was endowed with all the grace that was proper to her special dignity as Mother of God and associate of the divine Redeemer. She was endowed, not merely with sufficient grace, but in a superabundant way. However, since this fullness of grace is a relative fullness, growth was possible to Mary, for her capacity for more intense love of God could and did increase.

Merit increases with the greatness of the work that is done; in Mary we find works far greater than those of any other creature. Merit increases with the dignity and degree of grace of the one who merits; in Mary we find both fullness of grace and, as Pope Pius XI wrote, 'a dignity second only to God, a sort of infinite dignity, from the infinite good that God is.'[77] However, no works, however great they may be, would bring growth to their subject without love. Mary always acted with an unreserved maximum of love. Consequently, even small works of hers, such as household chores, would be more pleasing to God than the painful death of a martyr.[78] Our Lady grew by her merits, then, to the maximum degree intended by God. While Mary did not possesses the beatific vision on earth, she began her life with a more perfect charity than the greatest saints attain at the end of theirs. Her growth in charity was very rapid, because she was free from the slightest attachment to, or desire for, anything not perfectly directed to union with God. Her rapid growth was unimpeded by even the slightest personal obstacle.

A Christian grows in proportion to the greatness of his work, in proportion to his degree of grace, in proportion to his love. The greatness of Mary's work, a consent in the name of all mankind to become the Mother of the Redeemer, surpassed immeasurably any work that all creation had ever seen; her dignity was that of the one chosen to be the Mother of God; her own habitual grace had already been so great at the time of the Immaculate Conception that no one but God can comprehend it and yet had grown constantly since that moment; and now in her consent at the Annunciation there is the most absolute adherence to the will of God, an echo of the obedience of the Suffering Servant, of Christ Himself, made with unreservedly intense love. The increase in Mary's holiness is also reflected in her joining in prayer with the Apostles in the preparation for Pentecost. The personal Pentecost of Mary begins at the Annunciation in the Gospel: 'The Holy Spirit will come upon you' (Lk 1:35). Mary became the first and the most perfect icon of the Holy Spirit. Being completely transparent to His presence, she was totally filled by Him:

> In all things, from the Immaculate Conception to the *fiat* of the Incarnation (this *fiat* to which the Spirit has given a universal significance), from the first miracle of Jesus to his death, which was at once inspired by the Spirit and the source of the Spirit (Jn 19:30), from Pentecost to the last things, she is, in total dependence, the privileged place and image of the Spirit, the visible type and ideal realisation of the divine communion which he brings into being and perfects in the Church.[79]

In the life of the Mother of God, it is possible to distinguish two descents of the Holy Spirit. The first was when, by the power of the Holy Spirit, she conceived in her womb the Son of God in the Incarnation, and the second took place during the coming of the Holy Spirit on the Apostles at Pentecost. The former had the objective function of Mary's divine Motherhood, the latter was personal: a realization in her person of the degree of holiness that corresponded to her unique function.

Correlative to Mary's perfect love, she possessed also a great breadth of knowledge. Current discussion on Our Lady's knowledge tends to restrict it excessively, precisely because modern theological and biblical scholars have limited the knowledge of her Son. They ask whether Our Lady knew her Son was divine, or even that He was Messiah. They further ask the question: 'If she did know any of these things, when did she learn them?' The scholars who doubt Jesus' awareness of His Messianic dignity, are also led to conclude to ignorance in His Mother.[80] Among others, Pius XII affirmed of Christ a continual consciousness of His divinity and Messianic dignity.[81] Corresponding to Christ's universal knowledge, Mary must also have enjoyed a considerable gift of understanding, which Pope Paul VI implied, referring to her awareness of her role at the Annunciation: 'Mary taken into dialogue with God, gives her active and responsible consent, not to the solution of a contingent problem, but to that event of eternal importance, as the Incarnation of the Word has been rightly called.'[82]

The holiness of Mary is also reflected in her growth in faith, as well as in her readiness to link faith and reason. In the last of his *University Sermons* preached on the Feast of the Purification in 1843, Newman provided a penetrating analysis of the relations between faith and reason. His starting point was the scriptural passage: 'As for Mary, she treasured all these things and pondered them in her heart.' (Lk 2:19). Newman proposed that Mary's faith 'did not end in a mere acquiescence in Divine providences and revelations: as the text informs us, she "pondered" them.'[83] He shows how Mary is a model for relating faith and reason: 'She does not think it enough to accept, she dwells upon it; not enough to possess, she uses it; not enough to assent, she develops it; not enough to submit the Reason, she reasons upon it; not indeed reasoning first, and believing afterwards, with Zacharias, yet first believing without reasoning, next from love and reverence, reasoning after believing.'[84] The genius of Newman's idea is that Mary comes to symbolize not only the faith of the unlearned, but of the Doctors of the Church also, who need 'to investigate, and weigh, and define, as well as to profess the Gospel; to draw the line between truth and heresy; to anticipate or remedy the various aberrations of wrong reason; to combat pride and recklessness with their own arms; and thus to triumph over the sophist and the innovator.'[85]

The Holy Name of Mary

In Hebrew thought, the name of a person is intimately associated with the very nature content of the person,[86] thus the Holy Name of Mary is linked with her very being. Mary is a proper feminine name borne by only one person in the Old Testament, the sister of Moses and Aaron (Ex 15:20–21; Nb 12:1–5, 10, 15; Mi 6:4). In the Hebrew Massoretic text the name is *Miryām* (Mary), and the change in the first vowel to *Maryām* is probably the pronunciation in Aramaic-speaking Palestine during the two centuries preceding Christ. The name given to Mary was certainly divinely inspired to her parents St Joachim and St Anne.[87] As regards the meaning of the name given to Mary, St Jerome is the Father who started the tradition of saying that Mary means 'Star of the sea,' a fitting name for the Virgin Mother.[88] She may well be compared to a star; for, as a star beams forth its rays without any diminution of its own light, so too the Virgin gave birth to a Son with no loss to her virginity. The departing rays do not lessen the star's brightness, nor Mary's Son her inviolate maidenhood. She is, therefore, that noble star risen from Jacob and raised by nature above this great and wide sea. She shines with merits, she enlightens by her example. The Church, cast about upon the sea of this world in storms and tempests looks to the splendour of this star. More recent scholarship combined with twentieth-century archaeology has arrived at proposing that Mary means 'Highness' or 'the Exalted One.'[89] All of this points to Mary's central and greatest role, that of being Mother of God, which will be examined in the next chapter.

Notes

1   See chapter 3, pp. 56–58 above.
2   See Pope John Paul II, *Discourse at General Audience* (15 May 1996), 2.

3   In Patristic tradition there is a wide and varied interpretation of this expression. See, for example Origen, *In Lucam homiliae*, VI, 7 in *SC* 87, 148; Severianus of Gabala, *In mundi creationem*, Oratio VI, 10 in *PG* 56, 497f.; Basil of Seleucia, *Oratio 39, In Sanctissimae Deiparae Annuntiationem*, 5 in *PG* 85, 441–46; St Sophronius of Jerusalem, *Oratio 11, In Sanctissimae Deiparae Annuntiationem*, 17–19 in *PG* 87/3, 3235–3240; St John Damascene, *Homilia in Dormitionem*, 1, 70: *SC* 80, 96–101; St Jerome, *Epistola 65*, 9 in *PL* 22, 628; St Ambrose, *Expositio Evangelii secundam Lucam*, II, 9 in *CSEL* 32/4, 45f.; St Augustine, *Sermo 291*, 4–6 in *PL* 38, 131 8f.; Idem, *Enchiridion*, 36, 11 in *PL* 40, 250; St Peter Chrysologus, *Sermo 142* in *PL* 52, 579f.; Idem, *Sermo 143* in *PL* 52, 583; St Fulgentius of Ruspe, *Epistola 17*, VI 12 in *PL* 65 458; Later, in the Middle Ages, these Fathers were followed, for example, by St Bernard, *In laudibus Virginis Matris, Homilia III*, 2–3 in *S. Bernardi Opera*, IV, 1966, 36–38.

4   Origen, *Commentary on Luke*, 6 in *PG* 13, 1816.

5   St Justin Martyr, *Dialogue with Trypho the Jew*, 100 in *PG* 6, 710-711.

6   Tertullian, *The Flesh of Christ* 17, 4 in *PL* 2, 782.

7   St Irenaeus, *Against the heresies* Book 3, chapter 22, n. 4 in *PG* 7, 958–959. This idea is also found in the context of Irenaeus' theme of recapitulation: 'The Lord then was manifestly coming to his own things, and was sustaining them by means of that creation that is supported by himself. He was making a recapitulation of that disobedience that had occurred in connection with a tree, through the obedience that was upon a tree. Furthermore, the original deception was to be done away with – the deception by which that virgin Eve (who was already espoused to a man) was unhappily misled. That this was to be overturned was happily announced through means of the truth by the angel to the Virgin Mary (who was also [espoused] to a man) ... So if Eve disobeyed God, yet Mary was persuaded to be obedient to God. In this way, the Virgin Mary might become the advocate of the virgin Eve. And thus, as the human race fell into bondage to death by means of a virgin, so it is rescued by a virgin. Virginal disobedience has been balanced in the opposite scale by virginal obedience. For in the same way, the sin of the first created man received amendment by the correction of the First-Begotten' (*ibid.*, Book 5, chapter 19, n. 1 in *PG* 7, 1175–1176).

8   *Ascension of Isaiah*, 11.

9   *Odes of Solomon*, 19.

10 St Hippolytus, *Commentary on Psalm 22* in *PG* 10, 863.

11 St Ambrose, *Commentary on Psalm 118*, Sermon 22, 30 in *PL* 15, 1521.

12 St Augustine, *Nature and Grace* 36, 42 in *PL* 44, 267.

13 St Augustine, *Opus Imperfectum contra Julianum* Book 4, n. 122 in *PL* 45, 1418: 'quia ipsa conditio solvitur gratia renascendi.'

[14] St Cyril of Jerusalem, *Cathecheses*, 17, 6 in *PG* 33, 976.

[15] St Gregory Nazianzen, *Oratio* 38, n. 13 in *PG* 36, 325. See also Idem, *Oratio* 45, n. 9 in *PG* 36, 633.

[16] St Ephraem the Syrian, *Precationes ad Deiparam* 1–2 in *EM* 338–339. See also *Nisibene Hymns* 27, 8 in *EM* 429: 'You alone and Your Mother are more beautiful than any others, for there is no blemish in You nor any stains upon Your Mother.' See also *Hymns on the Nativity* 15, 23: 'Let women praise Her, the pure Mary, that as in Eve their mother great was their reproach, lo! in Mary their sister, greatly magnified was their honour.'

[17] St Ephraem the Syrian, *Oratio ad Deiparam* in *EM* 341.

[18] See St Ephraem, *Hymn 11 on the Nativity of Christ in the Flesh* in S. Ephraem Syrus, *Opera omnia quae extant graece, syriace, latine* Volume 2 (Rome: Vatican, 1740), pp. 429–430, where we read how Mary addresses Christ as follows: 'For I am Your sister, of the house of David the father of us Both. Again, I am Your Mother because of Your Conception, and I am Your Bride because of Your sanctification. I am Your handmaid and Your daughter, from the Blood and Water by which You have purchased me and baptised me.'

[19] See W. J. Burghardt, 'Mary in Eastern Patristic Thought' in J. B. Carol (ed.), *Mariology* vol. 2 (Milwaukee: The Bruce Publishing Company, 1955), p. 135.

[20] See chapter 5, pp. 115–116 below.

[21] Theodotus of Ancyra, *Homily 6, 11 (In sanctam Mariam Dei genitricem et in sanctam Christi nativitatem)* in *PG* 77, 1427.

[22] St Proclus of Constantinople, *Homily 1, 3* in *PG* 65, 683.

[23] Idem, *Homily 6, 17* in *PG* 65, 758.

[24] Theoteknos of Livias, *Encomium in Assumptionem Beatae Mariae Virginis,* 5–6 as found in A. Wenger, *L'Assomption de la Très Sainte Vierge dans la tradition byzantine de VIe au Xe siècle* (Paris: Institut Français d'Etudes Byzantines, 1955), pp. 272–291.

[25] St Andrew of Crete, *Sermon I on the Birth of Mary* in *PG* 97, 810.

[26] St Andrew of Crete, *Sermon I on the Dormition of Mary* in *PG* 97, 1067.

[27] St John Damascene, *Homily on the Nativity of the Blessed Virgin Mary,* 7 in *PG* 96, 671.

[28] St John Damascene, *Homily on the Nativity of the Blessed Virgin Mary,* 2 in *PG* 96, 663: 'O lumbos Ioachim beatissimos, ex quibus mundissimum semen iactus est! O praeclaram Annae vulvam, in qua tacitis accrementis ex ea auctus atque formatus fuit fetus sanctissimus.'

[29] St Maximus of Turin, *Homily 38* in *PL* 57, 310.

[30] St Fulgentius of Ruspe, *Sermo II de duplice nativitate Christi,* 6 in *PL* 65, 728.

[31] See St Andrew of Crete, *In conceptionem Sanctae Annae* in *PG* 97, 1307. This text for the feast of Our Lady's conception probably dates from the seventh or eighth century.

[32] St Anselm of Canterbury, *The Virgin Conception and Original Sin*, in *Complete Philosophical and Theological Treatises of Anselm of Canterbury* translated by J. Hopkins and H. Richardson (Minneapolis: The Arthur J. Banning Press, 2000), pp. 427–465. This treatise was possibly composed by his friend and disciple, the Saxon monk Eadmer of Canterbury.

[33] See St Anselm of Canterbury, *The Virgin Conception and Original Sin*, chapter 7, in *Complete Philosophical and Theological Treatises of Anselm of Canterbury*, pp. 439: 'For even if an infant be begotten by a corrupt concupiscence, there is no more fault in the seed than there is in the spittle or the blood should someone malevolently expectorate or malevolently shed some of his own blood. For what is at fault is not the spittle or the blood but the evil will.'

[34] See St Anselm of Canterbury, *The Virgin Conception and Original Sin*, chapter 11 in *Complete Philosophical and Theological Treatises of Anselm of Canterbury*, p. 443: 'For just as the clay of the earth had not received a nature or a will by whose operation the first man would be produced from it (even though the clay was that from which the first man could be created by God), so it was not by the operation of human nature and the human will that a woman was made from a man's rib or that a man was made from a woman alone. Rather, God, by His own power and will, created one man from the clay, created another man from a woman alone, and created a woman from a man alone.'

[35] See St Anselm of Canterbury, *The Virgin Conception and Original Sin*, chapter 8 in *Complete Philosophical and Theological Treatises of Anselm of Canterbury*, p. 439.

[36] Eadmer, *Tractatus de conceptione Beatae Mariae Virginis*, 9, in *PL* 159, 305.

[37] Eadmer, *Tractatus de conceptione Beatae Mariae Virginis*, 13, in *PL* 159, 306.

[38] Eadmer, *Tractatus de conceptione Beatae Mariae Virginis*, 10, in *PL* 159, 305. The famous expression is 'potuit plane et voluit; si igitur voluit, fecit.'

[39] See St Bernard of Clairvaux, *Letter 174 to the Canons of Lyons* in *PL* 182, 333–336.

[40] St Bernard of Clairvaux, *Letter 174 to the Canons of Lyons*, 7 in *PL* 182, 335: 'An forte inter amplexus maritales sanctitas se ipsi conceptioni immiscuit, ut simul et sanctificata fuerit, et concepta? Nec hoc quidem admittit ratio. Quomodo namque aut sanctitas absque Spiritu sanctificante, aut sancto Spiritui societas cum peccato fuit? aut certe peccatum quomodo non fuit, ubi libido non defuit?'

[41] St Albert the Great, *III Sententiarum*, distinction iii, part I, ad 1, Q. i.

[42] St Thomas Aquinas, *In I Sententiarum*, d. 44, q. 1, a. 3, ad 3: 'Item, videtur quod nec beata virgine: quia secundum Anselmum, decuit

ut virgo quam deus unigenito filio suo praeparavit in matrem, ea puritate niteret, qua major sub deo nequit intelligi. Sed nihil potest deus facere quod sibi in bonitate vel puritate aequetur. Ergo videtur quod nihil melius beata virgine facere possit.'

43 St Thomas Aquinas, *Summa Theologiae*, III, q. 27, a. 2.

44 *Ibid.*

45 St Thomas Aquinas, *Summa Theologiae*, III, q. 27, a. 1.

46 St Thomas Aquinas, *In salutationem angelica*, a. 1: 'Nam ipsa omne peccatum vitavit magis quam aliquis sanctus post Christum. Peccatum enim aut est originale, et de isto fuit mundata in utero; aut mortale aut veniale, et de istis libera fuit.'

47 See St Bonaventure, *Commentary on Book III of The Sentences*, d. 2, a. 1, q. 1: 'It must be said, that the flesh of the Blessed Virgin had not been sanctified before animation; not because God could not have purified the flesh of the Virgin before He could have animated it, but because sanctification has existence through some gratuitous, superadded gift, which indeed does not have existence in the flesh, but in the soul.'

48 Bl John Duns Scotus, *Questions in Libro III Sententiarum*, d. 3, q. 1, in *Opera Omnia* (Hildesheim: Georg Olms, 1968), Volume 7/1, pp. 92–93: 'imo excellentius beneficium est preservare a malo, quam permittere incidere in malum, et ab eo postea liberare. Videtur enim quod cum Christus multis animabus meruerit gratiam, et gloriam, et pro his sint Christo debitores, ut mediatori; quare nulla anima erit ei debitrix pro innocentia?'

49 *Ibid.*, pp. 94–97.

50 Bl John Duns Scotus, *Reportata Parisiensia*, Book 3, d. 3, q. 1, in *Opera Omnia* (Hildesheim: Georg Olms, 1969), Volume 11/1, pp. 432–433, in particular p. 433: 'Mediator perfectus praevenit omne peccatum actuale. Hoc concedunt omnes de beata Virgine: sed redemptio universalis est contra originale quam contra actuale: igitur ex hoc quod redemptor universalis, perfectius et immediatius praevenit originale, quam actuale.'

51 Bl John Duns Scotus, *Tractatus de Conceptione Mariae Virginis*, chapter V. 'Potuit, decuit, ergo fecit.'

52 See Mansi, 29, 183.

53 See Pope Sixtus IV, Constitution *Cum Praeexcelsa* in ND 704.

54 See Idem, Constitution *Grave nimis* in DS 1425–1426.

55 Council of Trent, Session V, *Decree on Original Sin* in ND 705.

56 Pope St Pius V, Bull *Ex omnibus afflictionibus* in ND [708]. Later in 1690, under Pope Alexander VIII, another Jansenist proposition was condemned which implied that at the Presentation of Our Lord in the temple, His Mother needed purification from sin. See DS 2324: 'The offering which the Blessed Virgin Mary made in the temple on the day of her purification with two young turtledoves, one as a

holocaust, the other as a sin offering, is sufficient evidence that she needed purification, and that her Son, who was presented, was also marked with the stain of His Mother, according to the words of the Law.'

57   Alexander VII, Brief *Sollicitudo omnium Ecclesiarum* in DS 2015–2017.

58   *Ibid.*, §1 in DS 2015.

59   Pope Bl Pius IX, Bull *Ineffabilis Deus* in DS 2803: 'Declaramus, pronuntiamus et definimus doctrinam quae tenet beatissimam Virginem Mariam in primo instanti suae conceptionis fuisse singulari Omnipotentis Dei gratia et privilegio, intuitu meritorum Christi Jesu Salvatoris humani generis, ab omni originalis culpae labe praeservatam immunem, esse a Deo revelatam, atque idcirco ab omnibus fidelibus firmiter constanterque credendam.'

60   S. L. Jaki, 'The Immaculate Conception and a Conscience Immaculate' in *Catholic Dossier* 6/6 (November/December 2000).

61   Pope Bl Pius IX, Bull *Ineffabilis Deus*. See also St Augustine, *De Natura et Gratia*, c. 36.

62   Cf. St Thomas Aquinas, *Summa Theologiae*, I, q. 51, a. 2; I, q. 77, a. 3 and I, q. 80, a. 2 as examples of a few instances of this axiom.

63   See Pope John Paul II, *Discourse at General Audience* (19 June 1996), 1.

64   See Origen, *Homilia 17 in Lucam* in *PG* 13, 1844–1845.

65   See St Basil, *Epistola* 260, n. 9 in *PG* 32, 965–968.

66   See St John Chrysostom, *Homilia in Matthaei Evangelium*, 27, 3 and 44, 1 in *PG* 57, 347 and 464f; see also Mt 12:46–50.

67   See St John Chrysostom, *Homilia in Ioannis Evangelium*, 21, 1 and 2 in *PG* 59, 130–131.

68   See St Thomas Aquinas, *Summa Theologiae*, III, q. 27, a. 4: 'In those words Chrysostom goes too far. They may, however, be explained as meaning that our Lord corrected in her, not the inordinate motion of vain glory in regard to herself, but that which might be in the thoughts of others.'

69   St Cyril of Alexandria, *Commentarius in Ioannis Evangelium*, Book 12 in *PG* 74, 661–664.

70   Council of Trent, Session VI, *Decree on Justification* in ND 706.

71   See Pope John Paul II, *Discourse at General Audience* (19 June 1996), 2. The expression used at the Council of Trent was *tenet*, that is, the Church *holds* this doctrine to be true.

72   See Pope John Paul II, *Discourse at General Audience* (19 June 1996), 2–4.

73   See CCC 377.

74   See St Thomas Aquinas, *Summa Theologiae*, III, q. 27, a. 3.

75   Prudentius, *Liber Apotheosis*, verses 571–572 in *CCL* 126, p. 97.

76   For the title Temple of the Holy Spirit, see St Isidore, *De ortu et obitu Patrum*, chapter LXVII, 111 in *PL* 83, 148; St Ildephonsus, *De virginitate perpetua sanctae Mariae*, chapter X in *PL* 96, 95; St Bernard, *In*

Assumptione B. Virginis Mariae: Sermo IV, 4 in *PL* 183, 428.

[77] Pope Pius XI, *Lux veritatis,* 25 December 1931 in *AAS* 23(1931), p. 513, citing St Thomas Aquinas, *Summa Theologiae* I, q. 25, a. 6.

[78] After all, it is not mere difficulty as such that increases the merit of a good work. The difficulty, however, often provides a benchmark of merit, serving as a kind of foil to evoke love; only great love can rise above great difficulties, though great love can rise even where there are no difficulties. See W. G. Most, 'Our Lady's Growth in Holiness' in *Cross and Crown* 14 (March 1962), pp. 79–91.

[79] R. Laurentin, 'Esprit Saint et théologie mariale' in *Nouvelle Revue Théologique* 89 (1967), p. 42.

[80] One example is Raymond Brown, who spends most of an entire book, *Jesus, God and Man* (New York: Macmillan, 1967), accumulating what he thinks are Scriptural instances for ignorance in Jesus. For example, on p. 57 Brown suspects Jesus did not know very much even about the afterlife: 'We cannot assume that Jesus shared our own sophistication on some of these questions. If Jesus speaks of heaven above the clouds ... how can we be sure that he knew that it was not above the clouds?' Another example is Karl Rahner who maintains that Christ's lack of knowledge is, in a sense a perfection: 'There is certainly a nescience which renders the finite person's exercise of freedom possible ... This nescience is ... more perfect for the exercise of freedom than knowledge, which would suspend this exercise.' See K. Rahner, 'Dogmatic Reflections on the Self-consciousness of Christ' in *Theological Investigations,* tr. K. H. Kruger (Baltimore: Helicon, 1966) Volume V, p. 202.

[81] Pope Pius XII, *Mystici Corporis,* 75: 'The most loving knowledge of this kind, with which the divine Redeemer pursued us from the first moment of the Incarnation, surpasses the diligent grasp of any human mind; for by that blessed vision which He enjoyed when just received in the womb of the Mother of God, He has all the members of the Mystical Body continuously and perpetually present to Himself ... In the manger, on the Cross, in the eternal glory of the Father, Christ has all the members of the Church before Him, and joined to Him far more clearly ... than a mother has a son on her lap, or than each one knows and loves himself.'

[82] Pope Paul VI, *Marialis Cultus,* 37: 'Haec enim, quasi ad colloquirum cum Deo admissa, *pro actuosa peculiaris officii sui conscientia,* non de re quadam adventitia, sed de saeculorum negotio, ut praeclare est Verbi incarnatio definita, actuose ac libere consentit.'

[83] J. H. Newman, 'The Theory of Developments in Religious Doctrine, 1843', in J. H. Newman, *Conscience, Concensus and the Development of Doctrine: Revolutionary Texts by John Henry Cardinal Newman,* ed. J. Gaffney, (New York: Image/Doubleday, 1992), 6–30; §2.

[84] *Ibid.,* §3

[85]   *Ibid.*

[86]   See J. L. McKenzie, 'Aspects of Old Testament Thought' in R. E. Brown, J. A. Fitzmeyer, R. E. Murphy, *The New Jerome Biblical Commentary* (Englewood Cliffs, N. J: Prentice-Hall, 2000), p. 1285.

[87]   See St Laurence of Brindisi, *Mariale* (Patavii: 1928), p. 177. See also M. J. Scheeben, *Mariology*, Volume 1 (New York: Herder, 1948), p. 6.

[88]   St Jerome, *Liber interpretationis hebraicorum nominum* in *PL* 23, 841–842. The problem is that it is likely that Jerome wrote *Stilla maris*, meaning 'a Drop from the sea', and copyists made the error of reading *Stella maris* signifying 'Star of the sea'. There is no Hebrew word for a star which resembles Our Lady's name, whereas a Hebrew word for a drop, *Mar* (Is 40:15), is similar to Mary.

[89]   See R. Kugelman, 'The Holy Name of Mary' in J. B. Carol (ed.), *Mariology* Volume 1 (Milwaukee: The Bruce Publishing Company, 1954), pp. 418–423. Philologically the name *Miryām* is derived from *Rwm* which signifies 'to rise up', 'to be high above' or 'to be exalted'. This root occurs in all Western Semitic languages.

CHAPTER 5

MOTHER OF GOD

Mary is the earthly paradise of Jesus Christ the new Adam, where He became man by the power of the Holy Spirit, in order to accomplish in her wonders beyond our understanding. She is the vast and divine world of God where unutterable marvels and beauties are to be found. She is the magnificence of the Almighty where He hid His only Son, as in His own bosom, and with Him everything that is most excellent and precious.

St Louis Grignon de Montfort,
Treatise on True Devotion to the Blessed Virgin

Development of the doctrine

The doctrine that Mary is the Mother of God is the central belief concerning Mary; all other truths flow from it or towards it. In the hierarchy of Mariological truths, Mary's being the Mother of God is the pivotal basis for her role in the economy of salvation.[1] Mary has been exalted by grace above all angels and men to a place second only to her Son, as the most holy Mother of God. From the earliest times the Blessed Virgin has been honoured under the title of Mother of God.[2] It is in view of her mission as the Mother of God that she is immaculately conceived.[3] It is due to her motherhood that she remains ever-virgin.[4] It is a result of her motherhood and consequent relationship to the Christ that she is assumed body and soul into heaven.[5]

In the New Testament, while the explicit title of *Theotokos*, or Mother of God, is not to be found, there are expressions which in essence contain this truth concerning Mary. Of her is written that she has conceived in her womb and borne a Son, named Jesus, who is Son of the Most High, holy and the Son of God (cf. Lk 1: 31–32, 35). Our Lady is also referred to as 'Mother of Jesus' (Jn 2:1,3; Ac 1:14) as well as 'Mother of the Lord' (Lk 1:43) or quite simply 'Mother' or 'His Mother' (Mt 2:11, 13, 14, 20, 21). The title 'Mother of God', already attested by Matthew in the equivalent expression 'Mother of Immanuel', God-with-us (cf. Mt 1:23), was explicitly attributed to Mary after a reflection that embraced about two centuries.[6]

Therefore, Mary does not only begin to be Mother in the year 431 when the Council of Ephesus made its solemn definition of Theotokos, just as Jesus does not only begin to be God when the First Council of Nicaea defined the doctrine of His divinity in the year 325. Instead, the Council of Ephesus was rather the occasion when the Church, in the face of heresy, having developed and made her faith explicit, defended this doctrine and reflected on its consequences. In this process which paved the way to the proclamation of Mary as *Theotokos*, three principal steps can be outlined. The first period involved the struggles against Docetism, Gnosticism, and Manichaeism in which the physical maternity of Mary was affirmed. The second period involved Christological controversies and here the metaphysical maternity of Mary was stressed. Finally, in the third period, theology acquired an awareness of the consequences of Mary's divine maternity. It should be stressed however, in a way which is consonant with the realist fabric of this work, that no real theological understanding of Mary's Motherhood can be achieved without the prior basis of her physical Motherhood.

The physical maternity of Our Lady

During the entire period when the Church was refuting the heresies of Docetism[7], Gnosticism[8] and Manichaeism[9] it was necessary to stress the physical maternity of Mary. These heresies, because of their rejection of matter as evil, or at least ambiguous, denied that Jesus Christ had a true and complete human body. The Docetists denied that the Saviour had a genuinely human body, or maintained that whatever body He had was not truly fashioned of flesh and blood from His Mother. Some of the exponents of Docetism affirmed that Jesus was born *through* the Virgin Mary and not *from* the Virgin Mary: in this way He was placed in her womb from heaven, and came forth from her as through a corridor, but not through true human generation. Tertullian sums up the Docetist error: 'He was born *through* a virgin, not *of* a virgin, and *in* a womb, not *of* a womb.'[10] On the other hand, the Gnostics introduced a distinction between Jesus as born of Mary and the Christ who descended into Jesus at baptism; they effectively denied that the Child born of Mary was God.[11] It was necessary to affirm against these errors that Jesus was truly the Son of the Virgin Mary, and fruit of her womb, and therefore that Mary was physically His Mother. In particular, around the end of the second century, St Irenaeus was clear in his affirmation of the divine maternity, against the errors of the Gnostics: 'Now, the Scriptures would not have testified these things of Him, if, like others, He had been a mere man. But the divine Scriptures do in both respects testify of Him that He had, beyond all others, in Himself that pre-eminent birth which is from the Most High Father, and also experienced that pre-eminent generation which is from the Virgin.'[12] Irenaeus also indicated that the Virgin Mary 'being obedient to His word, received from an angel the glad tidings that she would bear God.'[13] This proclamation that Mary was the physical Mother of Jesus served to highlight His humanity on the one hand and His divinity on the other. During this period, belief in Mary's divine motherhood was expressed in the creed of the Apostles. Within the form in use at the time of Hippolytus, around the year 215, the catechumens were asked if they believed in Jesus Christ who was 'born of the Holy Spirit and the Virgin Mary.'[14]

In a manner resembling the Gnostic error, the Manichaeans did not accept that Jesus was born of Mary. The great patristic champion of orthodoxy against the Manichaeans was St Augustine, who had for a time fallen a prey to them. Augustine opposed the Manichaean doctrine of a certain Faustus who held that Jesus was the 'Son of God', but in no sense could He be the Son of Mary. Faustus proposed that the virgin overshadowed by the Holy Spirit in the conception of Christ was not Mary, but the earth. Augustine taught the content of the truth that Mary was the Mother of God, yet without adopting that very expression. In his sermons, he does very clearly refer to Mary as God's Mother (*genitrici suae*).[15]

The metaphysical maternity of Our Lady

Some scholars maintain that the title *Theotokos* was attributed to Mary for the first time by Hippolytus in the first years of the third century: 'Joseph betroths Mary to himself and becomes a trustworthy witness to the Mother of God.'[16] Another early witness to the title *Theotokos*, is an Egyptian papyrus containing parts of the prayer *Sub tuum praesidium*, from the third century.[17] The formula has formed part of the Church's life of prayer for many centuries, but its discovery on this papyrus in Egypt in 1938 dates it to the second half of the third century. More certainly, the expression was used by Origen in the third century, along with other writers of the Alexandrian school, both before and after the First Council of Nicaea.[18] The evidence indicates that Alexandria played a special role in the development of the title *Theotokos*.

The first incontrovertible use of *Theotokos* lies in the letter of St Alexander, Bishop of Alexandria, announcing the deposition of Arius around the year 320 to Alexander, patriarch of Constantinople: 'After this we know of the resurrection of the dead, the first-fruits of which was our Lord Jesus Christ, who in very deed, and not merely in appearance, carried a body, of Mary Mother of God, who at the end times came to the human race to put away sin, was crucified and died, and yet without any detriment to His divinity, being raised from the dead, taken up into heaven, and seated at the right hand of Majesty.'[19] The witness of St Alexander of Alexandria and others of the Alexandrian school is of particular importance because it shows that the title of *Theotokos* was accepted in general use before the Nestorian controversy. St Athanasius, the successor of St Alexander of Alexandria, around the year 360 employed the expression *Theotokos* a number of times. He linked the divine maternity with the central truths of Christology: 'The Word begotten of the Father from on high, inexpressibly, inexplicably, incomprehensibly, and eternally, is He that is born in time here below of the Virgin Mary, the Mother of God.'[20]

In the middle of the fourth century, St Cyril of Jerusalem preached the truth of the divine Motherhood to his catechumens: 'The Father bears witness from heaven to His Son. The Holy Spirit bears witness, coming down bodily in the form of a dove. The archangel Gabriel bears witness, bringing the good tidings to Mary. The Virgin Mother of God bears witness.'[21] Syrian testimony of the expression is frequently exemplified in the works of St Ephraem. The following prayer is highly significant because Ephraem adopts all three principal words (*Deipara*, *Dei Genitrix*, *Mater Dei*) describing the divine maternity: 'Virgin Lady, bearer of God, blessed Theotokos, most blessed Mother of God, most pleasing to God, blessed above all, vessel of the divinity of the only-begotten Son, and of the invisible Father, bend down your ear, that you may hear the words spoken by my unclean and impure lips.'[22]

In the Western Church before the time of the Nestorian heresy, St Ambrose is the only author who explicitly attributed to Mary the title of Mother of God, and this was due to his knowledge of the Greek Fathers.[23] Around the year 380, he affirmed: 'The first thing which kindles ardour in learning is the greatness of the teacher. What is greater than the Mother of God? What more glorious than she whom Glory Itself chose?'[24] St Augustine, as has been seen defended the doctrine of the divine Maternity against the Manichaeans. His works are imbued with the doctrine, and he points out that though Elizabeth conceived a man, and Mary also a man, nevertheless 'Elizabeth conceived a man, Mary God and man.'[25] Augustine made it clear that Christ was anointed with the Spirit, not merely at His baptism but 'when the Word of God was made flesh, namely when human nature ... was joined to the Word of God in the womb of a Virgin, so as to from one Person with Him. For this reason we confess Him born of the Holy Spirit and the Virgin Mary.'[26] The doctrine, even if not the formula, of Mary Mother of God is also present in the writings of St Hilary of Poitiers (d.367) when he states simply that Mary 'was Mother of Our Lord according to the flesh.'[27] Hilary also affirmed that 'God is born from the womb of the Virgin.'[28]

St Basil the Great cited the expression *Mother of God* once in a Christmas homily, saying that 'those who love Christ refuse to listen to the idea that the Theotokos ever ceased to be a virgin.'[29] St Gregory of Nyssa, his younger brother, used the expression at least four times, of which the following excerpt is particularly beautiful: 'Just as, in the age of Mary the Mother of God, he (i.e. the devil) who had reigned from Adam to her time found, when he came to her and dashed his forces against the fruit of her virginity as against a rock, that he was shattered to pieces upon her, so in every soul which passes through this life in the flesh under the protection of virginity, the strength of death is in a manner broken and annulled, for he does not find the places upon which he may fix his sting.'[30] However, St Gregory Nazianzen, around the year 380, was perhaps the first to link the expression *Theotokos* to its Christological consequences. Probably, he was refuting the error of Diodore of Tarsus, who proposed the notion of two Sons of God, one eternal, and one born in time of the Virgin Mary. At the same time, Gregory directed his words against the error of Apollinaris, and reaffirmed the true faith against Docetist tendencies, and also provided a prophetic refutation of the error of Nestorius:

> If anyone does not believe that Holy Mary is Theotokos, he is severed from the Godhead. If anyone should assert that Christ passed through the Virgin as through a channel, but was not fashioned in her divinely and humanly – divinely because without the help of man, humanly because by the law of conception – he too is godless. If any assert that the Manhood was formed and afterward was clothed with the Godhead, he too is to be condemned. For this could not be a generation of God, but a shirking of generation. If anyone introduce the notion of two Sons, one of God the Father, the other of the Mother, and discredits the Unity and Identity, may he lose his part in the adoption promised to those who believe aright.[31]

It is significant that while the expression *Theotokos* was employed without hesitation, even before the Council of Ephesus, by the Alexandrian school of theology as well as that of the Cappadocians which was theologically close to Alexandria, the term was conspicuous by its absence from Antiochene literature. The Alexandrian school stressed the union of the divine with the human in Christ. Only when certain exponents of this school tried to explain this union in terms of a fusion of two natures into one, did the heresy of monophysitism emerge.

The word *Theotokos* was not unknown to the theologians of Antioch of the fourth century, but they seemed reluctant to adopt it. One reason may be that Arian misuse of the word could have aroused in the Antiochene theologians a reluctance to use it. Another reason may be that Apollinaris of Laodicea had been a strong defender of the term *Theotokos*. In defending the unity of Christ, he proposed that in Christ, the Word took the place of a human soul. The Christology of Antioch was often a reaction to the error of Apollinaris. In any case, it remains true that Nestorianism of the fifth century had fourth-century roots in Antioch. The school of Antioch exaggerated the separation of the divine and the human in Christ, explaining the union of divinity with humanity as a type of indwelling of God the Word in the man Jesus. They envisaged two physical persons in Christ, because He had two natures, and this was the root of the Nestorian heresy. Nestorius was born at Germanicia, a town in Syria, and he went to Antioch as a youth, later entering the monastic life, and then left it to apply himself to preaching. Nestorius had been a disciple of Theodore of Mopsuestia, who in his turn had been taught by Diodore, Bishop of Tarsus. Theodore and Diodore proposed that the Word of God dwelt in the man Jesus as in a temple, and so Mary was not considered to be the Mother of God.[32]

The Nestorian heresy put the expression *Theotokos* through the cauldron of trial, and it emerged victorious. Nestorius, as Patriarch of Constantinople, gave a series of sermons in which he defended Anastasius (his secretary) and Dorotheus (bishop of Marcianapolis) both of whom had been preaching that Mary should not be addressed as Mother of God. Nestorius proposed that Mary should be invoked as *Christotokos* (Mother of Christ) rather than *Theotokos* (Mother of God). The teaching of Nestorius aroused considerable disquiet among the faithful, who had already been invoking Our Lady under the title *Theotokos* for more than half a century. Even John, Patriarch of Antioch, a friend of Nestorius, pleaded with him to abandon his opposition to the expression *Theotokos*, indicating that many of the Fathers had used it.[33] The chief opponent of Nestorius was St Cyril of Alexandria, who demonstrated that the doctrine of Mary, Mother of God, was in continuity with tradition of the Fathers, who 'ventured to call the holy Virgin the Mother of God, not as if the nature of the Word or His divinity took its origin from the holy Virgin, but because of her was born that Sacred Body with a rational soul, to which the Word, being hypostatically united, is said to be born according to the flesh.'[34]

In 430, Pope Celestine I convoked a Synod at Rome to investigate the matter, the teaching of Nestorius was duly condemned, and the term *Theotokos* approved. Pope Celestine commissioned Cyril to carry out the sentence of excommunication against Nestorius, unless he recanted within ten days.[35] Cyril despatched to Nestorius his famous Letter of the Anathemas. Despite the fact that Universal Church had spoken in the expressions of Rome, Antioch and Alexandria, Nestorius remained obstinate in his error. The Emperor Theodosius II therefore decided, together with his co-emperor Valentinian III and with the agreement of Pope Celestine I, to convene a general council to meet at Ephesus in June 431. Despite imperial intimidation the assembly of bishops, presided over by St Cyril, gathered in the cathedral of Our Lady Theotokos at Ephesus, and solemnly proclaimed that Christ was the Second Person of the Blessed Trinity and that Mary was the Mother of God. The second letter of Cyril to Nestorius was declared to be in agreement with Nicaea, and approved by the Council. Here is to be found the basis for the doctrine of the divine maternity:

> The Word is said to have been begotten according to the flesh, because for us and for our salvation he united what was human to himself hypostatically and came forth from a woman. For he was not first begotten of the holy virgin, a man like us, and then the Word descended upon him; but from the very womb of his mother he was so united and then underwent begetting according to the flesh, making his own the begetting of his own flesh ... So shall we find that the holy fathers believed. So have they dared to call the holy virgin, *Mother of God*, not as though the nature of the Word or his Godhead received the origin of their being from the holy virgin, but because there was born from her his holy body rationally ensouled, with which the Word was hypostatically united and is said to have been begotten in the flesh.[36]

Although the *Letter of the Anathemas* was not proposed for the approval of the Council, it does have doctrinal authority in view of the fact that it was highly praised by the Second Council of Constantinople as a part of the acts of Ephesus.[37] In the first anathema, we read: 'If anyone does not confess that Emmanuel is God in truth, and therefore that the holy virgin is the Mother of God (for she bore in a fleshly way the Word of God become flesh), let him be anathema.'[38] Nestorius was solemnly deposed and stripped of his episcopal dignity.[39] The decrees of the Council of Ephesus were later ratified by the delegates of Pope Celestine. The night on which the decrees were promulgated, crowds of the faithful took to the streets and shouted enthusiastically, '*Hagia Maria Theotokos*', 'Holy Mary, Mother of God', and this cry continues to be one of the great hallmarks of Catholic orthodoxy. The proclamation of Mary as *Theotokos* by the Council of Ephesus, thus caused great joy among the local populace who accompanied the Fathers of the Council to their homes with lights and singing. The Council also brought about a great flowering of veneration towards the Mother of God in both East and West, expressed in liturgical feasts, icons, hymns and the construction of churches and basilicas, like that of St Mary Major's in Rome, built by Pope Sixtus III.

The Council of Ephesus stimulated a chorus of affirmation of the doctrine of the divine Motherhood in both East and West. In the West, just three years after Ephesus, Vincent of Lerins wrote: 'God forbid, therefore, that anyone should try to cheat Holy Mary of her privileges of divine grace and of her special glory. For by a unique favour of Him who is our Lord and God, but her Son, she is to be confessed Theotokos in the truest and most blessed way possible ... Holy Mary is Theotokos because ... in her sacred womb was accomplished this sacrosanct mystery, that by reason of a certain, matchless, unique unity of Person, even as the Word in flesh is flesh, so the Man in God is God.'[40]

Later, in the East, St John Damascene was an eloquent defender of the doctrine of *Theotokos*:

Moreover we proclaim the holy Virgin to be in strict truth the Mother of God. For inasmuch as He who was born of her was true God, she who bore the true God incarnate is the true Mother of God. For we hold that God was born of her, not implying that the divinity of the Word received from her the beginning of its being, but meaning that God the Word Himself, Who was begotten of the Father time-lessly before the ages, and was with the Father and the Spirit without beginning through eternity, took up His abode in these last days for the sake of our salvation in the Virgin's womb, and was without change made flesh and born of her. For the holy Virgin did not give birth to mere man but to true God: and not only God but God incarnate, Who did not bring down His body from Heaven, nor simply passed through the Virgin as a channel, but received flesh from her, of like essence to our own and subsisting in Himself. For if the body had come down from heaven and had not partaken of our nature, what would have been the use of His becoming man? For the purpose of God the Word becoming man was that the very same nature, which had sinned and fallen and become corrupted, should triumph over the deceiving tyrant and so be freed from corruption.[41]

John Damascene therefore professed that Mary is justly and truly called the Mother of God, and that this name encapsulates the whole economy of salvation. Also conversely, starting from the truth that Mary who bore Christ is the Mother of God, then it follows that He Who was born of her is God and likewise also man. For how could God, Who was before the ages, have been born of a woman unless He had become man? For the Son of Man must clearly be man Himself. However if He Who was born of a woman is Himself God, manifestly He Who was born of God the Father in accordance with the laws of an essence that is divine and knows no beginning, and He Who was in the last days born of the Virgin in accordance with the laws of an essence that has beginning and is subject to time, that is, an essence which is human, must be one and the same. The name in truth signifies the one subsistence and the two natures and the two generations of our Lord Jesus Christ. For the Word Himself became flesh, having been in truth conceived of the Virgin, but coming forth as God with the assumed nature which, as soon as He was brought forth into being, was deified by Him, so that these three things took place simultaneously, the assumption of our nature, the coming into being, and the deification of the assumed nature by the Word. John Damascene concludes that the holy Virgin is thought of and spoken of as the Mother of God, not only because of the nature of the Word, but also because of the deification of man's nature, the miracles of conception and of existence being wrought together, namely the conception the Word, and the existence of the flesh in the Word Himself. For the very Mother of God in some marvellous manner was the means of fashioning the Framer of all things and of bestowing manhood on the God and Creator of all, Who deified the nature that He assumed, while the union preserved those things that were united just as they were united, that is to say, not only the divine nature of Christ but also His human nature, not only that which is above us but that which is of us.[42]

The Council of Chalcedon in 451, made its own the expression *Theotokos*, in the context of its affirmation of the two natures in Christ:

> We all with one voice teach the confession of one and the same Son, our Lord Jesus Christ: the same perfect in divinity and perfect in humanity, the same truly God and truly man, of a rational soul and a body; consubstantial with the Father as regards his divinity, and the same consubstantial with us as regards his humanity; like us in all respects except for sin; begotten before the ages from the Father as regards his divinity, and in the last days the same for us and for our salvation from Mary, the virgin God-bearer (*Theotokos*) as regards his humanity.[43]

The significance of the title *Theotokos* was further explained by Pope John II in a letter to the Senate of Constantinople: 'We teach that it is right for Catholics to confess that the glorious and holy Mary, ever Virgin, is truly and properly Mother of God and Mother of God the Word incarnate from her.' The Pope further elaborated that this title cannot be understood either in a Nestorian or in a monophysite manner, since the Son of God was born from Mary truly and properly. Properly, 'lest one should believe that the Lord Jesus Christ received the name of God as a title of honour or as a favour as Nestorius foolishly taught; truly, lest one should believe that from the Virgin he took on a mere appearance of flesh or in some other way a flesh which was not real, as Eutyches irreverently declared.'[44]

The doctrine of the divine Motherhood was once again reaffirmed after it had become clear that the teaching of Theodore of Mopsuestia (d. 428) was also unsound. It took some time for the heresy latent in Theodore's writings to be uncovered, and his views were finally condemned at the Second Council of Constantinople in 553, which stated:

> If anyone declares that it can be only inexactly and not truly said that the holy and glorious ever-virgin Mary is the Mother of God, or says that she is so only in some relative way, considering that she bore a mere man and that God the Word was not made into human flesh in her, holding rather that the nativity of a man from her was referred, as they say, to God the Word as he was with the man who came into being; ... or if anyone says that she is the mother of a man or the Christ-bearer, that is the mother of Christ, suggesting that Christ is not God; and does not formally confess that she is properly and truly the mother of God, because he who before all ages was born of the Father, God the Word, has been made into human flesh in these latter days and has been born to her: let him be anathema.[45]

A persistent denial of the reality of Christ's human body

required further definitions of the Magisterium of the Church which also touched on the doctrine of Mary's divine maternity. In particular, the error of monothelitism, which proposed only one will in Christ, was simply an extension of monophysitism. The Lateran Council in 649 condemned this error, and at the same time affirmed the corporeal birth of Jesus Christ, from 'holy Mary, ever Virgin, Mother of God.'[46] This Lateran Council was authoritative if not a General Council. However, the same topic of two wills and two actions in Christ was taken up again by the third Council of Constantinople, which defined this doctrine, and also reiterated that Mary is 'properly and truly called Mother of God.'[47]

During more recent times the doctrine of the divine Motherhood has also been reaffirmed. One occasion was provided by the condemnation of Socianism, which basically denied the distinction of persons in the Godhead. Paul IV in his Constitution *Cum quorundam hominum* of 1555, which was confirmed in 1603 by Clement VIII in *Dominici gregis*, condemned several errors including that which denied that the Blessed Virgin was truly the Mother of God.[48] Then in 1743, Pope Benedict XIV required of the Maronites a Profession of Faith, in which adherence to the doctrine of the General Councils was involved, and by that token affirmation of the doctrine of the *Theotokos* formed part.[49]

In modern times, Pope Pius XI commemorated the fifteenth centenary of the Council of Ephesus with his encyclical *Lux Veritatis* on 25 December 1931. Against recent attempts to rehabilitate Nestorius, Pope Pius XI indicated that the traditional verdict stands: 'The Church, however, protests against this futile and temerarious attempt; for she has at all times acknowledged the condemnation of Nestorius as rightly and deservedly decreed; and has regarded the doctrine of Cyril as orthodox; and has counted the Council of Ephesus among the Ecumenical Synods, celebrated under the guidance of the Holy Spirit, and has held it in veneration.'[50]

More recently still, Pope John Paul II has insisted that the heritage of Ephesus enjoys permanent and perpetual value, and referred to the truth defined there 'concerning the Blessed Virgin, called to the unique and unrepeatable dignity of being the Mother of God, the Theotokos.'[51] The Pope excluded any compromise with the Nestorian error: 'In proclaiming Mary "Mother of God", the Church in a single phrase professes her belief regarding the Son and the Mother. This union was already seen at the Council of Ephesus; in defining Mary's divine motherhood, the Fathers intended to emphasize their belief in the divinity of Christ. Despite ancient and recent objections about the appropriateness of recognizing Mary by this title, Christians of all times, by correctly interpreting the meaning of this motherhood, have made it a privileged expression of their faith in the divinity of Christ and their love for the Blessed Virgin.'[52] The fundamental reason for the importance of the doctrine of the *Theotokos* is that the Christological doctrines rest upon it. The dogma of Mary's divine motherhood was for the Council of Ephesus and is for the Church like a confirmation of the dogma of the Incarnation, in which the Word truly assumes human nature into the unity of His person, without cancelling out that nature.[53]

Consequences of the divine Motherhood

Further reflection on the doctrine of Mary being Mother of God came about during the course of the Middle Ages. St Thomas Aquinas pointed out that the woman of whom any person is born is called his mother, for the reason that she supplies the matter for human conception. Hence the Blessed Virgin Mary, who provided the matter for the conception of the Son of God, should be called the true mother of the Son of God. As far as the essence of motherhood is concerned, the energy whereby the matter furnished by a woman is formed, does not enter into the question. She who supplied matter to be formed by the Holy Spirit is no less a mother than a woman who supplies matter that is to be formed by the energy latent in male seed. If anyone insists on maintaining that the Blessed Virgin ought not to be called the Mother of God because flesh alone and not divinity was derived from her, as Nestorius contended, he clearly is not aware of what he is saying. A woman is not called a mother for the reason that everything that is in her child is derived from her. Man is made up of body and soul; and a man is what he is in virtue of his soul rather than in virtue of his body. But no man's soul is derived from his mother. The soul is created directly by God. Consequently, just as any woman is a mother from the fact that her child's body is derived from her, so the Blessed Virgin Mary ought to be called the Mother of God if the body of God is derived from her. However, we have to hold that it is the body of God, if it is taken up into the unity of the person of God's Son, who is true God. Therefore all who admit that human nature was assumed by the Son of God into the unity of His person, must admit that the Blessed Virgin Mary is the Mother of God. Nestorius, who denied that the person of God and of the man Jesus Christ was one, was forced by logical necessity to deny that the Virgin Mary was the Mother of God.[54] The Angelic Doctor also focused on how Mary was affected by being the Mother of God, how this elevated her far above any other human creature: 'The Blessed Virgin, because she is the Mother of God, has a certain infinite dignity from the infinite good, which is God.'[55]

At the Reformation, even Luther insisted on the importance of Mary's divine Maternity:

The great thing is none other than that she became the Mother of God; in which process so many and such great gifts are bestowed upon her that no one is able to comprehend them. Thereupon follows all honour, all blessedness, and the fact that in the whole race of men only one person is above the rest, one to whom no one else is equal. For that reason her dignity is summed up in one phrase when we call her Mother of God; no one can say greater things of her or to her, even if he had as many tongues as leaves and blades of grass, as stars in heaven and sands on the seashore. It should also be meditated in the heart what that means: to be the Mother of God.[56]

While Luther had already left the Church when he wrote this, later he began to object to any special honour being paid to Mary. He still called her the Mother of God, but only 'because we cannot all be Mothers of God; otherwise she is on the same level as us.'[57] The history of Protestantism showed that while there was no explicit denial of the divine Maternity, the full import and consequences of the doctrine were not accepted and developed. In other words, the lack of due veneration offered to the Mother of God brought about a progressive dilution of the doctrine until the very divinity of Christ Himself was called into question.[58]

There was no such vacillation in the words of John Henry Newman regarding the doctrine of the divine Maternity: 'It is, then, an integral portion of the Faith fixed by Ecumenical Council, ... that the Blessed Virgin is Theotokos, ... or Mother of God; and this word, when thus used, carries with it no admixture of rhetoric, no taint of extravagant affection – it has nothing else but a well-weighed, grave, dogmatic sense, which corresponds and is adequate to its sound.'[59] Newman also re-echoed the idea of St Thomas pointing out that God is her Son, as truly as any one of us is the son of his own mother. Therefore, Newman adds, what can be said of any creature whatever, which may not be said of her? What can be overstated, so that it does not compromise the attributes of the Creator? God indeed might have created a more perfect and more admirable being than she is. He might have endowed that being, so created, with a richer gift of grace, of power, of blessedness: but in one respect she surpasses all even possible creations, namely that she is Mother of her

Creator. [60] Newman forcefully makes the profession of the Theotokos a test for the discernment of spirits: 'The confession that Mary is *Deipara*, or the Mother of God, is that safeguard wherewith we seal up and secure the doctrine of the Apostles from all evasion, and that test whereby we detect all the pretences of those bad spirits of "Antichrist which have gone out into the world." It declares that He is God; it implies that He is man; it suggests to us that He is God still, though He has become man, and that He is true man though He is God.'[61]

Also in the nineteenth century, Scheeben discussed the theology of the divine Motherhood, which he considered in terms of a relationship with the Word of God. The divine Motherhood is the distinguishing mark of Mary's person, and is more than a mere privilege or office conferred upon her by God. Rather it involves the highest service a creature can offer her Creator. In union with the Eternal Father she conceives His Son in her womb. The Son makes the perfect gift of Himself to Mary, giving Himself to be her Son, clothing Himself with her flesh in her womb.[62] Scheeben ascribes to Mary's divine Motherhood an ontological quality when he writes that Mary possesses the Word who gives Himself to her as her Son, and 'forms with her an organic oneness,' in which Mary is His closest associate and helper in the most intimate and permanent community of life.[63] Mary is Bride and Mother of the Word: Bride because she is Mother and Mother because she is Bride. These two aspects are indissolubly associated in Mary, and taken together constitute the supernatural hallmark of Mary's person.[64] Mary's bridal Motherhood is not merely an accidental or a moral relation; it is rather a 'hypostatic, substantial or essential distinguishing mark' of Mary's person, due to her spiritual union with the word dwelling in her with whom she is formed into one organic whole. The entire dignity and perfection of Mary is determined by this union.[65] The divine Person of Christ becomes 'grown together with her' as a fruit with its root, and dwells bodily in her. Mary is endowed with this substantial grace from the beginning of her existence, making her always the bride of the Person of the Word, so that this relation to His Person shapes her whole being, elevating it to the hypostatic order.

These considerations of the ontological basis for the divine Motherhood imply that Mary's being as Mother of God precede her action as Christ's disciple. In Mary, both being and action are important, but as elsewhere in theology, it is being that grounds action (*agere sequitur esse*). Therefore a question must be raised about recent attempts to use one of St Augustine's sermons to propose that Mary's discipleship is more important than her divine Motherhood: 'It is a greater thing for her that she was Christ's disciple than that she was His Mother. It is a happier thing to be His disciple than to be His Mother ... Her mind was filled more fully with Truth than her womb by His flesh ... Greater is that which is in her mind than that which she carried in her womb.' [66] These attempts, if not St Augustine's own perspective, are an exaggeration of the Western tendency to over-emphasize action at the expense of being. St Thomas Aquinas rightly interprets St Augustine's passage by setting it in the context that Mary must know about being Mother of God, that is the mystery must be announced to her. The Angelic Doctor points out that it was reasonable that it should be announced to the Blessed Virgin that she was to conceive Christ. First, in order to maintain a becoming order in the union of the Son of God with the Virgin, namely, that she should be informed in mind concerning Him, before conceiving Him in the flesh. Thus Augustine says 'Mary is more blessed in receiving the faith of Christ, than in conceiving the flesh of Christ'.[67] The whole point of Augustine's idea is to extend our relationship with Christ beyond the flesh and blood bonds of family ties. However, his hyperbolic use of language should not be taken to undermine the importance of the doctrine of the *Theotokos* which must be based on the physical aspect of Mary's maternity within a realist perspective. Another consequence of the ontological nature of Mary's divine Motherhood is that her excellence exceeds by its very nature that of the angels and saints. In that way, she is regarded as Queen of the Angels and Queen of all Saints, for she transcends the highest of the angels and the greatest of the saints.

St Louis Grignon de Montfort drew out the Trinitarian aspects of the doctrine of Mary, Mother of God. He hinted that in a certain sense, Mary shares in the Father's paternity: 'God the Father imparted to Mary his fruitfulness as far as a mere creature was capable of receiving it, to enable her to bring forth His Son and all the members of His mystical body.'[68] This idea was to be further developed by later theologians. Montfort indicated how Christ was Mary's Son: 'God the Son came into her virginal womb as a new Adam into his earthly paradise, to take his delight there and produce hidden wonders of grace.'[69] Mary's Motherhood, did not however stop with the mystery of the Incarnation, but continued on in Christ's earthly life. Christ glorified His independence and His majesty in depending upon His Mother in His conception, His birth, His presentation in the temple, and in the thirty years of His hidden life. Even at His death she had to be present so that He might be united with her in one sacrifice and be immolated with her consent to the eternal Father, just as formerly Isaac was offered in sacrifice by Abraham when he accepted the will of God. 'It was Mary who nursed Him, fed Him, cared for Him, reared Him, and sacrificed Him for us.'[70] Mary's maternal participation in Her Son's sacrifice forms the basis for the doctrine of Mary as Coredemptrix.[71] Montfort also showed how Mary is the spouse of the Holy Spirit: 'God the Holy Spirit, who does not produce any divine person, became fruitful through Mary whom He espoused. It was with her, in her and of her that He produced His masterpiece, God-made-man, and that He produces every day until the end of the world the members of the body of this adorable Head. For this reason the more He finds Mary His dear and inseparable spouse in a soul the more powerful and effective He becomes in producing Jesus Christ in that soul and that soul in Jesus Christ.'[72]

The divine Motherhood of Mary relates her in a most special way to God the Father, in a formal participation in the fecundity of His nature. This theological theme has its roots back in seventeenth century scholarship.[73] However, theologians have only given this question more detailed consideration in the twentieth century. This special relationship between the Mother of God and the First Person of the Blessed Trinity derives from the fact that the divine and human generations terminate in the one and the same Person of Christ. It is the one Person who is related as Son to God the Father and to the Virgin Mary. As Christ is the only-begotten of the One, so He is the only begotten of the other. Since the procession of the Son from the Father is an eternal action, one can propose that at the mysterious moment of the Incarnation, the two generations coincided, and Mary begot her Son being while He was being begotten by the Father.[74] Furthermore, all relation to the eternal Son with regard to generation is exclusively proper to the Eternal Father. Therefore one can enjoy this relationship to the Son only through a participation of what is specifically proper to the Father. Therefore Mary participates in the fecundity of the Father. It must be stressed that this is a gift of the Father, which brings with it the gift of the Son, who gives Himself formally as Son. The only reason that the Son of God could be the Son of Mary is precisely because His own personal being is to be Son. Further, the Holy Spirit also gives Himself according to His own personal function, realising in Mary the fecundity of the Father and the filiation of the Son. In this way, the Trinitarian dimension of Mary's divine Motherhood is expressed, at the same time respecting the truth of theology that the communication of the Father to Mary necessarily involves the communication of the other divine Persons. This is required so as to safeguard the doctrine that all the *ad extra* activities of God are common to the three Persons, which also maintains the status of

Our Lady as a creature.[75] Along these lines, if one maintains that the divine Motherhood is the most perfect
possible created assimilation to the divine Paternity, it
would seem to indicate that Mary's divine Motherhood is
necessarily a virginal motherhood. From this perspective,
the current chapter has examined one part of the arch
making up the doctrine of Mary, Virgin and Mother. The
coming chapter will uncover the other part.

Notes

[1] See Pope Pius XII, Encyclical Letter *Fulgens Corona*, 11, where he
    indicates that a dignity greater than that of Mother of God does not
    seem possible. Her position 'demands the fullness of Divine grace
    and a soul immune from stain, since it requires the greatest dignity
    and sanctity after Christ. Indeed, from this sublime office of the
    Mother of God seem to flow, as it were from a most limpid hidden
    source, all the privileges and graces with which her soul and life
    were adorned in such extraordinary manner and measure.'
[2] See Vatican II, *Lumen Gentium*, 66.
[3] See CCC 490.
[4] See CCC 499.
[5] See CCC 966.
[6] See Pope John Paul II, *Discourse at General Audience* (13 September
    1995), 4.
[7] *Docetism* was an error with several variations concerning the nature
    of Christ. Generally, it taught that Jesus only seemed (Greek *dokein* =
    to seem) to have a body, so that He was not really and truly incarnate.
    This error developed out of the dualistic philosophy which viewed
    matter as inherently evil, that God could not be associated with
    matter. The basic principle of Docetism was already refuted by St
    John the Apostle: 'This is the proof of the Spirit of God: any spirit
    which acknowledges Jesus Christ, come in human nature, is from
    God, and no spirit which fails to acknowledge Jesus is from God; it is
    the spirit of Antichrist, whose coming you have heard of; he is
    already at large in the world' (1 Jn 4:2–3). St Ignatius of Antioch (died
    around 100), St Irenaeus (115–190), and St Hippolytus (170–235)
    combatted the error in the early part of the second century. Docetism
    was condemned at the Council of Chalcedon in 451.
[8] *Gnosticism*, derived from the Greek word *gnosis* (knowledge)
    claimed a superior secret understanding of things. It was a system
    based on philosophical knowledge rather than on faith, where the

distinction between the eternal uncreated Supreme Being and all other beings was blurred or erased. The production of matter was expressed in terms of a downward emanation from God or as the work of a demiurge. The fact that the Gnostics belittled matter meant that they could not accept the Incarnation. Thus their knowledge of God was based on what they could acquire through their secret and elitist understanding of things rather than through revelation received from Christ. St Irenaeus in particular fought against this heresy.

9   *Manichaeism* is the name given to ideas linked with the dualist sect founded by Mani (216–276) who was born in Babylonia but then lived in Persia in the third century. The system consisted of a hybrid mixture of many religious elements, teaching that at the beginning of the cosmos there were two equal and opposite principles, good and evil or light and darkness. Through their fight for supremacy, the world was created. There were two levels of believers, and the fact that the members of the higher level (the 'elect') were forbidden to marry, to consume meat or wine and were not allowed to work indicated a belief that the material realm was evil. St Augustine was a follower of the Manichaean sect in his youth and after his conversion to Christianity refuted it in his writings.

10   See Tertullian, *De carne Christi*, chapter 20 in *CSEL* 70, 238

11   See St Irenaeus, *Adversus haereses*, Book 3, chapter 17, 1 in *PG* 7, 921.

12   St Irenaeus, *Adversus haereses*, Book 3, chapter 19, 2 in *PG* 7, 940.

13   St Irenaeus, *Adversus haereses*, Book 5, chapter 19, 1 in *PG* 7, 1175.

14   *The Apostolic Tradition of St Hippolytus*, 21, 15, ed. G. Dix (London: 1937), p. 36.

15   See St Augustine, *Sermo* 186, 1 in *PL* 38, 999: 'Quomodo Deus esse desisteret, cum homo esse coepit, qui genitrici suae praestitit ne desisteret virgo esse, cum peperit?' See also Idem, *Sermo* 195, n. 2 in *PL* 38, 1018.

16   St Hippolytus, *De benedictionibus Iacob*, chapter 1. However, since it does not appear in the Georgian translation of the text, the authenticity of the occurrence of the word *Theotokos* is debated. See also chapter 27, where Hippolytus wrote that Mary was literally pregnant with the Word of God, with God's Son. In another more obscure work, he wrote: 'They preached the advent of God in the flesh to the world, His advent by the spotless and God-bearing (*Theotokos*) Mary in the way of birth and growth, and the manner of His life and conversation with men, and His manifestation by baptism, and the new birth that was to be to all men, and the regeneration by the baptism.' See St Hippolytus, *A Discourse on the End of the World, and on Antichrist, and on The Second Coming of Our Lord Jesus Christ*, 1.

17   See C. H. Roberts (ed.), *Catalogue of the Greek and Latin Papyri in the*

John Rylands Library, Volume 3 (Cambridge: 1939), n. 470. However, while Roberts dates the prayer to the second half of the fourth century, other scholars like Vanucci date it to the third century. See G. Vannucci, 'La più antica preghiera alla Madre di Dio' in *Marianum* 3 (1941), pp. 97–101. See also M. J. Healy, 'The Divine Maternity in the Early Church' in *Marian Studies* 6 (1955), pp. 49–50. The prayers runs: 'We fly to your patronage, O holy Mother of God: despise not our petitions in our necessities, but deliver us from all evil, O glorious and blessed Virgin.'

[18] As regards Origen, see Socrates, *Historia Ecclesiastica* 7, 32 in *PG* 67, 811 who maintains that the former used the expression *Theotokos* in a part (now lost) of his *Commentary on St Paul's Letter to the Romans*.

[19] St Alexander of Alexandria, *Epistle to Alexander, Bishop of Constantinople*, 12 in *PG* 18, 568.

[20] St Athanasius, *De Incarnatione Dei Verbi et contra Arianos*, 8 in *PG* 26, 995.

[21] St Cyril of Jerusalem, *Catechetical Lectures* 10, 19 in *PG* 33, 685.

[22] St Ephraem the Syrian, *Precatio Secunda* in *EM* 339: 'Virgo Domina Deipara, benedicta Dei Genitrix, benedictissima Mater Dei, Deo gratissima, supra omnes benedicta, vas divinitatis Unigeniti filii immortalis, et invisibilis Patris, inclina aurem tuam, atque exaudi verba emissa a labiis meis sordidis, et impuris.'

[23] St Ambrose had studied in particular the works of Athanasius, Didymus, Gregory Nazianzen and Cyril of Jerusalem, all of whom had used the expression.

[24] St Ambrose, *De virginibus* lib. 2, cap. 2, n. 7 in *PL* 16, 209. See also Idem, *In Hexameron*, lib. 5, cap. 20, n. 65 in *PL* 14, 233; *Expositio evangelii secundum Lucam*, lib. 2, n. 26 and lib. 10, n. 130 in *PL* 15, 1561 and 1837.

[25] See St Augustine, *Sermo* 289, n. 2 in *PL* 38, 1308.

[26] St Augustine, *De Trinitate*, lib. 15, cap. 26, n. 46 in *PL* 42, 1093–1094.

[27] St Hilary, *Tractatus in Ps.131*, n. 8 in *PL* 9, 733.

[28] St Hilary, *Tractatus in Ps.126*, n. 16 in *PL* 9, 700. See also Idem, *De Trinitate* lib. 10, n. 17 in *PL* 10, 356.

[29] St Basil, *Homilia in sanctam Christi generationem*, 5 in *PG* 31, 1468.

[30] St Gregory of Nyssa, *De virginitate* cap. 13 in *PG* 46, 377. See also ibid., 19 in *PG* 46, 396; Idem, *In diem natalem Christi* in *PG* 46, 1136; Idem, *In Christi resurrectionem*, 5 in *PG* 46, 688.

[31] St Gregory Nazianzen, *Letter to Cledonius the Priest* 101 in *PG* 37, 177–180. See also St Gregory of Nyssa, *Epistola* 3 in *PG* 46, 1024, where he also condemned the theory of two Sons, one of God and the other of Mary: 'Let none of us dare to call the Holy Virgin, the Mother of God, 'Mother of man' also as some recklessly do.'

[32] See Diodore of Tarsus, *Contra Synousiastas* in *PG* 33, 1560. See also Theodore of Mopsuestia, *Contra Appollinarem* in *PG* 66, 993: 'He

who was born of the Virgin is the one who was formed of her substance, not the Word who is God. He who is of one nature with the Father has no mother.'

33 See John of Antioch, *Epistola ad Nestorium* in *PG* 77, 1455: 'None of the teachers of the Church has rejected the term *Theotokos*. Many indeed of the greatest among them have used it and those who did not use it have not censured those who did.'

34 St Cyril of Alexandria, *First Letter to Nestorius* in *PG* 77, 48–49.

35 See Pope Celestine I, *Letter to St Cyril of Alexandria* in *PL* 50, 463: 'Wherefore in virtue of the authority of Our See, and acting in Our stead, you will strictly enforce this sentence that he must either within ten days, to be numbered from the day of this decision, condemn his evil declarations in a written profession, and prove that he holds the same faith concerning the birth of Christ our God which is held by the Roman Church and that of Your Holiness and by the devotion of all; or if he will not do this, then Your Holiness to make provision for that Church, must know that he must by all means be removed from our body.'

36 St Cyril of Alexandria, *Second Letter to Nestorius* in TN 1, 43–44.

37 See Second Council of Constantinople, *Anathema 13 against the 'Three Chapters'* in TN 1,121.

38 Council of Ephesus, *Third Letter of Cyril to Nestorius*, Anathema 1 in TN 1, 59.

39 'Our Lord Jesus Christ, who has been blasphemed by him, has determined through this most holy synod that the same Nestorius should be stripped of his episcopal dignity and removed from the college of priests.' Council of Ephesus, *The judgement against Nestorius* in TN 1, 62.

40 Vincent of Lerins, *Commonitorium I*, cap. 15 in *PL* 50, 658.

41 St John Damascene, *An Exposition of the Orthodox Faith*, Book 3, chapter 12 in *PG* 94, 1028–1030.

42 *Ibid.*, in *PG* 94, 1029–1032.

43 Council of Chalcedon, Definition of the Faith in TN 1, 86.

44 Pope John II, *Letter to the Senate of Constantinople* in ND 617.

45 Second Council of Constantinople, 6th anathema against the 'Three Chapters' in TN 1, 116

46 The Lateran Council, in ND 627/4.

47 The Third Council of Constantinople, *Exposition of faith* in TN 1, 127.

48 See Pope Paul IV, Constitution *Cum quorundam hominum* in ND 707.

49 See Pope Benedict XIV, Constitution *Nuper ad nos* in DS 2528–2529.

50 Pope Pius XI, Encyclical Letter *Lux Veritatis*, 27.

51 Pope John Paul II, Apostolic Letter *A Concilio Constantinopolitano I* (For the 1600th Anniversary of the First Council of Constantinople and the 1550th Anniversary of the Council of Ephesus), 3.

[52]   Pope John Paul II, *Discourse at General Audience* (27 November 1996), 4

[53]   See Pope John Paul II, Encyclical Letter, *Redemptoris Mater*, 4

[54]   See St Thomas Aquinas, *Compendium of Theology*, Part 1, chapter 222.

[55]   St Thomas Aquinas, *Summa Theologiae*, I, q. 25, a. 6.

[56]   M. Luther, *Die Erklärung des Magnificat* in M. Luther, *Martin Luthers Werke* (Weimar: Böhlau), Volume 7, p. 546.

[57]   M. Luther, *Martin Luthers Werke* (Weimar: Böhlau), Volume 10, part 3, p. 316.

[58]   This denial came about in books like that of J. Hick, *The Myth of God Incarnate* (London: SCM, 1977).

[59]   J. H. Newman, *The Mother of God* edited with an Introduction and Notes by S. L. Jaki (Pinckney, MI: Real View Books, 2003), pp. 55–56.

[60]   *Ibid.*

[61]   J. H. Newman, 'The Glories of Mary for the Sake of her Son', in *Discourses Addressed to Mixed Congregations*, (London: Longmans, 1906), pp. 347–348.

[62]   See M. J. Scheeben, *Handbuch der katholischen Dogmatik*, Volume 3 (Freiburg in Breisgau: 1882), nn. 1589–1590.

[63]   *Ibid.*, n. 1588.

[64]   *Ibid.*, n. 1597.

[65]   *Ibid.*, nn. 1602, 1591.

[66]   St Augustine, *Sermon* 25, 7–8 in *PL* 46, 937–938. A similar idea is to be found in Idem, *De sancta virginitate*, 3 in *PL* 40, 397–398 : 'Therefore Mary is more blessed in receiving the faith of Christ, than in conceiving the flesh of Christ. For to a certain one who said, 'Blessed is the womb that bore You,' He Himself made answer, 'Blessed rather are those who hear the Word of God and keep it.' Lastly, to His brethren, that is, His kindred after the flesh, who believed not in Him, what profit was there in that being of kin? Thus also her nearness as a Mother would have been of no profit to Mary, had she not borne Christ in her heart after a more blessed manner than in her flesh.'

[67]   See St Thomas Aquinas, *Summa Theologiae III*, q. 30, a. 1.

[68]   St Louis Grignon de Montfort, *Treatise on True Devotion to the Blessed Virgin*, 17.

[69]   *Ibid.*, 18.

[70]   *Ibid.*

[71]   See chapter 7, pp. 187–201 below for a discussion of this topic.

[72]   St Louis Grignon de Montfort, *Treatise on True Devotion to the Blessed Virgin*, 20. However, Montfort clarifies his position on Mary as Spouse of the Holy Spirit in n. 21 by adding: 'This does not mean that the Blessed Virgin confers on the Holy Spirit a fruitfulness which he does not already possess. Being God, he has the ability to produce just like the Father and the Son, although he does not use this power

and so does not produce another divine person. But it does mean that the Holy Spirit chose to make use of our Blessed Lady, although he had no absolute need of her, in order to become actively fruitful in producing Jesus Christ and his members in her and by her.'

73   See S. de Saavedra, *Sacra Deipara, seu de eminentissima dignitate Deigenitricis immaculatissimae* (Lugduni: 1655), vest. 1, nn. 460–475.

74   See J. J. McGreevy, 'Divine Maternity' in K. McNamara (ed.), *Mother of the Redeemer. Aspects of Doctrine and Devotion* (Dublin: Gill and Son Ltd., 1959), pp. 75–76.

75   See Lateran IV, *Symbol of Lateran* in ND 19 and Council of Florence, *Decree for the Copts* in ND 325, where it is stated: 'Father, Son and Holy Spirit are not three origins of creation but one origin.'

CHAPTER 6

EVER A VIRGIN

Mary remained a virgin in conceiving her Son, a virgin in giving birth to Him, a virgin in carrying Him, a virgin in nursing Him at her breast, always a virgin.

St Augustine, *Sermon 186.*

The occurrence of miraculous births in the Scriptures usually foreshadowed a special divine mission for the child born in such circumstances, like Abraham, Samson and John the Baptist. However, these were cases of sterile or aged mothers being granted a miraculous gift of fertility. It is therefore completely fitting that the coming of Christ the Saviour should completely transcend the entry of those who prefigured Him in some way. The gift of fertility to hitherto sterile mothers was but a pale prefiguration of the gift of fruitful virginity bestowed on Mary, the Mother of God. The virginal conception is indicative also of the completely gratuitous nature of Christ's redemptive Incarnation. It is carried out without the aid of human agencies; it can only happen because God has freely chosen to intervene.

Although Our Lady's Motherhood and her virginity are dealt with in separate chapters they are really part of the same mystery of the Virgin Motherhood. When considering this privilege of Our Lady, so intimately united with her Motherhood, and with Christ's Incarnation, it has been customary to distinguish between virginity of the mind or of the spirit (*virginitas mentis*), virginity of the senses (*virginitas sensus*) and virginity of the body (*virginitas corporis*). While making these distinctions, we should remember that in theology it is helpful to distinguish in order to unite, to analyze in order to synthesize. The distinction is made in order to shed light on the mystery of Mary's virginity as a whole, remembering that each aspect is important in the realist perspective which this work proposes. In particular, recent attempts to exaggerate the spiritual aspect of Mary's virginity at the expense of the physical aspect could endanger the true doctrine concerning Mary's great privilege. Virginity of the mind is the determination of Our Lady to refrain from any thought word or action contrary to perfect chastity. Consideration of a vow of chastity made by Our Lady would come under this heading. Virginity of the senses describes Our Lady's complete freedom from disordered movements of the flesh, and is included in her freedom from concupiscence.[1] Virginity of the body refers to the virginal state of Our Lady's body, which excludes all damage to or violation of the generative organs, and all experience of venereal pleasure.[2]

The bodily virginity of Our Lady is further elaborated as virginity before the Birth of Christ, during his Birth and after His Birth (*virginitas ante partum, in partu,* and *post partum*). The doctrine of *virginitas ante partum* teaches the absence of marital relations between Our Lady and St Joseph up to the time of Christ's birth, and therefore affirms the virginal conception. The *virginitas in partu* includes the non-rupture of the hymen at the moment of birth, which takes place without any opening of the membranes or damage to Our Lady's body, and without pain. This description of the *virginitas in partu* involves a miraculous Birth, during which Christ passed from His Mother's womb, as He later passed from the closed sepulchre. At the same time, it was a true Birth. The teaching concerning *virginitas post partum* excludes marital relations, and thus the generation of other children, after the Birth of Christ. Taken together these truths constitute the perpetual virginity of the Blessed Virgin Mary. Often Western Patristic theology tended to focus on Mary's virginity in terms of its exemplary value, as is found in an affirmation of St Ambrose: 'Mary's life should be for you a pictorial image of virginity. Her life is like a mirror reflecting the face of chastity and the form of virtue. Therein you may find a model for your own life, showing what to improve, what to imitate, what to hold fast to.'[3] In Eastern Christendom, the Christological significance of this truth was emphasized, as St Gregory of Nyssa illustrates: 'It was fitting that He who became man to give all men incorruption should begin human life of an incorrupt Mother; for men are accustomed to call her incorrupt who is unwed.'[4]

Virginity before the Birth of Christ

A long-standing tradition indicates that Our Lady had, from an early age, made a vow of virginity. Mary asks a question of the angel who tells her of Jesus' conception and birth: 'But how can this come about, since I have no knowledge of man?' (Lk 1:34). The question clearly alludes to sexual intercourse of married persons, since 'knowledge' in this context is a hallowed Semitic expression for physical love. At first sight, Mary's words would seem merely to express only her present state of virginity: Mary would affirm that she does not 'know' man, that is, that she is a virgin. Nevertheless, the context in which the question is asked: 'But how can this come about?' and the affirmation that follows: 'since I have no knowledge of man', emphasize both Mary's present virginity and her intention to remain a virgin. Indeed, in her question, Mary did not look to the past, as if to say 'since up to this time, I have not known man.' If this had been the case, St Luke would have employed the past tense (aorist: *ouk egnon*) instead of the present absolute (*ouk gignosko*), which includes the intention of not making use of matrimonial relations in the future as well. The expression adopted, with the verb in the present tense, reveals the permanence and continuity of her state. Thus Mary's question sets her situation apart radically from the biblical accounts that relate the announcement of an extraordinary birth to a childless woman. Those cases concerned married women who were naturally sterile, to whom God gave the gift of a child through their normal conjugal life (1 Sm 1:19–20), in response to their anguished prayers (cf. Gn 15:2, 30:22–23, 1 Sm 1:10; Lk 1:13). Mary receives the angel's message in a different situation. She is not a married woman with problems of sterility; rather, by her own inspired choice she intends to remain a virgin. Therefore her intention of virginity, the fruit of her love for the Lord, appears to be an obstacle to the motherhood announced to her.

Mary's words and intentions appear improbable to some, since in the Jewish world virginity was considered neither a value nor an ideal to be pursued.[5] Many Old Testament writings confirm this in several well-known episodes. In the Book of Judges, for example, Jephthah's daughter who, having to face death while still young and unmarried, bewails her virginity, that is, she laments that she has been unable to marry (Jg 11:38). Marriage, moreover, by virtue of the divine command, 'Be fruitful and multiply' (Gn 1:28), is considered woman's natural vocation which involves the joys and sufferings that go with motherhood. Nevertheless, historically during the period in which Mary's decision came to maturity, a certain positive attitude to virginity began to appear in some Jewish circles. For example, the Essenes, of whom many important historical testimonies have been found at Qûmran on the shores of the Dead Sea, lived in celibacy or restricted the use of marriage because of community life and the search for greater intimacy with God.[6] It does not seem that Mary ever knew about these Jewish religious groups which practiced the ideal of celibacy and virginity. However, the fact that John the Baptist probably lived a celibate life and that in the community of his disciples it was held in high esteem would support the supposition that Mary's choice of virginity belonged to this new cultural and religious context. Nevertheless, the extraordinary case of the Virgin of Nazareth cannot simply be reduced completely to the mentality of her culture, thereby eliminating the uniqueness of the mystery that came to pass in her. From the very beginning of her life, Mary received a wondrous grace, recognized by the angel at the moment of the Annunciation in the exclamation 'Hail, Full of grace' (Lk 1:28). Mary was enriched with a perfection of holiness that, according to the Church's interpretation, goes back to the very first moment of her existence: the unique privilege of the Immaculate Conception influenced the whole development of the spiritual life of the young woman of Nazareth. Filled with the Lord's exceptional gifts from the beginning of her life, Mary was oriented to a total gift of self, body and soul, to God, in the offering of herself as a virgin.

Tradition has long held that Mary's virginal consecration to God took place at her presentation in the Temple. According to Exodus 13:2 and 13:12, all the Hebrew firstborn male children had to be presented in the Temple. This law would lead pious Jewish parents to observe the same religious rite with regard to other favourite children. This leads us to think that Joachim and Anne presented Mary their child in the Temple. The tradition of Mary's vow of virginity was first expressed by St Augustine.[7] Some of the Fathers, like St Gregory of Nyssa and St Germanus of Constantinople state that Joachim and Anne, faithful to a vow they had made, presented the child Mary in the Temple when she was three years old; that the child herself mounted the Temple steps, and that she made her vow of virginity on this occasion.[8] St Thomas Aquinas indicated that Mary had at least desired to make a vow of virginity before being betrothed to Joseph, and afterwards both made such a vow.[9] Pope John Paul II has recently reaffirmed the tradition of a early vow of virginity made by Our Lady.[10]

The Virginal Conception of Christ

The Gospel accounts (Mt 1:18–25; Lk 1:26–38) teach the virginal conception of Jesus as a divine work that surpasses all human understanding and possibility. The angel announced to Joseph about Mary his betrothed: 'She has conceived what is in her by the Holy Spirit. (Mt 1:20). This is the fulfilment of the divine promise given through the prophet Isaiah: 'The young woman is with child and will give birth to a son whom she will call Immanuel.' This is the rendering of the Hebrew text, where the Hebrew word translated by 'young woman' is *'almâh*. In the Greek Septuagint version, the Hebrew *'almâh* is rendered by 'virgin', which is correct, because the immediate context of the passage is an extraordinary sign, which would not be credible unless the young woman was also a virgin. The fact that Isaiah 7:14 is prophetically linked to Matthew 1:23, further reinforces the reading 'virgin' for the Hebrew *'almâh*, to give: 'Behold, a virgin shall conceive and bear a son' (Is 7:14).[11]

The virginal conception of Christ from Our Lady must be carefully distinguished from a freak of nature, or from a type of asexual reproduction. Thus it excludes every rationalist hypothesis of natural parthenogenesis and rejects the attempts to explain Luke's account (Lk 1:26–38) as the development of a Jewish theme or as the derivation of a pagan mythological legend.[12] Instead, Our Lady's virginity and Motherhood involve a supernatural gift, *the* Supernatural Gift, her Son. In the episode of the Annunciation, the Evangelist Luke calls Mary a 'virgin', referring both to her intention to persevere in virginity, as well as to the divine plan which reconciles this intention with her miraculous motherhood. The affirmation of the virginal conception is inseparably linked with the action of the Holy Spirit, and so the structure of the Lucan text resists any reductive interpretation. Its coherence does not validly support any mutilation of the terms or expressions which affirm the virginal conception brought about by the

Holy Spirit. The conception of Mary's Divine Son was brought about by divine intervention, and so the virginity of Mary is closely connected with the complete doctrine concerning Christ, God made man. Indeed where denials occur of some aspect or other of Mary's virginity, there also follow some corresponding tendency to deny Christ's divinity. Such denials have generally occurred in liberal Protestantism, in rationalism and in modernism.

In the first chapter of St John's Gospel there is also an indication of the virginal conception of Jesus.[13] In the early Church, the singular reading of John 1:12–13 was very common, as is conserved in the Jerusalem Bible: 'But to all who did accept Him He gave power to become children of God, to all who believe in the name of Him who was born not out of human stock or urge of the flesh or will of man but of God Himself.' The current reading, as proposed by the New Jerusalem Bible is: 'But to those who did accept Him He gave power to become children of God, to those who believed in His name who were born not from human stock or human desire or human will but from God himself.' The earlier reading is to be found in St Ignatius of Antioch, St Irenaeus, and Tertullian among others. Then, it disappeared from biblical texts, apart from one ancient Latin version, and the Greek manuscripts have the plural form. It has been proposed that the original form was singular, but was changed to plural under the influence of Gnostic heretics who wanted to give a more spiritual sense to the text, moving away from the real conception of Christ in the flesh to the spiritual conception of the faithful through baptism.[14] The reading of John 1:13 in the singular is a clear affirmation of the virginal conception of Jesus. It is also significant that if the plural reading is indeed due to a Gnostic influence, then once again it can be seen that a denial of the virginal conception goes hand in hand with a denial of the Incarnation. A growing number of scholars propose that the singular reading is correct also for reasons of internal coherence.[15] Other scholars accept the plural reading of the passage but maintain that triple negation ('not from human stock or human desire or human will') corresponds exactly to the faith of the Church concerning the virginal conception, indicating that John clearly refers to this doctrine. He does so making the birth of Jesus the *model* for the rebirth of Christians in baptism.[16]

A further Scriptural indication of the virginal conception is that this situation is communicated to Joseph after it had occurred. 'Her husband Joseph, being an upright man and wanting to spare her disgrace, decided to divorce her informally. He had made up his mind to do this when suddenly the angel of the Lord appeared to him in a dream and said, "Joseph son of David, do not be afraid to take Mary home as your wife, because she has conceived what is in her by the Holy Spirit"' (Mt 1:18–20). Joseph was not invited to give his assent prior to the conception of Mary's Son, the fruit of the supernatural intervention of the Holy Spirit and the co-operation of the mother alone. He is simply asked to accept freely his role as the Virgin's husband and his paternal mission with regard to her Child. The Scriptural picture deprives of any foundation several recent interpretations which understand the virginal conception not in a physical or biological sense, but only as symbolic or metaphorical: it would rather designate Jesus as God's gift to humanity. Another false opinion is that the account of the virginal conception is a *theologoumenon*, namely a way of expressing a theological doctrine (that of Jesus' divine Sonship) without any real doctrinal underpinning, effectively in a mythological portrayal.[17] The Gospels contain the explicit affirmation of a virginal conception of the biological order, brought about by the Holy Spirit. In the early centuries, the Church Fathers reflected on this truth and elaborated it. The faith expressed in the Gospels is thus confirmed without interruption in later tradition. The early Christian writers presuppose the assertion of a real, historical virginal conception of Jesus and are far from affirming a virginity that is only a moral quality or a vague gift of grace manifested in the Child's birth.[18]

The fact that St Mark's Gospel and the New Testament Letters and Epistles do not explicitly refer to Jesus' virginal conception, is no argument against this truth. Thus one cannot claim that we are merely dealing with legends or theological constructs without an historical basis. Faith in the virginal conception of Jesus is based on historical fact, for it met with the lively opposition, mockery or incomprehension of non-believers, Jews and pagans alike, so it could hardly have been motivated by pagan mythology or by some adaptation to the ideas of the age.[19] From the first formulations of her faith, the Church has confessed that Jesus was conceived solely by the power of the Holy Spirit in the womb of the Virgin Mary, affirming also the corporeal aspect of this event.[20] Early credal formulae affirmed the virginal conception of Jesus. For example, in the *Apostolic Tradition* of Hippolytus, around the year 215, it is recorded that the candidates for baptism were asked: 'Do you believe in Jesus Christ, the Son of God, who was born of the Virgin Mary by the Holy Spirit?'[21]

Shortly after the death of St John, St Ignatius of Antioch (AD 107) wrote: 'Mary's virginity and giving birth, and even the Lord's death escaped the notice of the prince of this world: these three mysteries worthy of proclamation were accomplished in God's silence.'[22] Ignatius also remarked that according to the flesh, Our Lord Jesus Christ was born from the stock of David, 'but if we look at the will and the power of God, He is the Son of God, truly born of a virgin.'[23] St Justin Martyr employed the parallel between Eve and Mary, to accentuate the virginal conception. Christ 'became man by the Virgin, in order that the disobedience which proceeded from the serpent might receive its destruction in the same manner in which it derived its origin. For Eve, who was a virgin and unde-filed, having conceived the word of the serpent, brought forth disobedience and death. But the Virgin Mary received faith and joy, when the angel Gabriel announced the good tidings to her that the Spirit of the Lord would come upon her, and the power of the Highest would over-shadow her.'[24]

Around the year 200, St Irenaeus was another witness to the virginal conception. He opposed the error of Cerinthus, 'who represented Jesus as having not been born of a virgin, but as being the son of Joseph and Mary according to the ordinary course of human generation, while nevertheless He was more righteous, prudent, and wise than other men.'[25] Irenaeus also wrote against the Ebionites, who were Jewish Christians, who had only partially converted to Christianity, possibly deriving from Essene groups. They did not accept Christ as the Son of God in the Trinitarian sense, and so did not accept His virginal conception. Irenaeus based his affirmation of the virginal conception upon his doctrine of recapitulation: 'Since Adam himself had his substance from untilled, and as yet virgin soil, and was formed by the hand of God, that is, by the Word of God …; so did He who is the Word, recapitulating Adam in Himself, rightly receive a birth, enabling Him to gather up Adam into Himself, from Mary, who was as yet a virgin.'[26] With a beautiful inter-pretation of an Old Testament prophecy, Irenaeus indicates how Christ came to be conceived by the power of the Holy Spirit: 'Daniel, foreseeing His advent, said that a stone, cut out without hands, would come into this world. For this is what "without hands" means, that His coming into this world was not by the operation of human hands, that is, of those men who are accustomed to stone-cutting; that is, Joseph took no part with regard to it, but Mary alone co-operated with the pre-arranged plan. For this stone from the earth derives existence from both the power and the wisdom of God.'[27]

A few years later, around 125, the philosopher Aristides of Athens in the earliest Christian apologetic, informed the emperor Hadrian that the birth of Jesus of a virgin, without human seed or human will, is an essential part of the Christian creed, alongside the divinity of Christ.[28] St Hippolytus (172–235), the disciple of St Irenaeus, also indicated that the virginal conception of Jesus was the common faith of the early Church, by affirming that Christ 'became incarnate in the Virgin's womb by the Holy Spirit.'[29] Hippolytus adopted on several occasions the image of the ark of the covenant for the Virgin Mary: 'At that time, the Saviour appeared and showed His own body to the world, born of the Virgin, who was the ark overlaid with pure gold, with the Word within and the Holy Spirit without; so that the truth is demonstrated, and the ark made manifest.'[30] Hippolytus proclaimed that the belief of the Church is in a virginal conception of Christ: 'The pious confession of the believer is that, with a view to our salvation, and in order to connect the universe with unchangeableness, the Creator of all things incorporated with Himself a rational soul and a sensible body from the all-holy Mary, ever-virgin, by an undefiled conception.'[31]

Origen was possibly a disciple of Hippolytus at the beginning of the third century, and is also a witness to the faith of the Church in Our Lady's virginity. Around the year 250, he countered the views of Celsus, a pagan, who attacked Christianity as a myth, proposing a purely natural origin for Jesus.[32] Origen regards this position of Celsus as 'street-corner abuse ... unworthy of any serious attention.'[33] Celsus also proposed another false idea which Origen rejected: 'If God had wished to send down His Spirit from Himself, what need was there to breathe it into the womb of a woman? For as one who knew already how to form men, He could also have fashioned a body for this person, without casting His own Spirit into so much pollution.' Origen retorted that Celsus made these remarks, because 'he knows not the pure and virgin birth, unaccompanied by any corruption, of that body which was to minister to the salvation of men. And in this he acts like those who imagine that the sun's rays are polluted by dung and by foul-smelling bodies, and do not remain pure amid such things.'[34] Above all, Origen linked the Christological faith of the Church with the virginal conception: 'It should not be that, believing a truth from one point of view, one should deny it from another: for example, there are those who believe that Jesus was crucified in Judaea, at the time of Pontius Pilate, but deny that He was born of the Virgin Mary: these people believe in Him on the one hand and yet do not believe in Him on the other.'[35]

Tertullian affirmed the virginal conception of Jesus as dogmatic truth, part of the rule of faith: 'This Word is called His Son, and, under the name of God, was seen in various ways by the patriarchs, heard at all times in the prophets, at last brought down by the Spirit and Power of the Father into the Virgin Mary, was made flesh in her womb, and, being born of her, went forth as Jesus Christ.'[36] However, Tertullian was not so clear regarding the virginity of Our Lady during Christ's birth and after His birth. St Augustine deepened the meaning of the virginal conception of Jesus: 'Her virginity also itself was on this account more pleasing and accepted, since it was not that Christ by being conceived in her, rescued it beforehand from a husband who would violate it, preserving it Himself; but, before He was conceived, chose it, already dedicated to God, as that from which to be born. This is shown by the words which Mary spoke in answer to the Angel announcing her conception: 'But how can this come about, since I have no knowledge of man?'[37]

The solemn definitions of faith by the Ecumenical Councils and the papal Magisterium followed the first brief formulae of faith and the teaching of the Fathers on the virginal conception. The Council of Chalcedon in the year 451, in its carefully formulated profession of faith and with its infallibly defined content, affirms that Christ was 'begotten . . . as to his humanity in the latter days, for us and for our salvation from Mary the Virgin Mother of God.'[38] In the year 649, the Lateran Council made a clear declaration concerning the virginal conception: 'If anyone does not, according to the Holy Fathers, confess truly and properly that the holy and ever virgin and immaculate Mary . . . without human seed, conceived by the Holy Spirit, God the

Word Himself, who before all time was born of God the Father... let him be condemned.'[39] This council was not ecumenical, but since it was conducted under the authority of Pope Martin I, and the teaching was given under pain of anathema, so its authority came to be regarded as very weighty. Pope Martin's successor Agatho conveyed the impression that the decisions of the Lateran Council were definitive, infallible and binding the faith.

In the same way, in the year 681, the third Council of Constantinople proclaimed that Jesus Christ was 'begotten ... as to his humanity, by the Holy Spirit and the Virgin Mary, she who is properly and in all truth the Mother of God.'[40] Other Ecumenical Councils (Constantinople II, Lateran IV and Lyons II) declared Mary 'ever-virgin', stressing her perpetual virginity.[41] These affirmations were taken up by the Second Vatican Council, which highlighted the fact that Mary 'through her faith and obedience ... gave birth on earth to the very Son of the Father, not through the knowledge of man but by the overshadowing of the Holy Spirit.'[42] In addition to the conciliar definitions, the definitions of the papal Magisterium concerning the Immaculate Conception of the Blessed Virgin Mary and the Assumption of the Immaculate and Ever-Virgin Mother of God extol Mary's virginity.[43] The description of Mary as 'Holy Ever-Virgin, Immaculate' draws attention to the connection between holiness and virginity. Mary wanted a virginal life because she was motivated by the desire to give her whole heart to God. The expression used in the definition of the Assumption, 'the Immaculate Ever-Virgin Mother of God', also implies the connection between Mary's virginity and her motherhood: two prerogatives miraculously combined in the conception of Jesus, true God and true man. Thus Mary's virginity is intimately linked to her divine motherhood and perfect holiness. Pope Paul VI reiterated in his profession of faith the dogma that the Son of God 'was incarnate of the Virgin Mary by the power of the Holy Spirit.'[44]

St Thomas Aquinas treated the doctrine of the virginal conception of Christ, giving, among others, three reasons why it was fitting that Christ should have been born of a virgin. First, in order to maintain the dignity of the Father Who sent Him. Since Christ is the true and natural Son of God, it was not fitting that He should have another father than God, lest the dignity belonging to God be transferred to another. Second, the virginal conception was consonant to a property of the Son Himself, Who is sent. The Son is the Word of God, and the Word is conceived without any interior corruption. Indeed, interior corruption is incompatible with perfect conception of the Word. Since therefore flesh was so assumed by the Word of God, as to be the flesh of the Word of God, it was fitting that it also should be conceived without corruption of the mother. Third, on account of the end of the Incarnation of Christ, which was that men might be born again as sons of God, 'not of the will of the flesh, nor of the will of man, but of God' (Jn 1:13), namely of the power of God, of which fact the very conception of Christ was to appear as exemplary.[45]

The virginal conception of Jesus was not really ever held in doubt until the advent of rationalism, modernism and liberalism in the nineteenth and twentieth centuries. The rationalist critique of Catholic theology, begun in the nineteenth century, aimed to examine doctrine from a positivist perspective. Positivism and scientism refuse to admit the validity of forms of knowledge other than those of the positive sciences and so these ideologies relegate religious, theological, ethical and aesthetic knowledge to the realm of mere fantasy.[46] The modernists based their thought on Kantian subjectivism and upon an evolutionary concept of truth. The modernist tendency towards a subjectivist and an evolutionary concept of truth coupled with a liberal approach to biblical criticism, led to an attempt to undermine the doctrine of the divine institution and divine and supernatural aspects of the Church. Instead, since one of the fundamental principles of modernism was historical development, this system proposed a development based on purely human and social factors.[47]

In similar fashion, Protestant theologians like W. Pannenberg wrote that the virginal conception of Jesus seemed to represent a diminution of Christ's humanity, since we cannot understand why He should come into this world in a manner different from other men.[48] J. A. T. Robinson, a liberal Anglican theologian, makes this point: 'To say that new life was fathered and quickened in Mary by the Spirit of God, is a profound way of expressing an inner truth about Jesus ... With regard to the biological details, I am prepared to keep an open mind. Nothing for me depends on them ... We are not bound to think of the Virgin Birth as a physical event, in order to believe that Jesus's whole life is "of God".'[49] The once-Catholic theologian H. Küng regards the generation of Jesus Christ by the work of the Holy Spirit and the virgin birth of Jesus as 'legends' adopted by the early Church to justify the post-Paschal title of Son of God to Jesus.[50] It is clear that Küng's denial of the virginal conception as an objective truth is of a piece with his denial of the divinity of Christ. Thus, in 1979, the Congregation for the Doctrine of the Faith declared he cannot be regarded any longer as a Catholic theologian, also because of the errors in his writings regarding the Blessed Virgin Mary.[51] Similarly, the New Dutch Catechism tended to exclude the biological aspect of the dogma of the Incarnation, and so with much vagueness and ambiguity, leaves the question of the virginal conception open to discussion or else insists on the symbolic meaning of the narratives which concern the virginal conception of Jesus.[52] The Church's reply to this equivocation was that the virginal conception of Jesus, which is in conformity with the mystery of the Incarnation itself, should be taught clearly; there is no excuse for abandoning the factual truth of this dogma, retaining only a symbolic interpretation.[53] More recently, Pope John Paul II affirmed that 'physical integrity is considered essential to the truth of faith of Jesus' virginal conception.'[54] Moreover, he pointed out that faith in the virginal conception of Jesus was firmly rooted in various milieux of the early Church. This deprives of any foundation several recent interpretations which understand the virginal conception not in a physical or biological sense, but only as symbolic or metaphorical. Instead, Scripture and Tradition contain the explicit affirmation of a virginal conception of the biological order, brought about by the Holy Spirit.[55] The meaning of this event is accessible only to faith, which understands in it the 'connection of these mysteries with one another' in the totality of Christ's mysteries, from His Incarnation to His Paschal Mystery.[56]

The eyes of faith can uncover in the context of a synthetic view of Revelation the mysterious reasons why God in His saving plan willed His Son to be born of a virgin. These reasons regard both the pneumatological perspective on the Person of Christ and His redemptive mission, and the welcome Mary gave that mission on behalf of all men. Mary's virginity manifests God's absolute initiative in the Incarnation. Jesus has only God as Father. Jesus is conceived by the Holy Spirit in the Virgin Mary's womb because He is the New Adam, who inaugurates the new creation: 'The first man, being made of earth, is earthly by nature; the second man is from heaven.' (1 Co 15: 47). From His conception, Christ's humanity is filled with the Holy Spirit, for God 'gives Him the Spirit without measure' (Jn 3:34). By his virginal conception, Jesus, the New Adam, ushers in the new birth of children adopted in the Holy Spirit through faith. From 'His fullness' as the head of redeemed humanity 'we have all received, grace upon grace' (Jn 1:16; cf. Col 1:18). Participation in the divine life arises 'born not from human stock or human desire or human will but from God Himself' (Jn 1:13). The acceptance of this life is virginal because it is entirely the Spirit's gift to man. The spousal character of the human vocation in relation to God (cf. 2 Co 11:2) is fulfilled perfectly in Mary's virginal motherhood. Mary is a virgin because her virginity is the efficacious sign of her faith untainted by any doubt, and of her undivided gift of herself to God's will. It is her faith that enables her to become the mother of the Saviour. At the same time virgin and mother, Mary is the symbol and the most perfect realization of the Church: 'the Church indeed ... by receiving the word of God in faith becomes herself a mother. By preaching and Baptism she brings forth sons, who are conceived by the Holy Spirit and born of God, to a new and immortal life. She herself is a virgin, who keeps in its entirety and purity the faith she pledged to her spouse.'[57]

Virginity during the Birth of Christ

A Scriptural allusion to the virginity of Our Lady during the Birth of Christ can be found in the exegesis of St Ambrose upon the text Luke 2:22–24, the Presentation of the Lord in the Temple, in relation to Ezechiel 44:2: 'The Lord said to me, "This gate will be kept shut. No one may open it or go through it, since the Lord God of Israel, has been through it. And so it must be kept shut."' For Ambrose, this gate is the Blessed Virgin Mary, 'of her it is written "the Lord shall pass through it", and it shall be closed after childbearing, because a virgin conceived and a virgin gave birth.'[58] Ambrose also pointed out that Isaiah (Is 7:14) did not only say that a virgin would conceive, he said that a virgin would give birth as well.[59] A further prophetic allusion to the miraculous nature of the Birth of Christ, as connected to Mary's virginity, is found is Isaiah 66:7: 'Before being in labour she has given birth. Before the birth pangs came, she has been delivered of a child.' A particular passage from the Song of Songs which has also been interpreted in an allegorical prefigurative way, indicated that the seals of Mary's virginity were not destroyed during childbirth: 'She is a garden enclosed, my sister, my promised bride; a garden enclosed, a sealed fountain' (Sg 4:12).[60]

Among the earliest Patristic witnesses to the special nature of Christ's Birth is St Ignatius of Antioch, writing around the year 107. The mystery of Christ's birth must be proclaimed aloud, he remarked, alongside that of His virginal conception.[61] An even clearer early testimony was offered by St Irenaeus: 'Emmanuel, born of the Virgin, exhibited the union of the Word of God with His own work-manship, declaring that the Word should become flesh, and the Son of God the Son of man, the pure One opening purely that pure womb which regenerates men unto God, and which He Himself made pure.'[62]

Despite these and other early Patristic affirmations of Our Lady's virginity during childbirth, all was not plain sailing for this doctrine. Tertullian, in his attempt to counter the doctrine of Docetists, Marcionites and Gnostics, who all undermined the humanity of Christ, presented the birth of Christ as simply normal, often with brutal realism: 'She was a virgin, so far as her husband was concerned; she was not a virgin, so far as her child-bearing was concerned.'[63] In the East, the Cappadocian Father St Gregory of Nyssa first clearly highlighted Our Lady's virginity during childbirth. He started from the analogy between Eve and Mary, so that the Mother of Life begins pregnancy with joy and finished childbearing through joy.[64] He enunciated the principle that since Mary had experienced no sensual pleasure in conceiving Jesus, she also underwent no labour pains in giving birth to Him: 'Her pregnancy was without coition, her childbed unde-filed, her travail free from pain ... His birth alone was without labour, just as His formation was without union.'[65] Gregory sees in the Burning Bush (Ex 3:2) a prefiguration of Mary's virginity. Like the bush which was aflame but not consumed, Mary brought the Light to the world but was not corrupted,[66] for the Light 'kept the burning bush incorrupt; the sprout of her virginity was not withered by her childbearing.'[67]

For some of the Fathers, the passage Luke 2:23 presented an obstacle to the doctrine of the virginity of

Our Lady during Christ's Birth. It runs 'Every male that opens the womb shall be consecrated to the Lord.'[68] For Origen, it is normally intercourse that opens the womb of a woman. However, in the case of Our Lady, 'the womb of the Lord's Mother was unlocked at the time of her child-bearing; for before the Birth of Christ no male touched in the slightest that holy womb, worthy of all esteem and veneration.'[69] It is not clear in Origen what this 'unlocking' at the time of Christ's Birth involved. However, Origen alludes to the tradition that after the Birth of Christ, Mary went in to the temple to worship and stood in the place reserved for virgins.[70] It seems that Origen understood physical virginity only as the absence of marital inter-course, and therefore did not fully consider the question of what constituted virginity at childbirth. Amphilochius of Iconium arrived at a solution to the conundrum presented by Luke 2:23. He remarked, like Origen, that it is normally by intercourse that a woman's womb is opened, but it the case of Our Lady it was the Saviour who opened her womb. However, Amphilochius then added that as regards Mary's virginity, the gates were not opened, for this is Ezekiel's 'gate of the Lord,' where He goes in and out and still the gate is closed (Ez 44:2). He concludes that the Incarnate Word 'opened the Virgin's womb without intercourse; He came forth in an inexpressible manner.'[71] The way was thus paved for considering the Birth of Christ a true and *miraculous* Birth which preserved the integrity of His Mother.

St John Chrysostom is unequivocal in his proclamation of the virginity of Mary in childbirth. Mary gave birth 'without experiencing corruption.' After her childbearing, 'pure and holy' as it was, she is a virgin still, and this is a 'supernatural' thing. The Son's inexpressible birth of a virgin parallels His unutterable generation from the Father. In being born of her, God 'preserves her womb unchanged, and maintains her virginity unharmed' where 'the seal of her virginity' is 'unblemished.'[72] In St Ephraem's *Hymns on Blessed Mary*, Our Lady's virginity in childbearing is a constant theme. She gives birth without pain; her body abides intact; she gives of her milk without loss of virginity; she is the 'closed gate' of Ezechiel; the seals of her virginity are as inviolate as the seals of Christ's sepulchre, inviolate even in death.[73] Concerning the painless nature of this birth, Ephraem wrote: 'Just as the Lord made His entrance when the doors were closed, in the same way did He come forth from the Virgin's womb, because this virgin really and truly gave birth without pain.'[74] Theodotus of Ancyra took a slightly different perspective regarding the relation between Christ's birth and his exit from the tomb. He said that the risen Christ opened the door of His tomb, but did not open the door of His Mother's womb when He was born.[75]

Around the beginning of the Nestorian controversy in 428, Nilus of Ancyra defended Mary's virginity during childbirth against those who denied her this privilege: 'In His birth Our Lord Christ opened the undefiled womb; after His birth He sealed the womb by His own wisdom, power, and wondrous activity. He did not break the seals of her virginity at all.'[76] It is with the Council of Ephesus (431), and probably as a result of that Council, that the last lingering doubts on Our Lady's virginity in parturition disappear from orthodox circles. Afterwards, St John Damascene (675–750) formulates very clearly and carefully the virginity of Mary during the birth of Christ, so as to stress also that the birth is a real one: 'Just as He who was conceived kept her who conceived still a virgin, in like manner also He who was born preserved her virginity intact, only passing through her and keeping her closed. The conception, indeed, was through the sense of hearing, but the birth through the usual path by which children come ... For it was not impossible for Him to have come by this gate, without injuring her seal in any way.'[77] John Damascene also made it clear that Christ's Birth was painless; 'for as pleasure did not precede it, pain did not follow it.'[78]

In the West, doctrine on the virginity of Our Lady during the Birth of Christ flowered during the fourth century. While St Hilary of Poitiers was very clear concerning the virginity of Mary *post partum*, he did not treat of the question of her virginity during the Birth.[79] However, around the same time, St Zeno of Verona clearly affirmed that Mary was a virgin in her conception of Christ, a virgin in giving birth, and a virgin after His birth.[80] St Ambrose of Milan was very much part of this milieu, and had to combat the errors of a certain Jovinian. The latter, after having followed an ascetical life, launched a scathing attack on virginity. Despite the fact that he was condemned by Pope Siricius, he appealed to the secular authorities, claiming that the supporters of virginity were Manichaeans. While he did not negate the virginal conception, Jovinian denied the virginity of Mary during and after the Birth of Christ, and St Ambrose called a Synod to counter this error. This Synod maintained that the denial of Mary's virginity during the Birth of Christ undermined belief in Christ's Birth itself. Ambrose took a strong lead in advocating the virgin birth also in his writing and preaching:

> This is the Virgin who conceived in the womb, this the Virgin who gave birth to a Son ... For Isaiah did not say that a virgin would merely conceive; he said that a virgin would give birth as well. Now, what is that gate of the sanctuary, that outer gate looking to the East, which remains shut and no one, it says, shall pass through it save the God of Israel alone (Ez 44:2)? ... This gate is blessed Mary; of her it is written that the Lord shall pass through it and it shall be closed after childbearing, because a virgin conceived and a virgin gave birth.[81]

St Jerome was another great defender in the West of Mary's virginity. On several occasions he clearly proclaimed the virginity of Our Lady during the birth of Christ:

> Christ is a virgin, and the mother of our Virgin is herself ever a virgin; she is mother and virgin. Although the doors

were shut, Jesus entered within; in the sepulchre that was Mary, which was new and hewn in hardest rock, no one was laid before or after ... She is the eastern gate of whom Ezechiel speaks, always shut and full of light, which closing on itself brings forth from itself the Holy of Holies; whereby the Sun of justice ... enters in and goes out. Let them tell me how Jesus entered [the Cenacle] when the doors were shut ... and I will tell them how holy Mary is both mother and virgin, virgin after childbirth and mother before marriage.[82]

In Jerome's eyes, Our Lord could somehow 'open the womb' of Mary without violating her virginity.

The picture provided by Jerome concerning the virginity of Mary during Christ's Birth was sharpened by St Augustine, St Peter Chrysologus, and Pope St Leo the Great. For Augustine, Mary is a virgin before and during wedlock, virgin in her pregnancy, virgin in giving to Christ of her milk. In taking birth of her, He did not steal virginity from her.[83] In brief, 'she conceives and is a virgin; she gives birth and is a virgin.'[84] Peter Chrysologus sees Mary's virginal integrity as strengthened through childbirth, which is the crown of her virginity.[85] Christ comes forth in such fashion that the virginal gate does not swing open, and so Our Lady realizes in Bethlehem the garden enclosed, the sealed fountain of the Song of Songs (Sg 4:12).[86] Pope Leo the Great declares that Mary's womb is a mother's womb, but the birth of Jesus is a virgin birth.[87] It is the incorruption of Christ that kept intact the integrity of Mary.[88] In his *Tome to Flavian* in 449 which expressed the rule of faith, Leo stated that birth from a virgin is included among the truths of faith universally believed: 'He was conceived by the Holy Spirit in the womb of the Virgin Mother, who gave Him birth without losing her virginity just as she conceived Him without losing her virginity.'[89] In 521, Pope St Hormisdas explained that 'the Son of God became Son of man, born in time in the manner of a man, opening his mother's womb to birth and, through God's power, without dissolving his mother's virginity.'[90] This tradition was finally ratified in 649 by the Lateran Council when it condemned anyone and everyone who 'does not, according to the Holy Fathers, confess truly and properly, that ... Mary ... without loss of integrity brought Him forth.'[91] The word *integrity*, which means the state of being untouched, denotes a physical reality or state. It rules out lesions, blood and similar things. The Greek text, which is of equal authority, has *aphthoros*, meaning without corruption. The eleventh council of Toledo in 675 proclaimed Mary's virginity during Childbirth: 'The Virgin Birth is neither grasped by reason nor illustrated by example. Were it grasped by reason, it would not be wonderful; were it illustrated by example, it would not be unique.'[92]

St Thomas Aquinas was most clear in his formulation of Mary's virginity during the Birth of Christ. He stated that her virginity was not violated in the act of giving birth. Christ's body, which appeared to the disciples when the doors were closed, could by the same power come forth from the closed womb of His mother. The Angelic Doctor pointed out that it was not seemly that He, who was born for the purpose of restoring what was corrupt to its pristine integrity, should destroy integrity in being born.[93] The Angelic Doctor stated that we must assert without any doubt whatever that the Mother of Christ was a virgin even in Christ's Birth. This virginity was very appropriate for three reasons. First, because this was in keeping with the nature of Christ's Birth, for He is the Word of God. For the word is not only conceived in the mind without corruption, but also proceeds from the mind without corruption. Therefore in order to show that body to be the body of the very Word of God, it was fitting that it should be born of a virgin incorrupt. Second, it is fitting as regards the effect of Christ's Incarnation: since He came for this purpose, that He might take away our corruption. Therefore it would have been unseemly that in His Birth He should have corrupted His Mother's virginity. Third, it was fitting that He Who commanded us to honour our father and mother should not in His Birth lessen the honour due to His Mother.[94]

During the middle of the twentieth century, the physical nature of Mary's virginity during the birth of Christ was called into question. Mitterer affirmed that two traits given in tradition connected with Mary's virginity *in partu*, namely the absence of pains of childbirth and preservation of the hymen, did not belong to the essence of virginity and that any lack of them implied a diminution of motherhood.[95] Similarly, Galot sees the birth of Christ as happening in an ordinary way, like any other birth of a child. It was the complete bodily birth of a child. Jesus therefore opened His mother's womb with all the usual blood of a birth. According to Galot, a normal birth is compatible with virginal integrity without corruption or sin. Such a birth cannot preclude virginity because it cannot be identified with a sexual act. Galot also argued for painful delivery and rupture of the hymen.[96] Graver still was Campenhausen's position which regarded the dogma of Mary's virginity in childbirth as rooted in the ascetical influence of early monks, in Augustine's supposedly negative attitude towards sexuality, and in the Church's insistence on clerical celibacy.[97] While Rahner affirmed the substance of the doctrine on Mary's virginity *in partu*, he does not back this up by specifying what this virginity involves.[98] On the other hand, Jaki's realist approach highlights the importance of specifying some concrete details about the miraculous nature of Christ's Birth.[99]

In June 1960, the Holy Office drew up a decree on this matter but did not publish it officially. It was sent to a certain number of bishops and religious superiors as a *monitum* or warning:

> This supreme Congregation has often observed recently, and with deep concern, that theological works are being published in which the delicate question of Mary's virginity *in partu* is treated with a deplorable crudeness of

expression and, what is more serious, in flagrant contradiction to the doctrinal tradition of the Church and to the sense of respect the faithful have. Consequently in its plenary session of Wednesday, the twentieth of this month [July 1960], it seemed necessary to the eminent Fathers of the Holy Office, by reason of their serious responsibility to watch over the sacred deposit of Catholic doctrine, to see to it that for the future the publication of such dissertations on this problem be prohibited.[100]

The Second Vatican Council gave further weight to the Lateran Council, repeating the word 'integrity', and referring in a note to the text of the Lateran: 'This union of the Mother with the Son in the work of salvation is evident from the time of the virginal conception of Christ even to His death ... also when the Mother of God brought forth her Firstborn, who did not diminish His mother's virginal integrity but sanctified it.'[101] Citing once again the Lateran Council in 649, Pope John Paul II reaffirmed the doctrine of Mary's virginity during Christ's birth: 'Mary was therefore a virgin before the birth of Jesus and she remained a virgin in giving birth and after the birth.'[102] John Paul II also stated that 'of the three, the affirmation of her virginity "before giving birth" is, undoubtedly, the most important, because it refers to Jesus' conception and directly touches the very mystery of the Incarnation.'[103] By this the Pope did not wish to diminish the importance of Mary's virginity during and after the birth of Christ, but rather stressed that her virginity *in partu* and *post partum* are related to the virginal conception.

In the whole question, a delicate balance is required to preserve the true Motherhood of Mary in a real yet miraculous birth of Christ, in order to dispel any suspicion of Docetism. At the same time, it is necessary to avoid reducing Mary's virginity during birth to a merely symbolic issue. It seems clear that any attempt to undermine the virginity of Our Lady during Birth takes away from the unique nature of Christ's Birth, as well as paving the way for a purely spiritual concept of virginity. The notion of virginity is applied to Mary in a special sense. While in the case of other women, virginity would only be lost through intercourse, it would have been lost by Our Lady through the rupture of the hymen through an ordinary birth. Therefore the virginity of Mary would exclude the rupture of the hymen and also exclude pain in childbirth, which is a consequence of original sin.

Virginity after the Birth of Christ

A third phase of Mary's virginity concerns her life after Bethlehem, and the Church's doctrine here indicates that Mary did not have conjugal relations after the birth of Jesus, that she did not have any children besides Jesus. Against this doctrine, the objection is sometimes raised that the Bible mentions brothers and sisters of Jesus (Cf. Mk 3:31–35; 6:3; 1 Cor 9:5; Gal 1:19). The Church has always understood these passages as not referring to other children of the Virgin Mary. In fact James and Joseph, 'brothers of Jesus', are the sons of another Mary, a disciple of Christ, whom St Matthew significantly calls 'the other Mary' (Mt 13:55; 28:1; cf. Mt 27:56). Those referred to as the brothers of Jesus are His blood relations at the level of cousin, according to the ancient Semitic way of thinking as also found in the Old Testament.[104] If Mary had given birth to other children, it becomes difficult to explain why Jesus is emphatically called 'Son of Mary' (Mk 6:3) noting especially there is no mention of Joseph. In the same manner, Mary is never referred to as the mother of the brethren of Jesus. If Mary had other children, then Jesus, as He was dying on the Cross, would not have entrusted Mary to the care of St John. Many Protestants hold that Mary gave birth to Jesus as a virgin and then had James, and maybe other sons and daughters with Joseph. In accord with Church Fathers writing after the New Testament era, the Catholic and Orthodox Churches teach

Mary's perpetual virginity, which means she and Joseph never had marital relations. Some Orthodox think Joseph had James by his first wife, and after she died he married Mary, whose only child was the virgin-born Jesus. Thus, James was Jesus' half-brother. The Catholic position is that James was merely Jesus' close relative, perhaps the son of Clopas (traditionally said to be Joseph's brother) or a cousin on Mary's side.

St Luke's Gospel states that Mary 'gave birth to a Son, her first-born' (Lk 2:7). In biblical Greek, the word for first-born (πρωτότοκος) in no way implies that the Virgin Mary subsequently had other children, but rather stresses the dignity and rights of the Child. This expression 'first-born' is used in a way which parallels what is found in the Letter to the Hebrews: 'when He brings the First-born into the world, He says: Let all the angels of God pay Him homage' (Heb 1:6). The formula is predicated of the Word being the *only* Son of the Father and of Jesus Christ being the *only* Son of His Mother Mary. A further difficulty in the proposal that Jesus had blood brothers would be their descendants' claim upon very close blood ties with Him, and this would undermine Christ's statement that the Kingdom is not based on such ties but on hearing the Word of God and keeping it (cf. Lk 11:28). For anyone who does the will of Christ's Father in Heaven is His brother and sister and mother (cf. Mt 12:50).

Western Christianity faced the question of Our Lady's perpetual virginity only gradually. Some very few Fathers were problematic in their view of the question. For example, Tertullian regarded the Mother of Jesus as mother of other children as well after the Birth of Christ.[105] St Hilary of Poitiers marked an important watershed in rejecting the errors of those who held that Mary had marital relations with Joseph after Jesus' birth; for Hilary these are 'irreligious individuals, utterly divorced from spiritual teaching.' He himself is aware that, whenever Scripture speaks of Mary and Joseph in the same breath, Mary 'is called Mother of Christ, because that is what she was; not "wife of Joseph," because she was not.' For Hilary, the brothers of Jesus were children of Joseph by a former marriage; were that not so, Jesus would not have been compelled to entrust His Mother to John from the Cross.[106] Hilary's forceful language expresses his deep conviction concerning the perpetual virginity of Mary, that is rooted in her dignity as Mother of the Saviour. In the face of error, Zeno of Verona offered an important formula, which was already an expression of Mary's perpetual virginity: 'O marvellous mystery! Mary conceived as virgin incorrupt; after conception she gave birth as a virgin; after childbirth she remained a virgin.'[107]

During the decade between 383 and 392 it became necessary to defend further the doctrine of Mary's virginity *post partum*. The key antagonists in this struggle were primarily Helvidius and Bonosus. Helvidius did not make the tactical blunder of affirming that virginity is inferior to marriage and he did not appear to attack the Virgin Mary. He simply asserted that marriage and virginity are equal in honour, that Mary is doubly admirable for having been, in turn, virgin and mother of a family: virgin until the birth of Jesus, then mother of the brothers and sisters of Jesus spoken of in Scripture. St Jerome defended the faith, and in the year 383 in his work *Adversus Helvidium* developed the thesis that virginity is superior to marriage; his key proof was that Mary would never have dreamed of relations with any man, no matter who.[108] As witnesses to this doctrine, Jerome cited the Fathers Ignatius, Polycarp, Irenaeus, and Justin. For Jerome, the Lord's brethren are children not of Mary but of her sister. He concludes in reply to Helvidius:

> But as we do not deny what is written, so we do reject what is not written. We believe that God was born of the Virgin, because we read it. That Mary was married after she brought forth, we do not believe, because we do not read it. Nor do we say this to condemn marriage, for virginity itself is the fruit of marriage; but because when we are

dealing with saints we must not judge rashly. If we adopt possibility as the standard of judgement, we might maintain that Joseph had several wives because Abraham had, and so had Jacob, and that the Lord's brethren were the issue of those wives, an invention which some hold with a rashness which springs from audacity not from piety. You say that Mary did not remain a virgin. I claim still more; I claim that Joseph himself was a virgin for Mary's sake, so that from a virgin wedlock a virgin Son might be born.[109]

The other adversary, Bonosus, Bishop of Naissus (Nis in present-day Yugoslavia), proposed around the year 390 that Mary had had more than one child.[110] St Ambrose replied to this error. Adopting several Old Testament symbols of Mary's perpetual virginity like the 'closed gate' of Ezechiel, the 'enclosed garden' and 'sealed fountain' of the Song of Songs, he explained the New Testament texts misinterpreted by Bonosus (Mt 1:18–25).[111] The brothers of Jesus are not children of Mary; they may have been Joseph's. In any case, the term 'brother' need not be interpreted in the literal modern sense of the word.[112] Bonosus was condemned by his fellow bishops of Illyricum, and this condemnation was approved in a celebrated letter whose author may be Pope Siricius but is more probably Ambrose himself.[113] The text runs: 'Your Reverence was perfectly justified in rebuking him [i.e. Bonosus] on the score of Mary's children, and you had good reason to be horrified at the thought that another birth might issue from the same virginal womb from which Christ was born according to the flesh. For the Lord Jesus would never have chosen to be born of a virgin if He had ever judged that she would be so incontinent as to contaminate with the seed of human intercourse the birthplace of the Lord's body, that court of the Eternal King.'[114]

The condemnation of Bonosus consolidated the proclamation of the truth of Mary's virginity after Christ's Birth. St Augustine often repeats the basic truth that Our Lady 'conceived as a virgin, she gave birth as a virgin, she remained a virgin.'[115] The same truth is also echoed by such western Fathers as St Peter Chrysologus and St Leo the Great. For St Peter Chrysologus, Mary was a virgin who conceived, a virgin who gave birth and she remained a virgin.[116] Pope St Leo the Great wrote: 'For when God was born in the flesh, God Himself was the Father, as the archangel witnessed to the Blessed Virgin Mary ... The origin is different but the nature like: not by intercourse with man but by the power of God was it brought about: for a Virgin conceived, a Virgin gave birth, and a Virgin she remained.'[117] The definitive pronouncement of the Lateran Council, in the year 649, came in the wake of the declarations of many Fathers: 'If anyone does not, according to the Holy Fathers, confess truly and properly that the holy and ever virgin and immaculate Mary ... after His birth preserved her virginity inviolate, let him be condemned.'[118]

In the Christian East, there was an early tradition that St Joseph was a widower, with children by his former wife, and too advanced in years to have conjugal relations. This idea can be found in a fragment from Clement of Alexandria: the Jude who wrote the Catholic Epistle was 'a brother of Joseph's children,' and so 'the brother of James.'[119] Also in the Alexandrian school, Origen firmly rejected the notion that Mary should have had any other children: 'no one whose mind on Mary is sound would claim that she had any child save Jesus.'[120] Origen had this to say about the 'brothers of Jesus':

> Some say that the brothers of Jesus are children of Joseph by a former wife, who had lived with him before Mary. They are motivated by a tradition of the so-called Gospel according to Peter, or the Book of James. Now, those who say this wish to preserve the dignity of Mary in virginity to the end, that the body chosen to minister to the Word ... might not know intercourse after the Holy Spirit had come upon her and the power from on high had overshadowed her. And I think it reasonable that Jesus was, in regard of men, the first-fruits of the purity that resides in chastity,

and Mary in regard of women; for piety forbids us to
ascribe to someone else besides her the first-fruits of
virginity.[121]

The fundamental inspiration for the conviction of Origen
and many contemporary Christians that Mary remained a
virgin to the end was theological: a firmly rooted faith that
by the Incarnation the body of Our Lady had been irrevo-
cably consecrated to the Holy Spirit and to the Word.
Furthermore, St Basil, Bishop of Caesarea in Cappadocia
rejected a discourse of the famous Arian, Eunomius, in
which the latter declared that Joseph and Mary had
marital relations after the birth of Jesus. St Basil rebutted
the thesis of Eunomius in a Christological key, saying that
'lovers of Christ refuse to lend their ear to the idea that the
Mother of God ever ceased to be a virgin.'[122] Similarly,
Ephraem counteracted the error of those 'who dare to say
that Mary was Joseph's wife after the Saviour's birth.' His
answer resembles that of Origen: 'How could this be, that
she who was the home where the Spirit dwelt, she whom
God's power overshadowed, should become wife of
mortal man? ... As she conceived in purity, so did she
abide in sanctity.'[123] The very fact that Jesus gave Mary to
John on Calvary proves that the 'brothers' were not her
children.[124]

The perpetual Virginity of Mary

An important step came in the East with St Epiphanius and
his profession that Mary was ever virgin. In 374, he records
the heresy of the Antidicomarianites that Mary had intercourse with Joseph after the birth of Jesus.[125] In 377, he
replies by reproducing a letter addressed some years before
to Christians in Arabia. The letter castigates the opinion as
novelty, audacity, madness and totally ungodly. Mary has
always been known as the Virgin and this is her name of
honour. The brothers of Jesus were children of Joseph by a

former marriage. Jesus was Mary's only Child, and Epiphanius insists that she was 'ever virgin.'[126] About 390, St John Chrysostom taught in Antioch that Mary remained a virgin her whole life long. He presents her virginity after Bethlehem as a deduction from Scripture, whereas the virginal conception is a truth taught explicitly therein.[127] Later, in the seventh century, St John Damascene affirmed: 'The ever virgin One thus remains even after the birth still a virgin, having never at any time up till death consorted with a man ... For could it be possible that she, who had borne God and from experience of the subsequent events had come to know the miracle, should receive the embrace of a man.'[128] The expression 'ever virgin' or *aeiparthenos* in Greek became the standard expression in the Church, signifying the total consecration of Mary in body and soul during her whole existence, to the Holy Trinity.

Various statements of the Magisterium indicated that the perpetual virginity of Mary was part and parcel of the faith. The Council of the Lateran in the year 649 defined: 'If anyone does not, according to the Holy Fathers, confess truly and properly that the holy and ever virgin and immaculate Mary is really and truly the Mother of God, inasmuch as she, in the fullness of time, and without human seed, conceived by the Holy Spirit, God the Word Himself, who before all time was born of God the Father, and without loss of integrity brought Him forth, and after His birth preserved her virginity inviolate, let him be condemned.'[129] In the year 1215, the Fourth Lateran Council professed that Jesus Christ was 'conceived from Mary ever Virgin with the co-operation of the Holy Spirit.'[130] In the year 1555, Paul V condemned various heresies of the Unitarians and Socinians and in this context affirmed that Our Lady maintained intact her virginity 'before the birth, during the birth and perpetually after the birth.'[131]

St Thomas Aquinas gave four beautiful theological reasons why, without any hesitation, we must abhor the error that Christ's Mother, after His Birth, was carnally known by Joseph, and bore other children. These reasons place the virginity of Our Lady after Christ's Birth in a Christological perspective. For, in the first place, the error is derogatory to Christ's perfection: for as He is in His Godhead the Only-Begotten of the Father, being thus His Son perfect in every respect, so it was becoming that He should be the Only-begotten Son of His Mother, as being her perfect offspring. Second, this error is an insult to the Holy Spirit, whose 'shrine' was the virginal womb, in which He had formed the flesh of Christ: it was unbecoming that this womb should be desecrated by intercourse with man. Third, this error is derogatory to the dignity and holiness of God's Mother: for thus she would seem to be most ungrateful, were she not content with such a Son; and were she, of her own accord, by carnal intercourse to forfeit that virginity which had been miraculously preserved in her. Fourthly, it would be tantamount to an imputation of extreme presumption in Joseph, to assume that he attempted to violate her whom by the angel's revelation he knew to have conceived by the Holy Spirit. St Thomas concludes that the Mother of God, as she was a virgin in conceiving Him and a virgin in giving Him birth, remained a virgin ever afterwards.[132] The perpetual virginity of Mary is an expression also of her intimate discipleship with the Father, the Son and the Holy Spirit, which we examine in the next chapter.

Notes

[1] This has already been discussed in chapter 4, pp. 93–94 above.
[2] See B. H. Merkelbach, *Mariologia* (Paris: 1939), p. 216.
[3] St Ambrose, *The Virgins* 2:2:6 in *PL* 16, 208.
[4] St Gregory of Nyssa, *In diem natalem Christi* in *PG* 46, 1135–1136.
[5] Indeed some scholars, while not denying the possibility of a vow under the inspiration of the Holy Spirit, nevertheless deny the fact, yet still claim to maintain Catholic doctrine concerning Mary's virginity. For an example of these, see K. Rahner, 'Le principe fondamentale de la théologie Mariale' in *Recherches de Sciences Religieuses* 44 (1954), p. 517, n. 73. Also M. Schmaus, 'Mariology' in

K. Rahner (ed.), *Encyclopaedia of Theology* (The Concise Sacramentum Mundi) (New York: The Seabury Press, 1975), p. 895, who hazards that 'many theologians now assume that Mary resolved on a life of virginity only at the moment of the annunciation.'

6 See S. Lyonnet, *Le récit de l'annonciation et la maternité divine de la Sainte Vierge* (Rome: Pontificio Istituto Biblico, 1954), p. 7. Furthermore, in Egypt there was a community of women who, associated with the Essene spirituality, observed continence. These women, the *Therapeutae*, belonging to a sect described by Philo of Alexandria (*De Vita Contemplativa*, 21–90), were dedicated to contemplation and sought wisdom.

7 See St Augustine, *De sancta virginitate* 4 in *PL* 40, 398: 'This is shown by the words which Mary spoke in answer to the Angel announcing her conception to her. She said: "But how can this come about, since I have no knowledge of man?" Assuredly she would not say this, unless she had beforehand vowed herself unto God as a virgin.' See *Idem, Sermon* 225, 2 and *Sermon* 291, 5 in *PL* 38, 1097, 1318.

8 See St Gregory of Nyssa, *In diem natalem Christi* in *PG* 46, 1140f., and St Germanus of Constantinople, *Oratio IV. In praesentatione Sanctissimae Deiparae* in *PG* 98, 313.

9 See St Thomas Aquinas, *Summa Theologiae*, III, q. 28, a. 4: 'It was fitting that her virginity should be consecrated to God by vow. Nevertheless because, while the Law was in force both men and women were bound to attend to the duty of begetting, since the worship of God was spread according to carnal origin, until Christ was born of that people, the Mother of God is not believed to have taken an absolute vow of virginity, before being espoused to Joseph, although she desired to do so, yet yielding her own will to God's judgment. Afterwards, however, having taken a husband, according as the custom of the time required, together with him she took a vow of virginity.'

10 See Pope John Paul II, *Discourse at General Audience* (24 July 1996).

11 See chapter 2, pp. 39–42 and chapter 3, pp. 52–53, 58 above.

12 See Pope John Paul II, *Discourse at General Audience* (10 July 1996), 1. Natural biological parthenogenesis has been observed in many lower animals, especially insects such as aphids. In many social insects, like the honey bee and the ant, parthenogenesis gives rise to male drones, while fertilized eggs produce female workers and queens. Some larger animals, like some lizards, can reproduce through parthenogenesis. Parthenogenesis has also been artificially induced in frogs and snakes, although it quite often results in abnormal development.

13 See Pope John Paul II, *Discourse at General Audience* (10 July 1996), 1: 'The Church has constantly held that Mary's virginity is a truth of

faith, as she has received and reflected on the witness of the Gospels of Luke, of Matthew and probably also of John.'

14 See A. Serra, 'Vergine' in S. De Fiores and S. Meo, *Nuovo dizionario di mariologia* (Milano: Paoline, 1986), p. 1431.

15 See I de la Potterie, 'Maternità di Maria e Maternità della Chiesa seconda la tradizione giovannea' in AA.VV., *Il Salvatore e la Vergine Madre* (Roma/Bologna: Marianum/Dehoniane, 1981), p. 275.

16 See C. K. Barrett, *The Gospel according to John* (London: SPCK, 1962), p. 137.

17 See Pope John Paul II, *Discourse at General Audience* (10 July 1996), 3. The error is, for example, expressed by R. McBrien in his *Catholicism* (London: Geoffrey Chapman, 1994), p. 542.

18 See Pope John Paul II, *Discourse at General Audience* (10 July 1996), 4.

19 See St Justin, *Dialogue with Trypho* 99, 7 in *PG* 6, 708–709; see also Origen, *Contra Celsum* 1, 32, 69 in *PG* 11, 720–721.

20 See *CCC* 496.

21 St Hippolytus, *Apostolic Tradition* in ND 2.

22 See St Ignatius of Antioch, *Epistle to the Ephesians* 19, 1 in *SC* 10 (Paris: Cerf, 1945), pp. 64–65.

23 St Ignatius of Antioch, *Epistle to the Smyrnaeans* 1, 1 in *SC* 10 (Paris: Cerf, 1945), pp. 120–121.

24 St Justin, *Dialogue with Trypho*, 100 in *PG* 6, 709–711. See also n. 43, where Justin remarks: 'Now it is evident to all, that in the race of Abraham according to the flesh no one has been born of a virgin, or is said to have been born [of a virgin], save this our Christ.'

25 St Irenaeus, *Adversus haereses*, Book 1, chapter 26, n. 1 in *PG* 7, 686.

26 St Irenaeus, *Adversus haereses*, Book 3, chapter 21, n. 10 in *PG* 7, 954–955.

27 St Irenaeus, *Adversus haereses*, Book 3, chapter 21, n. 7 in *PG* 7, 953. See Daniel 2:34.

28 See Aristides, *Apologia*, c. 7 in *EM* 6.

29 St Hippolytus, *De Benedictionibus Patriarcharum* in *EM* 119.

30 St Hippolytus, *Fragmentum in Danielem*, 6 in *PG* 10, 648. See also Idem, *Sermonum Fragmentum* 6, in *PG* 10, 866: 'But the Lord was without sin, being of imperishable wood in respect of His humanity,— that is to say, being of the Virgin and the Holy Spirit, covered, as it were, within and without with the purest gold of the Word of God.' See also Idem, *Fragmenta in Proverbia* in *PG* 10, 625: 'Christ, the wisdom and power of God the Father, has built His house, namely His nature in the flesh derived from the Virgin.'

31 St Hippolytus, *Discourse against Beron and Helix*, Fragment 8 in *PG* 10, 840.

32 Celsus blasphemously proposed that Jesus was the result of a union of Mary with a Roman soldier. Origen refers to this in *Contra Celsum* Book 1, chapters 28 and 32, saying that Celsus maintained that 'when

she was pregnant she was turned out of doors by the carpenter to whom she had been betrothed, as having been guilty of adultery, and that she bore a child to a certain soldier named Panthera.' Origen pointed out that Celsus and others blindly concocted these fables to deny His miraculous conception by the Holy Spirit.

33 Origen, *Contra Celsum* Book 1, chapter 39 in *PG* 11, 733.

34 Origen, *Contra Celsum* Book 6, chapter 73 in *PG* 11, 1407–1408.

35 Origen, *Commentaria in Evangelium Ioannis*, Tomus XX, 24 in *PG* 14, 641–644.

36 Tertullian, *The Prescription against Heretics*, 13 in *PL* 2, 26.

37 St Augustine, *On Holy Virginity* chapter 4, 4 in *PL* 40, 398.

38 Council of Chalcedon in ND 614.

39 Lateran Council (649), *Condemnatio errorum de Trinitate et de Christo*, canon 3 in DS 503.

40 Third Council of Constantinople in DS 555.

41 See the respective definitions in DS 423, 801, 852.

42 Vatican II, *Lumen Gentium*, 63.

43 See Pope Bl Pius IX, Bull *Ineffabilis Deus* in DS 2803, and Pope Pius XII, Apostolic Constitution *Munificentissimus Deus* in DS 3903.

44 Pope Paul VI, *Profession of Faith* (30th June 1968), 11.

45 See St Thomas Aquinas, *Summa Theologiae*, III, q. 28, a. 1. Another reason which St Thomas proposed is not so strong, namely that it was not possible in a nature already corrupt, for flesh to be born from sexual intercourse without incurring the infection of original sin. This proposition seems to deny the Immaculate Conception of Mary, who was born from sexual intercourse, but was preserved from original sin.

46 See Pope John Paul II, Encyclical Letter *Fides et Ratio*, 88.

47 See P. Haffner, *The Mystery of Reason* (Leominster: Gracewing, 2002), pp. 238–239.

48 See W. Pannenberg, *The Apostle's Creed in the light of today's questions* (Philadelphia: Westminster Press, 1972), p. 72.

49 J. A. T. Robinson, *But That I Can't Believe* (London: Collins Fontana, 1967), p. 25.

50 See H. Küng, *On Being a Christian* (New York: Doubleday, 1976), pp. 453–457.

51 See Congregation for the Doctrine of the Faith, Declaration *Christi ecclesia* regarding certain aspects of the theological doctrine of Professor Hans Küng (Declaratio de quibusdam capitibus doctrinae theologiae professoris Ioannis Küng, qui, ab integra fidei catholicae veritate deficiens, munere docendi, qua theologus catholicus, privatus declaratur), 15 December 1979, in *AAS* 72 (1980), pp. 90–92.

52 See *A New Catechism: Catholic Faith for Adults* (New York: 1973), pp. 74ff.

[53] See Papal Commission of Cardinals, *Declaration on The New Catechism* (15th October 1968), II, 3.

[54] Pope John Paul II, *Discourse at General Audience* (10 July 1996), 5.

[55] See *ibid.*, 3.

[56] See *CCC* 498 and Vatican I, *Dei Filius*, 4 in DS 3016.

[57] Vatican II, *Lumen gentium*, 64. See also St Augustine *On Holy Virginity* cap. 6, 6 in *PL* 40, 399: 'That one woman is both mother and virgin, not in spirit only but even in body. In spirit, she is mother, not of our Head, who is our Saviour himself-of whom all, even she herself, are rightly called children of the bridegroom-but plainly she is the mother of us who are his members, because by love she has cooperated so that the faithful, who are the members of that head, might be born in the Church. In body, indeed, she is the Mother of that very Head.'

[58] St Ambrose, *Epistle 42*, n. 4 in *PL* 16, 1174. See also Idem., *De istitutione virginis* cap. 8, n. 52 in *PL* 16, 320. It is significant that this exegesis is mentioned in a footnote to Vatican II, *Lumen Gentium*, 57.

[59] See St Ambrose, *Epistle 42*, n. 4 in *PL* 16, 1174.

[60] See St Jerome, *Adversus Iovinianum*, lib. 1, n. 31 in *PL* 23, 265.

[61] See St Ignatius of Antioch, *Epistle to the Ephesians* 19, 1 in *Sources Chrétiennes* 10 (Paris: Cerf, 1945), pp. 64–65.

[62] St Irenaeus, *Adversus haereses*, Book 4, chapter 33, n. 11 in *PG* 7, 1080. The key Latin expression is: 'purus pure puram aperiens vulvam.' It seems likely that the adverb and not the verb merits the stress.

[63] Tertullian, *De carne Christi*, chapter 23 in *CSEL* 70, 246–247. 'Et virgo, quantum a viro; non virgo, quantum a partu.' See also Tertullian, *Adversus Marcionem*, Book 3, chapter 11 in *CSEL* 47, 394: 'Birth will not be worse for Him than death ... If Christ truly suffered all of this, to be born was something less for Him.' However, Tertullian nuanced his position somewhat, allowing for the possibility of virginity in childbirth in *De virginibus velandis*, chapter 6 in *PL* 2, 898.

[64] See St Gregory of Nyssa, *In Cantica canticorum*, sermon 13 in *PG* 44, 1053.

[65] St Gregory of Nyssa, *In Cantica canticorum*, sermon 13 in *PG* 44, 1053. See also Idem, *In Christi resurrectionem*, oratio 1 in *PG* 46, 604.

[66] See Idem, *In diem natalem Christi* in PG 46, 1136.

[67] Idem, *De vita Moysis* in *PG* 44, 332.

[68] In the Vulgate, the passage is 'omne masculinum adaperiens vulvam sanctum Domino vocabitur.' However, in some new translations like the New Jerusalem Bible, the problem is skirted because the text simply runs: 'Every first-born male must be consecrated to the Lord.'

[69] Origen, *Homilia 10 in Lucam* in *EM* 144.

70 See Origen, *Commentarium in Mathaeum*, Tract 23 in *EM* 135.
71 Amphilochius of Iconium, *Oratio 2: In occursum Domini*, n. 2 in *PG* 39, 48.
72 St John Chrysostom, *In natalem Christi diem* in *PG* 56, 387–393.
73 See St Ephraem, *Hymni de beata Maria*, 1, 2; 2, 3; 4, 7; 4, 10; 5, 1–2; 6, 2; 7, 6; 8, 3; 10, 2; 11, 4; 11, 6; 12, 1; 15, 2; 15, 5; 18, 20.
74 St Ephraem, *Explanatio evangelii concordantis*, cap. 2, n. 6.
75 Theodotus of Ancyra, *Homilia 5*, n. 1 in *EM* 1196: '[... Christus] resurgens e sepulchro sepulchra aperuit; natusque e vulva vulvam non aperuit. Ex morte enim ac terrae sinu emergens monumenta aperit; nascens vero ex Virgine uterum non aperuit: sed et nascitur et Virginis sinum clausum relinquit.'
76 Nilus of Ancyra, *Epistolae*, lib. 1, ep. 270 in *PG* 79, 181.
77 St John Damascene, *De Fide orthodoxa*, Book 4, cap. 14 in *EM* 1920.
78 *Ibid.*, in *EM* 1919.
79 See St Hilary of Poitiers, *Commentary on St Matthew*, I, 3–4 in *PL* 9, 921–922.
80 See St Zeno of Verona, *Tractatus 8*, Book 2 in *PL* 11, 414–415, where the beautiful formula is to be read: 'O magnum sacramentum! Maria Virgo incorrupta concepit, post conceptionem virgo peperit, post partum virgo permansit.'
81 St Ambrose, *Epistola 42*, n. 4 in *PL* 16, 1174. See also *De institutione virginis*, cap. 8, n. 52: '... virginali fusus est partu, et genitalia virginitatis claustra non solvit' in *PL* 16, 320. Ambrose proposed the same doctrine to the people in his sermons; cf. *Expositio evangelii secundum Lucam*, lib. 2, n. 43 in *PL* 15, 1568–1569, where we read: 'Nupta peperit, sed virgo concepit; nupta concepit, sed virgo generavit.'
82 St Jerome, *Epistola 49*, n. 21 in *CSEL* 54, 386. See also Idem, *Dialogus contra Pelagianos*, liber 2, n. 4 in *PL* 23, 563: 'only Christ opened the closed gates of her virginal womb, and yet the gates remained unfailingly closed.'
83 See St Augustine, *Sermon 188*, n. 4 in *PL*, 38, 1004.
84 Idem, *Sermon 189*, n. 2 in *PL*, 38, 1005; cf. Idem, *Sermon 191*, nn. 3–4 in *PL* 38, 1010–1011.
85 See St Peter Chrysologus, *Sermon 142* in *PL* 52, 581 and *Sermon 175* in *PL* 52, 658.
86 See St Peter Chrysologus, *Sermon 154* in *PL* 52, 589.
87 See St Leo the Great, *Sermon 24*, cap. 1 in *PL* 54, 204.
88 See Idem, *Sermon 22*, cap. 2 in *PL* 54, 196.
89 Pope St Leo the Great, *Tome to Flavian*, cap. 2 in ND 609 and DS 291. In the Latin, one notices that both aspects of Mary's virginity are on the same level: 'illum ita salva virginitate edidit, quemadmodum salva virginitate concepit.'
90 Pope St Hormisdas, Letter *Inter ea quae*, cap. 10 in DS 368.

[91] Lateran Council (649), *Condemnatio errorum de Trinitate et de Christo*, canon 3 in DS 503.

[92] Eleventh Council of Toledo, *Symbol of Faith* in *DS* 533: 'Qui partus Virginis nec ratione colligitur, nec exemplo monstratur; quod si ratione colligitur, non est mirabile; si exemplo monstratur, non erit singulare.'

[93] St Thomas Aquinas, *Compendium theologiae*, Part I, chapter 225.

[94] Idem, *Summa Theologiae*, III, q.28, a.2.

[95] See A. Mitterer, *Dogma und Biologie der heiligen Familie* (Vienna: 1952), pp. 98–130 and 'Marias wahre Jungfräulichkeit und Mutterschaft in der Geburt' in *Theologische-praktische Quartalschrift* 108 (1960), pp. 188–93. Mitterer was followed by C. E. L. Henry, 'A Doctor Considers the Birth of Jesus,' in *Homiletic & Pastoral Review* 54 (1953), pp. 219–233.

[96] See J. Galot, *Maria la donna nell'opera di salvezza* (Roma: Pontificia Università Gregoriana, 1984), p. 159, and Idem, 'La virginité de Marie et la naissance de Jésus' in *Nouvelle Revue Théologique* 82 (1960), pp. 449–469.

[97] See H. von Campenhausen, *The Virgin Birth in the Theology of the Ancient Church*, (London: SCM Press, 1964).

[98] See K. Rahner, 'Virginitas in partu' in *Theological Investigations*, vol. 4 (Baltimore: Helicon, 1966), pp. 134–162.

[99] See S. L. Jaki, *The Virgin Birth and the Birth of Science* (Front Royal, VA: Christendom Press, 1990).

[100] Several journals did publish it. It appeared in Italian in *Ephemerides Mariologicae* 11 (1961), p. 138 and *Marianum* 23 (1961), p. 336 and in French in *La Vie des Comunautés Religieuses* (Montreal) 18 (1960), #8. R. Laurentin, in *A Short Treatise on the Virgin Mary* (Washington: AMI Press, 1991) translated the decree on pp. 328–329, in the form cited above.

[101] Vatican II, *Lumen Gentium*, 57.

[102] Pope John Paul II, *Discourse at General Audience*, 28 January 1987.

[103] Pope John Paul II, *Discourse at General Audience*, 28 August 1996, 2.

[104] See chapter 3, pp. 51, 54–55 above where this has already been discussed. See also Gn 13:8; 14:16; 29:15.

[105] See Tertullian, *Adversus Marcionem*, lib. 3, cap. 11 in *CSEL* 47, 393; Ibid., Lib. 4, cap. 19 in *CSEL* 47, 482–483; Idem, *De carne Christi*, cap. 7 in *CSEL* 70, 208–212.

[106] See St Hilary, *Commentarius in Matthaeum*, cap. 1, nn. 3-4 in *PL*, 9, 921–922.

[107] St Zeno, *Tractatus*, lib. 2, tr. 8, 2 in *PL* 11, 414–415; cf. *Tractatus*, lib. 1, tr. 5, 3 in *PL* 11, 303.

[108] St Jerome, *Adversus Helvidium* in *PL* 23, 193-216.

[109] St Jerome, *Adversus Helvidium*, n. 19 in *PL* 23, 213; cf. *ibid.*, n. 17 in

PL 23, 211. The brothers of Jesus are described as 'fratres propin-
quitate, non natura.'
110 St Ambrose gives an account of the errors of Bonosus, who was not
   alone in denying the perpetuity of Mary's virginity. See St Ambrose
   De institutione virginis, cap. 5, n. 35 in *PL* 16, 328.
111 Cf. St Ambrose, *De institutione virginis*, cap. 5, n. 36 ff. in *PL* 16,
   329ff.
112 Cf. *Ibid.*, cap. 6, n. 43 in *PL* 16, 331. St Ambrose also argues from the
   fact that Christ entrusted Mary to John on Calvary in *De institutione
   virginis*, cap. 7, nn. 46–48 in *PL* 16, 332–333.
113 *De Bonoso* in *PL* 16, 1222–1224; also in *PL* 13, 1176–1178, as Pope
   Siricius, *Epistola 9, Ad Anysium Thessalonicensem aliosque Illyrici epis-
   copos*. The relevant note in *PL* 16 refuses to choose from among the
   authors suggested while the monitum in *PL* 13 ascribes the letter to
   Siricius. F. Homes Dudden believes that 'the style and the matter
   indicate Ambrosian authorship'. See *The Life and Times of St Ambrose*
   (Oxford, 1935), Volume 2, p. 402, note 4.
114 *De Bonoso*, n. 3 in *PL* 16, 1223–1224; 13, 1177.
115 St Augustine, *Sermon 190*, n. 2 in *PL* 38, 1008; see also *Sermon 196*, n.
   1 in *PL* 38, 1019: 'Virgo concepit, miramini; virgo peperit, plus
   miramini; post partum, virgo permansit.'
116 Cf. St Peter Chrysologus, *Sermon 97* in *PL* 52, 521: 'Virgo concipit,
   virgo parturit, virgo permanet.'
117 Pope St Leo the Great, *Sermon 22*, cap. 2 in *PL*, 54, 195: 'divina
   potestate subnixum est, quod virgo conceperit, quod virgo
   pepererit, et virgo permanserit.'
118 Lateran Council (649), *Condemnatio errorum de Trinitate et de Christo*,
   canon 3 in DS 503.
119 Clement of Alexandria, *Adumbrationes in epistolam Iudae* in *PG*, 9, 731.
120 Origen, *Commentaria in Evangelium Ioannis*, Tomus 1, Praefatio, n. 6
   in *EM* 151.
121 Origen, *Commentaria in Evangelium secundum Matthaeum*, Tomus 10,
   17 in EM 132.
122 St Basil, *Homilia in sanctam Christi generationem*, n. 5 in *PG* 31,
   1468.
123 St Ephraem, *Explanatio evangelii concordantis*, cap. 2 in *EM* 295.
124 See *ibid*.
125 St Epiphanius, *Ancoratus*, n. 13. in *PG* 43, 39–42.
126 Cf. St Epiphanius, *Panarion*, haeresis 78, nn. 5–24 in *PG* 42, 705–738
   and Idem, *Ancoratus*, n. 120 in *PG* 43, 233–234.
127 St John Chrysostom, *Homilia 5 in Matthaeum*, n. 3 in *PG* 57, 58.
128 St John Damascene, *De Fide orthodoxa*, Book 4, cap. 14 in *EM* 1920.

[129]   Lateran Council (649), *Condemnatio errorum de Trinitate et de Christo*, canon 3 in DS 503.
[130]   Lateran IV, Chapter I on the Catholic Faith in ND 20.
[131]   Pope Paul V, Constitution *Cum quorundam hominum* in DS 1880.
[132]   See St Thomas Aquinas, *Summa Theologiae*, III, q. 28, a. 3.

CHAPTER 7

DISCIPLE OF HER SON

Who can her Rose be? It could be but One:
Christ Jesus, our Lord – her God and her Son.
In the Gardens of God, in the daylight divine
Shew me thy Son, Mother, Mother of mine.
What was the colour of that Blossom bright?
White to begin with, immaculate white.
But what a wild flush on the flakes of it stood,
When the Rose ran in crimsonings down the Cross-wood.
In the Gardens of God, in the daylight divine
I shall worship the Wounds with thee, Mother of mine.

Gerard Manley Hopkins, 'Rosa Mystica'

Mary, the First Disciple

The discipleship of Mary has been in some ways an acquisition of recent theology. Recent deeper Biblical insights have increased our awareness of Mary as the model of faithful discipleship.[1] Nevertheless the fact that Our Lady is her Son's disciple is based on her divine Motherhood, in such a way that there can be no tension between these two aspects of Mary's life. From the reality that Our Lady is Mother of God stem all the other aspects of her mission; aspects that are well illustrated by the titles with which the community of disciples of Christ in every part of the world honour her.[2] The Western concept of Mary as follower of Christ is based also on her obedience to her Son. However, in the West, this obedience has sometimes been conceived in an excessively moral sense and reduced simply to carrying out commands. Instead, what is required is the consideration of Mary's total gift of correspondence to God's economy of salvation. At the same time, Mary's obedience is both a contrast to and a healing of Eve's disobedience.

The account of Mary's discipleship begins with a reflection on her obedience as the New Eve compared with the disobedience of the first Eve. This parallel is treated by several early Fathers of the Church, both from the East and from the West, such as St Irenaeus, St Justin and Tertullian.[3] In particular, Irenaeus (120–202), adopting his theory of recapitulation, in which the Eve–Mary parallel is set side by side with the Adam–Christ analogy, formulates the contrast as follows:

> By the obedience that took place on a tree the Lord recapitu-
> lated the disobedience that took place on a tree; and, to the
> destruction of that seduction whereby the betrothed virgin
> Eve was evilly seduced, the glad tidings of truth were
> happily brought by an angel to Mary, virgin espoused. For,
> as Eve was seduced by the utterance of an angel to flee God
> after disobeying His word, so Mary by the utterance of an
> angel had the glad tidings brought to her, that she should
> bear God in obedience to His word. And whereas Eve had
> disobeyed God, Mary was persuaded to obey God, that the
> Virgin Mary might become patroness of the virgin Eve. And
> as the human race was sentenced to death by means of a
> virgin, by means of a virgin is it saved. A virgin's disobedi-
> ence is balanced by a virgin's obedience.[4]

St Irenaeus views the function of Mary as the Second Eve in relation to man's Redemption. The co-operation of the first Eve with Satan in effecting man's spiritual death is matched and outstripped by Mary's co-operation with God in effecting man's return to life. Her co-operation and discipleship involved activity of the moral order and went beyond it: she gave Gabriel and God a free consent. Her obedience was not compelled, but with clear vision and unfettered will, she placed herself at God's disposal for the accomplishment of His designs.

Theodotus of Ancyra (d. 438) introduces a concept of ministry in discipleship carried out by Mary:

> In place of the virgin Eve, who had ministered to death, a virgin was graced by God and chosen to minister life ... This woman, worthy of her Creator, divine providence has given us as procurer of blessings, not provoking to disobedience but showing the way to obedience ... not holding out death-bringing fruit but offering life-giving bread ... It is not [Gabriel says] conception in iniquities or conception in sins that I shall announce to you; it is rather joy that I shall expound to you, joy that softens the sorrow which stems from Eve.[5]

Those who were Apostles and fellow workers of Christ are to be distinguished from those who simply followed Him as disciples. Among these disciples can be enumerated the women who had followed Jesus from Galilee and looked after him (Mt 27:55) and Joseph, a rich man of Arimathaea who followed Jesus secretly (Mt 27:57). Above all, Mary the Mother of God is Jesus' first and principal disciple. She was the first of His disciples in time, because even when she found her adolescent Son in the temple she received from Him lessons that she kept in her heart (cf. Lk 2:51). Thus, in a sense, Mary as Mother became the first 'disciple' of her Son, the first to whom He seemed to say: 'Follow me,' even before He addressed this call to the Apostles or to anyone else (cf. Jn 1:43).[6] She was the first disciple above all else because no one has been 'taught by God' (cf. Jn 6:45) in such depth. She was 'both mother and disciple,' as St Augustine said of her.[7] St Augustine's proposal that Mary's discipleship was more important for her than her Motherhood has been taken up again in recent times. However, an objection to that view could be posed by saying that her discipleship is based on her Motherhood, since being is the basis for action (*agere sequitur esse*). In the course of her Son's preaching Mary received His words, and He declared blessed those who heard and kept the word of God (cf. Mk 3:35; Lk 11:27f.) as she was faithfully doing (cf. Lk 2:19; 51).[8] As the perfect disciple, the Virgin Mary heard the Word of God and kept it, to the lasting joy of the messianic generations who call her blessed.[9] Indeed, Mary, who always adapted herself to God's will, was the first to merit the words of praise that Christ spoke to His followers: 'Anyone who does the will of my Father in heaven is my brother and sister and mother' (Mt 12:50).[10]

As a believing disciple of Jesus, Mary can be called daughter of the Church, and our sister as well. For, like us, she has been redeemed by Christ, although in an eminent and privileged way.[11] Mary is worthy of imitation because she was the first and the most perfect of Christ's disciples.[12] Mary, the handmaid of the Lord, remained throughout her earthly life faithful to what this name expresses. She confirmed that she was a true 'disciple' of Christ, who strongly emphasized that His mission was one of service: the Son of Man 'came not to be served but to serve, and to give His life as a ransom for many' (Mt. 20:28). In this way, Mary became the first of those who, 'serving Christ also in others, with humility and patience lead their brothers and sisters to that King whom to serve is to reign.'[13] As regards discipleship,

> the figure of the Blessed Virgin does not disillusion any of the profound expectations of the men and women of our time but offers them the perfect model of the disciple of the Lord: the disciple who builds up the earthly and temporal city while being a diligent pilgrim towards the heavenly and eternal city; the disciple who works for that justice which sets free the oppressed and for that charity which assists the needy; but above all, the disciple who is the active witness of that love which builds up Christ in people's hearts.[14]

Therefore, Mary of Nazareth, the first disciple, willingly put herself at the service of God's plan by the total gift of self. Having lived with Jesus and Joseph in the hidden years of Nazareth, and been present at her Son's side at the key moments of His public life, the Blessed Virgin Mary teaches unconditional discipleship and diligent service.[15] During the apostolic life of Jesus, Mary was in many ways a hidden disciple, who nevertheless was seen in key particular moments. Christ's first sign, given at Cana (cf. Jn 2:1–12), when He changed water into wine and opened the hearts of the disciples to faith, was effected thanks to the intervention of Mary, the first among believers.[16]

Mary as Exemplar of faith

Mary's faith is evident from the moment of the Annunciation when she replied to the angel Gabriel: 'Behold the handmaid of the Lord; be it done to me according to your word' (Lk 1:38). Mary is called to believe in a virginal motherhood, for which the Old Testament mentions no precedent. In fact, the well-known prophecy of Isaiah: 'Behold, a young woman shall conceive and bear a son, and shall call his name Immanuel' (7:14), although not excluding such a view, was explicitly interpreted in this sense only after Christ's coming and in the light of the Gospel revelation. Mary is asked to assent to a truth never expressed before. She accepts it with a simple yet daring heart. With the question: 'How can this be?', she expresses her faith in the divine power to make virginity compatible with her exceptional and unique Motherhood.[17]

Mary's faith grew and developed. One situation where this is evident is the finding of the boy Jesus in the Temple (Lk 2:41–52). Through this episode, Jesus prepares His Mother for the mystery of the Redemption. During those three dramatic days when the Son withdraws from them to stay in the temple, Mary and Joseph experience an anticipation of the Triduum of His Passion, Death and Resurrection. Letting His Mother and Joseph depart for Galilee without telling them of His intention to stay behind in Jerusalem, Jesus brings them into the mystery of that suffering which leads to joy, anticipating what He would later accomplish with His disciples through the announcement of His Passover.[18] For Mary, finding Jesus on the third day means discovering another aspect of His person and His mission. His Mother asked Jesus: 'Son, why have you treated us so? Behold, your father and I have been looking for you anxiously' (Lk 2:48). This question indicates precisely the pain of the growth in faith. Jesus' reply, in the form of a question, is highly significant: 'How is it that you sought me? Did you not know that I must be in my Father's house?' (Lk 2:49). This response discloses the mystery of His Person to Mary and Joseph in an unexpected, unforeseen way, inviting them to go beyond appearances and unfolding before them new horizons for His future. In this reply to His anguished Mother, the Son immediately reveals the reason for His behaviour. Mary had said: 'Your father', indicating Joseph; Jesus replies: 'My Father', meaning the heavenly Father. Referring to His divine origin, He indicates that He must be concerned about all that regards His Father and His plan and stresses that His Father's will is the only norm requiring His obedience.[19] The fact of Mary's invitation to a growth in faith is also indicated in the words of the Evangelist indicating that Mary did not fully 'understand the saying which He spoke to them' (Lk 2:50) and yet at the same time 'kept all these things in her heart' (Lk 2:51). The Mother of Jesus associated these events with the mystery of her Son, revealed to her at the Annunciation, and pondered them in the silence of contemplation, offering her co-operation in the spirit of a renewed 'fiat'. In this way the first link is forged in a chain of events that will gradually lead Mary beyond the natural role deriving from her motherhood, to put herself at the service of her divine Son's mission. At the temple in Jerusalem, in this prelude to His saving mission, Jesus associates His Mother with Himself; no longer is she merely the One who gave Him birth, but the Woman who, through her own obedience to the Father's plan, can co-operate in the mystery of Redemption.[20]

In the episode of the wedding at Cana, St John presents Mary's first intervention in the public life of Jesus and highlights her faith co-operation in her Son's mission. At the beginning of the account the Evangelist tells us that 'the Mother of Jesus was there' (Jn 2:1), and, as if to suggest that her presence was the reason for the couple's invitation to Jesus and His disciples, he adds 'Jesus also was invited to the marriage, with His disciples' (Jn 2:2). With these remarks, John seems to indicate that Mary presents the Saviour to the world at Cana, as she did in the Incarnation.[21] Turning to Jesus with the words: 'they have no wine' (Jn 2:3), Mary expresses her concern to Him about this situation, expecting Him to solve it with an extraordinary sign. The choice made by Mary shows the courage of her faith, since until that moment we have no record of public miracles worked by Jesus. Jesus' answer to Mary's words, 'O woman, what have you to do with me? My hour has not yet come' (Jn 2:4), appears to express a refusal, as if putting His Mother's faith to the test. The expression rather shows how Jesus put Mary's co-operation on the level of salvation which, by involving her faith and hope, required her to go beyond her natural role of mother. The formulation Jesus gives: 'My hour has not yet come' (Jn 2:4), is also full of significance. It refers to the first miracle in which Christ's messianic power would be revealed. This 'hour' is also linked with the Passion event. In any case her trust in her Son is rewarded. At Cana, Mary's faith in Jesus' as yet unrevealed power causes Him to perform His 'first sign', the miraculous transformation of water into wine. She precedes in faith the disciples who, as John says, would believe after the miracle: Jesus 'manifested His glory; and His disciples believed in Him' (Jn 2:11). Thus, Mary strengthened the faith of Jesus' disciples by obtaining this miraculous sign.[22]

Jesus, whom she has left totally free to act, works the miracle, recognizing his Mother's courage and docility: 'Jesus said to them, 'Fill the jars with water'. And they filled them up to the brim' (Jn 2:7). Thus their obedience also helps to procure wine in abundance. Mary's request: 'Do whatever He tells you', keeps its ever timely value for the disciples and for Christians of every age. It is an exhortation to trust without hesitation, especially when one does not understand the meaning or benefit of what Christ asks.[23]

Mary as Associate of Christ

By being His first disciple, Mary was the associate of Christ in all His Life and Ministry. Mary was unimpeded by sin and was able to dedicate herself wholeheartedly, which she in fact did, to God's saving will. She devoted herself totally by the grace of Almighty God, as a hand-maid of the Lord, to the person and work of her Son, serving the mystery of Redemption. Her co-operation was free, so she was not merely passively engaged by God, but was actively associated in the economy of man's salvation through faith and obedience.[24] The Blessed Virgin Mary was on this earth 'above all others and in a singular way the generous associate and humble handmaid of the Lord. She conceived, brought forth and nourished Christ. She presented Him to the Father in the temple, and was united with Him by compassion as He died on the Cross.'[25] This union of the mother with the Son in the work of salvation is revealed from the time of Christ's virginal conception up to His death, as she co-operated by her obedience, faith, hope and burning charity in the work of the Saviour in giving back supernatural life to souls.[26] Mary is the Mother of Jesus Christ and His closest associate in the new economy of salvation. She participated in her Son's sacrifice for our Redemption in such intimate fashion that He designated her the mother not only of John the Apostle but also of the human race, which he represented.[27]

The Gospels provide few details of Mary's life; but they do delineate a remarkable portrait of the woman who gave herself wholeheartedly to her Son and His mission in perfect faith, love and obedience.[28] By accepting the Annunciation, she became intimately associated with all the saving mysteries of Jesus' life, death, and Resurrection. From the time of the Annunciation, she was the living chalice of the Son of God made man.[29] Through her life of faith on earth, and now through her union with the risen Christ, the Mother of Jesus is the supreme example of loving association with the Saviour in His mission of redeeming mankind.[30]

The beginning of Jesus' mission also meant separation from His Mother, who did not always follow her Son in His travels on the roads of Palestine. Jesus deliberately chose separation from His Mother and from family affection, as can be inferred from the conditions He gave His disciples for following Him and for dedicating themselves to proclaiming God's kingdom. Nevertheless, Mary sometimes heard her Son's preaching. We can assume that she was present in the synagogue at Nazareth when Jesus, after reading Isaiah's prophecy, commented on the text and applied it to Himself (cf. Lk 4:18–30). She must have suffered greatly on that occasion, after sharing the general amazement at 'the gracious words which proceeded out of His mouth' (Lk 4:22), as she observed the harsh hostility of her fellow citizens who drove Jesus from the synagogue and even tried to kill Him. The drama of that moment is evident in the words of the Evangelist Luke: 'They rose up and put Him out of the city, and led Him to the brow of the hill on which their city was built, that they might throw Him down headlong. But passing through the midst of them He went away' (4:29–30). Realizing after this event that there would be other trials, Mary confirmed and deepened her total obedience to the Father's will, offering Him her suffering as a mother and her loneliness. According to the Gospels, Mary had the opportunity to hear her Son on other occasions as well. First at Capernaum, where Jesus went after the wedding feast of Cana, 'with His mother and His brothers and His disciples' (Jn 2:12). For the Passover, moreover, she was probably able to follow Him to the temple in Jerusalem, which Jesus called His Father's house and for which He was consumed with zeal (cf. Jn 2:16–17). Finding herself later among the crowd and not being able to approach Jesus, she hears Him replying to those who had told Him that she and their relatives had arrived: 'My mother and my brethren are those who hear the word of God and do it' (Lk 8:21).[31]

These words of Christ express great praise to His Mother by affirming a far loftier bond with her than would arise from family ties.[32] As the messianic mission of her Son grew clearer to her eyes and spirit, her Motherhood was increasingly shaped by that new dimension which was to constitute her salvific role beside her Son.[33] Indeed, in listening to her Son, Mary accepts all his words and faithfully puts them into practice. We can imagine that, although she did not follow Jesus on His missionary journey, she was informed of her Son's apostolic activities, lovingly and anxiously receiving news of His preaching from the lips of those who had met Him. Separation did not mean distance of heart, nor did it prevent the Mother from spiritually following her Son, from keeping and meditating on His teaching as she had done during Jesus' hidden life in Nazareth. Her faith in fact enabled her to grasp the meaning of Jesus' words before and better than His disciples, who often did not understand His teaching, especially the references to His future Passion (cf. Mt 16:21–23; Mk 9:32; Lk 9:45).[34]

Following the events in her Son's life, Mary shared in His drama of experiencing rejection from some of the chosen people. This rejection first appeared during His visit to Nazareth and became more and more obvious in the words and attitudes of the leaders of the people. Through this suffering borne with great dignity and humility, Mary shares the journey of her Son 'to Jerusalem' (Lk 9:51) and, more and more closely united with Him in faith, hope and love, she co-operates in the salvation which He brings about.[35]

Mary was also associated in revealing Christ. For some Fathers of the Church, the first revelation of the Holy Trinity in the New Testament took place at the Annunciation: 'You, O Mary, are resplendent with light in the sublime spiritual kingdom! In you the Father, who is without beginning and whose power has covered you, is glorified. In you the Son, whom you bore in the flesh, is adored. In you the Holy Spirit, who has brought about in your womb the birth of the great King, is celebrated. And it is thanks to you, O Full of grace, that the holy and consubstantial Trinity has been able to be known in the world.'[36] Through her hidden and at the same time incomparable sharing in the messianic mission of her Son, Mary was called in a special way to bring close to people that love which He had come to reveal: the love that finds its most concrete expression embracing the suffering, the poor, those deprived of their own freedom, the blind, the oppressed and sinners. Mary revealed God's mercy in an exceptional way, and made possible with the sacrifice of her heart, her own sharing in revealing God's mercy. This sacrifice is intimately linked with the Cross of her Son. Her sacrifice is a unique sharing in the revelation of mercy, that is, a sharing in the absolute fidelity of God to His own love, to the covenant that He willed from eternity and that He entered into in time with humanity; it is a sharing in the revelation that was definitively fulfilled through the Cross. It was precisely this merciful love, which is manifested above all in contact with moral and physical evil, that the heart of Mary, the Mother of the crucified and risen One shared in an exceptional way.[37]

From this consideration flows the devotion to Our Lady of Sorrows. Traditionally, the *Seven Sorrows of Mary* comprise the prophecy of Simeon (Lk 2:33–35), the flight into Egypt (Mt 2:13–15), the loss of the Child Jesus in the Temple (Lk 2:41–52), the meeting of Jesus and Mary on the Way of the Cross (Jn 19:17), the Crucifixion (Jn 19:25–30), the taking down of the Body of Jesus from the Cross (Jn 19:31–37), and the burial of Jesus (Jn 19:38–42). The

prophecy of Simeon in one sense initiated Mary's participation in Jesus' redemptive Passion:

> When David, in the midst of all his pleasures and regal
> grandeur, heard, from the Prophet Nathan, that his son
> should die, he could find no peace, but wept, fasted, and
> slept on the ground. Mary with the greatest calmness
> received the announcement that her Son should die, and
> always peacefully submitted to it; but what grief must she
> continually have suffered, seeing this amiable Son always
> near her, hearing from Him words of eternal life, and
> witnessing His holy demeanour! Abraham suffered much
> during the three days he passed with his beloved Isaac,
> after knowing that he was to lose him … Not for three
> days, but for three and thirty years had Mary to endure a
> like sorrow![38]

During the Passion and Death of Christ, every torture
inflicted on the body of Jesus was a wound in the heart of
his Mother. In this sense, Our Lady suffered more than a
martyr. This is a new kind of martyrdom, a Mother
condemned to see an innocent Son, and one whom she
loves with the whole affection of her soul, cruelly
tormented and put to death before her own eyes.[39]

Just as Mary shared intimately in her Son's Passion, it
would follow that she also shared in the fruits of His
Resurrection. The specific sharing which is her
Assumption into glory will be treated later.[40] Concerning
the episodes in which Our Lady experienced her Son's
Resurrection, the biblical accounts do not mention Mary;
but neither do they attempt to give a complete account of
all that Jesus did or said: 'There were many other signs
that Jesus worked in the sight of the disciples, but they are
not recorded in this book' (Jn 20:30). There remains pious
tradition as to how Mary was a witness to this event.
Having suffered at the foot of the Cross, it seems most
probable that she would have also witnessed the joys of
His Resurrection. George of Nicomedia infers from Mary's
share in Our Lord's sufferings that before all others and

more than all she must have shared in the triumph of her Son.[41] St Ambrose states expressly: 'Mary therefore saw the Resurrection of the Lord; she was the first who saw it and believed. Mary Magdalen too saw it, though she still wavered.'[42] Later authors like Rupert of Deutz, Eadmer, St Ignatius of Loyola and Suarez all propose that the risen Christ appeared to His blessed Mother.[43] Furthermore, it is consonant with the closeness of Mary to her Son that the risen Christ should have appeared first to His Blessed Mother. Though the Gospels do not expressly state this, it may be supposed that Mary was present when Jesus showed himself to a number of disciples in Galilee and at the time of His Ascension (cf. Mt 28:7, 10, 16; Mk 16:7). Pope John Paul II also affirmed this tradition: 'The Gospels do not tell us of an appearance of the risen Christ to Mary. Nevertheless, as she was in a special way close to the Cross of her Son, she also had to have a privileged experience of his Resurrection.'[44]

Mary as Coredemptrix

Simeon's prophecy found its fulfilment principally during the time of Our Lord's suffering and Death. Mary's role as disciple and associate of Christ thus came to a climax during the Passion of Our Lord.[45] Mary's action as Coredemptrix is but a logical consequence of her discipleship. Many theologians acknowledge Mary's role as Coredemptrix.[46] While many Protestant and other Christian writers have no difficulty expressing some acceptance of Mary's discipleship, they do not make the step which leads from discipleship to coredemption. Some Christian writers from outside the Catholic tradition are however supportive of this truth, like J. Macquarrie who writes: 'It is Mary who has come to symbolise that perfect harmony between the divine will and the human response, so that it is she who gives meaning to the expression Corredemptrix.'[47]

Christ fulfils His role as Mediator by the Redemption of the human race. Some Scripture texts, notably 1 Timothy 2:5 and Acts 4:12, are invoked by Protestant critics against the Catholic teaching of all secondary agents of mediation in general, and of Our Lady in particular: 'For there is only one God, and there is only one mediator between God and humanity, Himself a human being, Christ Jesus, who offered Himself as a ransom for all' (1 Tm 2:5–6). Thus they assert Christ is the sole Mediator in a way which excludes subordinate mediation, since there is no salvation in any other name but His (Ac 4:12). In Catholic theology, on the other hand, extending the term 'mediator' to those other than Christ involves the use of analogy, by which one and the same word is expressive of concepts that are partly the same and partly different. Moreover, when the Apostle Paul proposes that we are all God's fellow workers (1 Co 3:9), he maintains the real possibility for man to co-operate with God. The collaboration of believers, which obviously excludes any equality with Him, is expressed in the proclamation of the Gospel and in their personal contribution to its taking root in human hearts.[48] Christ is the one supreme, necessary and adequate Mediator between God and men; He alone offered the sacrifice which in accordance with the mandate of His Father was the price of our Redemption, and which made condign, sufficient, superabundant satisfaction for the injury wrought by the sin of Adam; but this unique mediation does not exclude secondary and subordinate mediators, nor is there anything in the thought of St Paul to imply such exclusion. 'No creature could ever be counted along with the Incarnate Word and Redeemer; but just as the priesthood of Christ is shared in various ways both by His ministers and the faithful, and as the one goodness of God is radiated in different ways among His creatures, so also the unique mediation of the Redeemer does not exclude but rather gives rise to a manifold co-operation which is but a sharing in this one source.'[49]

The fact that God is our Father does not exclude the

existence of earthly fathers; the fact that Christ is the one High Priest does not prevent His sharing His priesthood with the apostles and their successors throughout the centuries; no more does the unique and necessary media-tion of Christ rule out a mediation which is subordinate and dependent. Mary's Coredemptive activity is, in this context, part and parcel of her discipleship:

> Thus the Blessed Virgin advanced in her pilgrimage of faith, and faithfully persevered in her union with her Son unto the cross. There she stood, in keeping with the divine plan, enduring with her only begotten Son the intensity of His suffering, joining herself with His sacrifice in her mother's heart, and lovingly consenting to the immolation of this victim, born of her: to be given, by the same Christ Jesus dying on the cross, as a mother to His disciple, with these words: 'Woman, behold your son.'[50]

Next is necessary to clarify what constitutes the Redemption. Since original sin was an offence against God, so the reparation, in order to be adequate had to be made by a Person who was divine.[51] Thus the Word was made flesh, lived His life among us and died the Victim for sin on the Cross. While it is true that every action of the God-man Christ was of infinite moral value, nevertheless, as Scripture and Tradition testify beyond doubt, it was by His final sacrifice of the Cross that Christ achieved the Redemption of mankind. By that oblation sins were forgiven, grace was again available to man and with it, the possibility of assimilation to the image and likeness of God and incorporation into the Church, the Body of Christ. The Redemption involves the concept of humanity being ransomed from sin and death (cf. Mt 10:45; 20:28; Gal 3:13; 1 Co 6:20; 7:23). There are several aspects contained in the doctrine of Redemption. The first consid-ers Christ as Representative, in which He takes the place of human beings: 'For the love of Christ overwhelms us when we consider that if one Man died for all, then all have died' (2 Co 5:14).[52] The second idea involves Christ as

Victim, whereby His Redemption forgives the punishment which man should have had to undergo: 'For our sake He made the sinless One a victim for sin, so that in Him we might become the uprightness of God' (2 Co 5:21).[53] Consideration of Christ as Victim also involves the concept of Redemption as the payment of a debt, or expiation: 'they are justified by His grace as a gift, through the redemption which is in Christ Jesus, whom God put forward as an expiation by His blood, to be received by faith' (Rm 3:24–25).[54] Third, Christ is the Priest and Mediator, and the Redemption can be conceived as a physical and mystical solidarity. Here, the idea is that all humanity forms a unit, a community, of which the humanity of Christ forms part. However, in Him, human nature is joined in one Person to the divinity. So His redemptive power is mediated from His divinity through His humanity to all humanity to heal it: 'For in Him all the fullness of God was pleased to dwell, and through Him to reconcile to Himself all things, whether on earth or in heaven, making peace by the blood of His cross' (Col 1:19–20).[55] The Redemption should be framed within a Covenant perspective, in which the obedient death of Christ was the Covenant condition. Without obedience, the Passion and Cross of Christ would have been a tragedy, not a Redemption. Therefore, in the Redemption, which is of infinite and universal value, are found the aspects of covenant, sacrifice, and the restoration of a relationship between God and humanity. Our Lady participates in all aspects of the Redemption, but in a way which is particular to her.

A way forward to founding a theology of Marian coredemption involves making various distinctions, so as to see the complete picture, and in order to affirm that no single individual can ever be imagined who has ever contributed like Mary, or will ever contribute so much, toward reconciling man with God.[56] One essential distinction lies between the objective and the subjective Redemption. The *objective Redemption* is, as has just been described, the once-for-all acquisition by the sacrifice of Calvary of the claim to all grace and forgiveness. The *subjective Redemption* is the distribution of that grace and forgiveness throughout all ages after Calvary. In both phases of Redemption, Christ has admitted others who act as co-operators with Him. Here we will consider how Mary co-operated in the objective Redemption as Coredemptrix. Later on, we will explain how Our Lady, co-operates in the subjective Redemption as Mediatrix.[57] Pope Leo XIII indicated that Mary was a minister of both aspects of the Redemption: 'For thereafter, by the divine plan, she so began to watch over the Church, so to be present to us and to favour us as Mother, that she who had been the minister of accomplishing the mystery of human redemption, would be likewise the minister of the dispensation of that grace, practically limitless power being given to her.'[58]

A further distinction now needs to be made between the *remote co-operation* in the objective redemption, whereby the Mother of the Redeemer, in faith and obedience furnished Him with the flesh and blood in which He could die, and the *immediate co-operation* which is an actual participation in the sacrifice of Calvary. As regards the remote co-operation, Mary by her free acceptance of the angel's message became the Mother of God, and brought Him into the world at Bethlehem. She nurtured and cared for Him as an infant, and figured with Him in many of the mysteries of His life. Mary presented Him in the Temple, and suffered the sorrow of losing Him when He was twelve years old, when the Child vindicated the claims of His Father's business. She was present at Cana, where the power of her influence was testified to by the miracle which changed the water into wine. Finally, she was present at Calvary where she offered immediate co-operation in the Redemptive sacrifice of Christ.

The question now arises, as to what kind of co-operation Mary offered in the actual sacrifice on Calvary. Various ideas have been proposed. The first is that Our Lady may be conceived in the capacity of co-offerer and co-priest with Christ the great High Priest, in which case her co-operation in Redemption would be physical and immediate. Such a possibility, however, has no foundation in fact. If it is said that Mary offered the sacrifice of the Cross, this would imply that she was endowed with the character of a priest, and tradition has rejected this possibility. Indeed, several of those who misguidedly propose the ordination of women support the thesis that Mary shared in the ministerial priesthood of Christ.[59] Already in the Patristic period, St Epiphanius opposed a strange Marian cult offered by the Collyridian sect, where a liturgical rite, bearing some resemblance to the Eucharistic sacrifice was offered by women. Epiphanius wrote that in the Old Covenant, 'no woman ever exercised the priesthood.' He then stated that in the Christian era, 'if women had received that mandate to offer to God a priestly worship or to attend to the performance of a regulatory function in the Church, Mary herself would have deserved to carry out the priestly ministry in the New Covenant.'[60] Instead, Mary's priesthood is of a kind with that enjoyed by all who are baptized in Christ. The Church has always been wary of devotions to Mary as Priest, and in 1916 the Holy Office forbade the use of images of Mary portraying her as such. In 1927 the Holy Office forbade the devotion to Mary Virgin Priest altogether.[61] Instead, it is more theologically sound to regard Mary as being the Associate of Christ, the High Priest, like Eve was the helpmate to Adam (Gn 2:18). In this way her role transcends that of a simple participation in the royal priesthood of the people of God; it is something more.[62]

Second, one might conceive the possibility of Our Lady persuading Christ to offer the sacrifice that was required for our Redemption. In this hypothesis, the Redemption would be in part the immediate effect of Mary's moral co-operation with Christ. Just as at Cana, Christ's miracle was immediately due to the plea of His Mother in the words, 'They have no wine,' so conceivably Christ's sacrifice might have been due to her request that we were all in need of' Redemption. Apart from other considerations, there is a particular objection against this supposition. Christ's sacrifice, as we know, was entirely in obedience to the will of His Father. So far as the evidence of Scripture and Tradition goes, that mandate was independent of Mary's prayers and wishes. We have but to recall the incident of the loss in the Temple, when the Christ-child explained His absence from His parents by the reply that He was about His Father's business.

A third option is that Our Lady would have co-operated immediately in Redemption since her receptivity and compassion on Calvary constituted, together with the sacrifice of Christ, the total price of Redemption. Receptivity is precisely the quality which is characteristic of woman, and Mary exercised this to a supreme degree. In such a case her compassion, which literally means suffering with Christ, together with Christ's sacrifice, would have been ordained by the Father as the total adequate principle whereby the injury of original sin was to be repaired and grace restored. It is proposed that Our Lady collaborated in this immediate way in the act of Christ, so that she is entitled to the title Coredemptrix.

The basis in Tradition for justifying this title begins with the idea of Mary as the New Eve. As has already been seen, many early Fathers like St Justin and St Irenaeus proposed this theme.[63] Just as St Paul had spoken of Christ as the New or Second Adam, the Fathers teach there was also a New or Second Eve. Just as the first Eve really contributed to bringing down the damage of original sin on our race, so the New Eve, Mary, really contributed to reversing that damage. St Augustine actually used the expression co-operation in regard to Mary's role: '... certainly she is the Mother of His members, which we are; for she co-operated in love that the faithful might be born in the Church.'[64]

During the Middle Ages, further progress was made in understanding the part played by Mary in the Redemption. Eadmer regarded Mary as the Reparatrix of the lost world.[65] St Bernard of Clairvaux (died 1153), developed the idea of Mary offering Christ as Victim to the Father, and in this sense represented a step forward in the doctrine of Marian coredemption.[66] A disciple and friend of St Bernard, Arnold of Chartres, shed light particularly on Mary's offering in the sacrifice of Calvary: 'Whoever then was present on the Mount of Calvary might see two altars, on which two great sacrifices were consummated; the one in the body of Jesus, the other in the heart of Mary.'[67] St Bonaventure took this a step further. He adopted the Eve-Mary parallel from the Fathers, saying that just as Adam and Eve were the destroyers of the human race, so Jesus and Mary were its repairers.[68] Bonaventure also considered how Mary merited reconciliation for the entire human race.[69] Furthermore, he specified that 'she paid the price [of Redemption] as a woman brave and loving – namely, when Christ suffered on the cross to pay that price in order to purge and wash and redeem us, the Blessed Virgin was present, accepting and agreeing with the divine will.'[70] He stated precisely how Mary shared in the Sacrifice of Calvary: 'there was but one altar, that of the Cross of the Son, on which, together with this Divine Lamb, the victim, the Mother was also sacrificed.'[71] Participation in the sacrifice of Christ was also the line adopted by John Tauler (d. 1361), in his development of Mary's role. God accepted her oblation on Calvary as a pleasing sacrifice for the utility and salvation of the whole human race, and made her a sharer of all of His merits and afflictions, and so she co-operated with Him in the restoration of men to salvation.[72] The word Coredemptrix first figured in the fourteenth century at least in a hymnal in Salzburg, Austria.[73] Then, there are reasons to believe that the expression Coredemptrix appeared in the year 1521 in the sermons of Alain de Varènes.[74] Lanspergius, or John Justus of Landsberg, (1489–1539) formulated the doctrine in such a way that the idea of Mary's co-operation was expressed in coredemption: 'Christ was pleased that she, the cooperatress in our Redemption, and whom He had determined to give us for our Mother, should be there present; for it was at the foot of the Cross that she was to bring us forth as her children.'[75]

By the sixteenth century the concept began to enjoy theological currency, as for example in the writings of F. Suárez (1548–1617): 'For just as Christ, because He redeemed us, is our Lord and King by a special title, so the Blessed Virgin also (is our queen), on account of the unique manner in which she assisted in our redemption, by giving of her own substance, by freely offering Him for us, by her singular desire and petition for, and active interest in, our salvation.'[76] In the second half of the seventeenth century, Quirino de Salazar applied to Mary the title of 'Redemptrix' which he had proposed in virtue of the intimate analogy between Christ and Mary.[77] Later, great figures like St Alphonsus Liguori (1696–1787) had no hesitation in expressing the basic truth that 'if Mary's lips were silent, her heart was not so, for she incessantly offered the life of her Son to Divine Justice for our salvation.'[78]

The Ordinary Magisterium during the past century or so has increasingly highlighted Mary's immediate co-operation in the objective Redemption. Pope Leo XIII indicated how Mary progressed from being the Handmaid of the Lord to being a sharer in the laborious expiation for the human race. 'Hence we cannot doubt that she greatly grieved in soul in the most harsh anguishes and torments of her Son. Further, that divine sacrifice had to be completed with her present and looking on, for which she had generously nourished the victim from herself. Finally this is more tearfully observed in the same mysteries: There stood by the Cross of Jesus, Mary His Mother... of her own accord she offered her Son to the divine justice, dying with Him in her heart, transfixed with the sword of sorrow.'[79] Pope St Pius X made a particularly significant advance in the doctrine of Marian coredemption:

But when the final hour of her Son came, His Mother stood
by the cross of Jesus, not just occupied in seeing the dread
spectacle, but actually rejoicing that her Only-Begotten
was being offered for the salvation of the human race ...
from this common sharing of sufferings and will, she
merited to become most worthily the Reparatrix of the lost
world, and so the dispensatrix of all the gifts which were
gained for us by the death and blood of Jesus ... Since she
was ahead of all in holiness and union with Christ, and
was taken up by Christ into the work of human salvation,
she merits congruously, as they say, what Christ merited
condignly, and is the chief minister of the dispensation of
graces.[80]

St Pius X designates Mary as the chosen partner of Christ
in the work of Redemption, and due to her unified suffering and purpose with the Redeemer, Mary became the
'reparatrix,' the female restorer with Christ, of the world
lost by sin. St Pius X made the most important distinction
between the Redemption obtained by Christ which He
merits for us in the order of justice (*de condigno*), and the
co-operation by which Mary merits in the order of appropriateness or fittingness (*de congruo*).[81]

In 1908, the Sacred Congregation for Rites responded
positively to the request of the Prior General of the
Servites, concerning the possibility of giving a special
status to the feast of the Seven Dolours of Our Lady, that
it increasingly arouse devotion towards 'the coredemptive
mercy for the human race.'[82] In 1914, the Holy Office
permitted an indulgenced prayer, referring to Mary as the
Coredemptrix of the human race.[83] In 1918, Pope Benedict
XV effectively affirmed the content of the doctrine of
Marian coredemption: 'With her suffering and dying Son
she suffered and almost died, so did she surrender her
mother's rights over her Son for the salvation of human
beings, and to appease the justice of God, so far as
pertained to her, she immolated her Son, so that it can be
rightly said, that together with Christ she has redeemed
the human race.'[84]

Pope Pius XI, used the expression Coredemptrix on three occasions during his pontificate. Most significant was when he closed the Jubilee Year of 1935: 'O Mother of piety and mercy, who as Coredemptrix stood by your most sweet Son suffering with Him when He consummated the Redemption of the human race on the altar of the Cross... preserve in us, we beg, day by day, the precious fruits of the Redemption and of your compassion.'[85] Pope Pius XI made it clear that it was appropriate to invoke Mary under the title of Coredemptrix in relation to Christ her Son, the Saviour of mankind:

> Given the nature of His action, the Redeemer would have associated His Mother with His work. For this reason we invoke her under the title of Coredemptrix. She gave us the Saviour, she accompanied Him in the work of Redemption as far as the Cross itself, sharing with Him the sorrows of the agony and of the death in which Jesus consummated the Redemption of mankind. And immediately beneath the Cross, at the last moments of His life, she was proclaimed by the Redeemer as our Mother, the Mother of the whole universe.[86]

Pope Pius XII also taught the doctrine of the coredemption by Our Lady: 'It was she, the second Eve, who, free from all sin, original or personal, and always more intimately united with her Son, offered Him on Golgotha to the Eternal Father for all the children of Adam, sinstained by his unhappy fall, and her mother's rights and her mother's love were included in the sacrifice. Thus she who, according to the flesh, was the mother of our Head, through the added title of pain and glory became, according to the Spirit, the mother of all His members.'[87] Pius XII also re-echoed the relationship between the co-operation of Mary in the Redemption and her role of Mediatrix of the graces already won through the Redemption in these words: 'For having been associated with the King of Martyrs in the ineffable work of human Redemption, as Mother and Cooperatrix, she remains forever associated with Him, with an almost unlimited power, in the distribution of graces which flow from the Redemption.'[88] Pius XII linked the concept of Christ's Kingship and Our Lady's Queenship with the Redemption: 'Certainly, in the full and strict meaning of the term, only Jesus Christ, the God-Man, is King; but Mary, too, as Mother of the divine Christ, as His associate in the Redemption, in His struggle with His enemies and His final victory over them, has a share, though in a limited and analogous way, in His royal dignity.'[89] The Pope also proposed the theological notion of *recapitulation* as an important key for understanding Mary's involvement in the Redemption. Mary played an active role in the work of salvation, and was, in God's plan, associated with Jesus Christ, the source of salvation itself, in a manner comparable to that in which Eve was associated with Adam, the source of death. Therefore, the work of our salvation was accomplished by a kind of recapitulation, in which a virgin was instrumental in the salvation of the human race, just as a virgin had been closely associated with its death. Likewise, Our Lady had been chosen to be Mother of God in order that she might become a partner in the Redemption of the human race.[90]

The Second Vatican Council, while not explicitly adopting the expression Coredemptrix, taught the doctrine: 'So also the Blessed Virgin advanced in her pilgrimage of faith, and faithfully bore with her union with her Son even to the cross, where, in accord with the divine plan, she stood, vehemently grieved with her Only-Begotten, and joined herself to His Sacrifice with a motherly heart, lovingly consenting to the immolation of the victim born of her.'[91] Her coredemptive activity was expressed also in this form: 'In conceiving Christ, in giving birth to Him, in feeding Him, in presenting Him to the Father in the Temple, in suffering with her Son as He died on the cross she co-operated in the work of the Saviour in an altogether singular way, by obedience, faith, hope and burning love, to restore supernatural life to souls.'[92]

Pope John Paul II has often expressed the doctrine of Mary Coredemptrix, in various aspects. One is that co-operation was by way of obedience, which links closely with Redemption as the covenant condition. Co-operation by way of obedience is clearly active.

> How great, how heroic then is the obedience of faith shown by Mary in the face of God's 'unsearchable judgements'! How completely she 'abandons herself to God without reserve, 'offering the full assent of the intellect and the will' to Him whose 'ways are inscrutable ... Through this faith, Mary is perfectly united with Christ in his self-emptying ... At the foot of the Cross Mary shares through faith in the shocking mystery of this self-emptying. This is perhaps the deepest 'kenosis' of faith in human history. Through faith the Mother shares in the death of her Son, in His redeeming death ... as a sharing in the sacrifice of Christ – the new Adam – it becomes in a certain sense the counterpoise to the disobedience and disbelief embodied in the sin of our first parents.[93]

The value of Christ's Passion and Death depended on His obedience to the will of the Father (cf. Rm 5:19) for that obedience was the condition of the New Covenant, the essential interior disposition of the great sacrifice. Moreover, Mary's co-operation consisted in the obedience of faith, and so was a share in the covenant condition, in His obedience; hence her obedience became 'the counter-poise to the disobedience and disbelief embodied in the sin of our first parents.'

Pope John Paul II has used the expression Coredemptrix on at least five occasions. The most important and often cited was on 31 January 1985, in an address at the Marian shrine in Guayaquil, Ecuador: 'Mary goes before us and accompanies us. The silent journey that begins with her Immaculate Conception and passes through the "yes" of Nazareth, which makes her the Mother of God, finds on Calvary a particularly important moment. There also, accepting and assisting at the sacrifice of her Son, Mary is the dawn of Redemption;... Crucified spiritually with her crucified Son (cf. Ga 2:20), she contemplated with heroic love the death of her God, she lovingly consented to the immolation of this Victim which she herself had brought forth ... In fact, at Calvary she united herself with the sacrifice of her Son that led to the foundation of the Church; her maternal heart shared to the very depths the will of Christ "to gather into one all the dispersed children of God" (Jn 11:52) ... In fact, *Mary's role as Coredemptrix* did not cease with the glorification of her Son.'[94]

The Catechism stated that Mary was 'associated more intimately than any other person in the mystery of Christ's redemptive suffering.[95] The full doctrine of coredemption would conclude Mary's proximate, immediate, objective, active and universal co-operation with Christ the Redeemer. Current theology continues to take an interest in Mary's coredemptive role. For Balthasar, Mary had a core-demptive part to play, and Mary renews her 'fiat' from a position of both proximity to the Crucified One and distance from him: 'Hidden behind the multitude of sinners, embracing them all, she is objectively closest to Him: she makes His suffering possible and guarantees its goal. Now, however, He can only see her as the farthest from Him; this is how He *must* see her. He is forsaken *absolutely*, and the only way of fellowship with Him is to take leave of Him and plunge into forsakenness. He must withdraw from His mother just as His Father has with-drawn from Him: "Woman, behold your Son."'[96] Moreover, the fact that the Son is accompanied by a witness to God's atoning action means that the revelation of the Trinity on the Cross cannot be expounded on the basis of the Crucified Christ alone. This witness, the Mother of the Lord, is an icon of the fruitful receptivity by which the Son greets the love of the Father in the Holy Spirit. It is because she witnesses in her poverty, the humiliation of which the Magnificat speaks, standing behind sinners and with them, that she is able to receive the measureless outpouring of the Son on the Cross in His sacrifice of praise and petition to the

Father, and receive it in such a way that she becomes the Bride of the Lamb and the Womb of the Church, in a 'nuptial relationship that begins in the utter forsakenness and darkness they both experience.'[97]

Laurentin explains that the expression Coredemptrix has been used by the Popes and therefore requires respect. It would be gravely temerarious to attack its legitimacy.[98] For Gherardini, the truth of Marian Coredemption meets totally and in an amply verifiable way the conditions by which a doctrine is and must be considered Church doctrine. Its foundation is indirect and implicit, yet solid, in the Scriptures; extensive in the Fathers and Theologians; unequivocal in the Magisterium. It follows, therefore, that the Coredemption belongs to the Church's doctrinal patrimony.[99] The prefix 'co' does not mean equal, but comes from the Latin word, 'cum' which means 'with'. The title of Coredemptrix applied to the Mother of Jesus never places Mary on a level of equality with Jesus Christ, the divine Lord of all, in the saving process of humanity's Redemption. Rather, it denotes Mary's singular and unique sharing with her Son in the saving work of Redemption for the human family. Having seen how Mary co-operated in Christ's Redemption, we now turn to examine how she shared in the fruits of the same Redemption by her Assumption into heaven.

Notes

1. See National Conference of US Bishops, *Behold Your Mother* (1973), 81.
2. See Pope John Paul II, *Discourse at General Audience*, 7 January 2004, 3.
3. See chapter 4, pp. 75–76 above for the relevant texts.
4. St Irenaeus, *Adversus haereses*, Book 5, chapter 19, n. 1 in *PG* 7, 1175–1176. See also *ibid.*, Book 3, chapter 22, n. 4 in *PG* 7, 958–959.
5. Theodotus of Ancyra, *Homilia 6, In sanctam Mariam Dei genitricem et in sanctam Christi nativitatem*, nn. 11–12 in *EM* 1201.
6. See Pope John Paul II, Encyclical Letter *Redemptoris Mater* (1987), 20.
7. See Pope John Paul II, *Catechesi Tradendae*, 73. See also St Augustine, *Sermo 25*, 7 in *PL* 46, 937–938.

[8]   See Vatican II, *Lumen Gentium*, 58.

[9]   See National Conference of US Bishops, *Behold Your Mother* (1973), 78.

[10] See Pope Paul VI, *Signum Magnum*, 23.

[11] See National Conference of US Bishops, *Behold Your Mother* (1973), 114. See also Paul VI, *Address on the Feast of the Purification* (2nd February 1965).

[12] See Pope Paul VI, *Marialis Cultus*, 35.

[13] See Pope John Paul II, Encyclical Letter *Redemptoris Mater*, 41. See also Vatican II, *Lumen Gentium*, 36.

[14] Pope Paul VI, *Marialis Cultus*, 37.

[15] See Pope John Paul II, *Vita Consacrata* (1996), 18, 28.

[16] See Pope John Paul II, *Rosarium Virginis Mariae* (2002), 21.

[17] See Pope John Paul II, *Discourse at General Audience* (3 July 1996), 3.

[18] See Pope John Paul II, *Discourse at General Audience* (15 January 1997), 2.

[19] *Ibid.*, 2–3. This reference to his total dedication to God's plan is highlighted in the Gospel text by the words: 'I must be', which will later appear in His prediction of the Passion (cf. Mk 8:31).

[20] *Ibid.*, 4.

[21] See Pope John Paul II, *Discourse at General Audience* (26 February 1997), 1. See Idem, *Redemptoris Mater*, 21.

[22] See Pope John Paul II, *Discourse at General Audience* (26 February 1997), 2.

[23] See *Ibid.*, 4.

[24] See Vatican II, *Lumen Gentium*, 56.

[25] Vatican II, *Lumen Gentium*, 61.

[26] See Vatican II, *Lumen Gentium*, 57 and 61.

[27] See Pope Paul VI, Apostolic Exhortation *Signum Magnum*, 8 and 10.

[28] See National Conference of US Bishops, *Behold Your Mother*, 69.

[29] See *Ibid.*, 131.

[30] See *Ibid.*, 18, 66.

[31] See Pope John Paul II, *Discourse at General Audience* (12 March 1997), 1–2.

[32] See chapter 3, pp. 53–54, 63 above.

[33] See Pope John Paul II, *Redemptoris Mater*, 20.

[34] See Pope John Paul II, *Discourse at General Audience* (12 March 1997), 2.

[35] See *Ibid.*, 3.

[36] St Gregory Thaumaturgus, *Homilia 2 in Annuntiatione Virginis Mariae* in *PG* 10, 1169.

[37] See Pope John Paul II, *Dives in Misericordia*, 9.

[38] St Alphonsus de Liguori, *The Glories of Mary* (Rockford, Illinois: Tan, 1977), p. 422.

[39] See St Alphonsus de Liguori, *The Glories of Mary*, p. 443.

40 See chapter 8 below.
41 See George of Nicomedia, *Oratio IX* in *PG* 100, 1500.
42 St Ambrose, *De Virginitate*, III, 14 in *PL* 16, 283.
43 See Rupert of Deutz, *De divini officio*, VII, 25 in *PL* 159, 306; Eadmer, *De excellentia Virginis Mariae*, c.6 in *PL* 159, 568; St Ignatius of Loyola, *Spiritual exercises*, On the resurrection, First apparition; Suárez, *De mysteriis vitae Christi*, XLIX, I.
44 Pope John Paul II, *Discourse at the Marian shrine in Guayaquil, Ecuador* (31 January 1985), in *IG* 8/1 (1985), pp. 318–319.
45 See, J. Alfaro, *Cristologia e Antropologia* (Assisi: Cittadella, 1973), p. 234.
46 See J. Galot, *Maria, la donna nell'opera della salvezza* (Roma: Editrice Pontificia Università Gregoriana, ²1991).
47 J. Macquarrie, *Mary for All Christians* (London: Collins, 1990), p. 113.
48 See Pope John Paul II, *Discourse at General Audience* (9 April 1997), 1.
49 Vatican II, *Lumen Gentium*, 62.2.
50 Vatican II, *Lumen Gentium*, 58. See Jn 19:26–27.
51 See St Thomas Aquinas, *Summa Theologiae*, III, q. 1, a. 2: 'For an adequate satisfaction it is necessary that the act of him who satisfies should possess an infinite value and proceed from one who is both God and Man.'
52 See G. O'Collins, *The Calvary Christ* (London: SCM, 1977), pp. 106–109, who discusses the weaknesses inherent in the use of the expression 'substitution'. See also St Athanasius, *On the Incarnation*, 9: 'He takes to Himself a body capable of death that it, by partaking of the Lord who is above all, might be worthy to die instead of all … All are considered to have died in Him.'
53 See St Athanasius, *On the Incarnation*, 8. Christ died so that 'the law involving the ruin of men might be undone, inasmuch as its power was fully spent in the Lord's body.'
54 St Athanasius, *On the Incarnation*, 9: 'The Word of God … by offering His own temple and corporeal instrument for the life of all, satisfied the debt by His death.' St Anselm further developed the idea of Redemption as a debt which man had incurred through original sin.
55 See St Athanasius, *Second Oration Against the Arians*, 70: 'Such a union was made so He might join what was by nature divine with what was by nature human, so (human) salvation and divinization might be secure.'
56 See Pope Leo XIII, Encyclical Letter *Fidentem Piumque*, 3.
57 See chapter 9, pp. 254–266 below.
58 Pope Leo XIII, Encyclical Letter *Adiutricem populi*, (5th September 1895) in *ASS* 28 (1895), pp. 130–131.
59 See, for example, J. Wijngaards, *The Ordination of Women in the Catholic Church* (London: Darton, Longman and Todd, 2001).

[60]   St Epiphanius, *Haeresis 79*, 2–4 in *PG* 42, 741–745.

[61]   Holy Office, *Decree* (29 March 1916) in *AAS* 8 (1916), p. 146: 'After mature examination the Eminent Cardinals, general inquisitors of the Holy Office, have decided that images of the Blessed Virgin Mary wearing priestly vestments are not approved.' See also the letter from Cardinal Merry del Val to the Bishop of Adria, and in a later elucidation by the Cardinal, which was published in the *Palestra del Clero* 6 (1927), p. 611: 'The Holy Office no longer wants any question of a devotion to the Virgin Priest. The explanations you offer in your periodical satisfy us and you do not need to return to the subject ... You respond well to the intention of the Holy Office by leaving this question entirely alone, a question which less enlightened minds would not be able to exactly understand.'

[62]   See J. M. Samaha, 'The Sacerdotal Quality of Mary's Mission' in *Immaculata Mediatrix* 2/2 (2002), pp. 197–207.

[63]   See chapter 4, pp. 75–76 above and the current chapter, pp. 176–177 above.

[64]   St Augustine, *On Holy Virginity* 6, 6 in *PL* 40, 399: ' ... plane Mater membrorum eius, quod nos sumus; quia cooperata est charitate, ut fideles in Ecclesia nascerentur.'

[65]   Eadmer, *De excellentia Virginis Mariae*, chapter 9 in *PL* 159, 573. The phrase is 'Reparatrix perditi orbis.'

[66]   See St Bernard, *Homilia II super Missus est* in *PL* 183,62; *Sermo III de Purificatione Beatae Mariae* in *PL* 183, 370; *Sermo II in Festo Pentecostes* in *PL* 183, 328.

[67]   Arnold of Chartres, *De VII verbis Domini in cruce*, tractatus 3 in *PL* 189, 1694: 'Nimirum in tabernaculo illo duo videres altaria, aliud in pectore Mariae, aliud in corpore Christi. Christus carnem, Maria immolabat animam.'

[68]   See St Bonaventure, *Sermo 3 de Assumptione* in *Opera Omnia* (Collegio San Bonaventura: Quaracchi, 1885), Volume 9, p. 695.

[69]   See Idem, *Commentarius in III Librum Sententiarum Petri Lombardi*, dist. 4, a. 3, qu. 3, conclu., in *Opera Omnia*, Volume 3, p. 115.

[70]   Idem, *Collatio 6 de donis Spiritus Sancti*, n. 5, n. 15, n. 16, n. 17, in *Opera Omnia*, Volume 5, p. 486.

[71]   Idem, *Stimulus amoris*, part 1, chapter 3.

[72]   See J. Tauler, *Sermo pro festo Purificationis Beatae Mariae Virginis*; *Oeûvres complètes*, (Paris: 1911), Volume 6, ed. E. P. Noel, pp. 253, 259.

[73]   See Prayer book of St Peter's in Salzburg, in G. M. Dreves, *Analecta hymnica medii aevi*, (Lipsia: Reisland, 1905), t.46, 126 n. 79:, where the following hymn is cited:

> Pia, dulcis et benigna
> Nullo prorsus luctu digna

Si fletum hinc eligeres
Ut compassa Redemptori,
Captivato transgressori
Tu *Corredemptris* fieres.

Loving, sweet, and kind,
Wholly undeserving of any sorrow,
If henceforth you chose weeping,
As one suffering with the Redeemer,
For the captive sinner,
Coredemptrix would you be.

[74] See R. Laurentin, *Le titre de Corédemptrice. Etude historique* (Rome-Paris: 1951), pp. 10–11.

[75] Iohannes Iustus Lanspergius, *In Passionem agonemque Christi Iesu Salvatoris nostri*, homilia 48 in *Opera* (Coloniae Agrippinae: 1693), III, p. 112. 'Voluit enim eam Christus ... cooperatricem nostrae Redemptionis sibi adstare, quam futuram nobis constituerat dare misericordiae matrem. Debebat enim piissima Christi mater sub cruce nos parere filios adoptionis, ut quae naturalis – hoc est, corporalis – esset mater Christi, esset adoptione atque spiritualiter omnium quoque nostra mater: ut quomodo nos Christo sumus incorporati, unde mystica eius vocamur membra, ita Mariae simus quoque propterea filii, non carne, sed adoptione ... Quomodo caput Christus, ita nos corporis eius membra, et filii sumus Mariae.'

[76] F. Suárez, *De mysteriis vitae Christi*, disp. XXII, sect. II (ed Vivès, XIX, 327).

[77] Q. Salazar, *In Proverbis*, 1. (Cologne: 1621), p. 627: 'Quia id habuit commune cum Christo ut vere et proprie redemptionis nostrae dedisse atque attulisse dicatur ... , propterea ... redemptrix, reparatrix, Mediatrix, au(c)trix et causa salutis nostrae appellatur.'

[78] St Alphonsus de Liguori, *The Glories of Mary*, p. 448.

[79] Pope Leo XIII, Encyclical Letter *Iucunda Semper*, (8th September 1884) in *ASS* 27 (1884), p. 178.

[80] Pope St Pius X, Encyclical Letter *Ad diem illum*, (2 February 1904), 12–14.

[81] *Meritum de condigno* (condign merit) *ex toto rigore justitiae* (equality between the meritorious action and its reward, as well as between the persons giving and receiving the reward) is a type of merit ('a right to a reward') that can be obtained only by Jesus Christ in the light of His divine nature. The redemptive act by Jesus Christ on the Cross was both satisfactory (removing the relationship of guilt between the human race and God) and meritorious (establishing a right to a reward from Almighty God, which is always at the same time presupposing a gift of grace from God). On the other hand,

meritum de congruo (congruous merit) is a right to a reward based on its appropriateness or fittingness, along with the generosity of the person granting the reward.

82   Sacred Congregation of Rites, *Response to the Prior General of the Servites* in *ASS* 41 (1908), p. 409.

83   Holy Office, *Decree* in *AAS* 6 (1914), p. 108.

84   Pope Benedict XV, Apostolic Letter *Inter Sodalicia* (1918) in *AAS* 10 (1918), p. 182.

85   Pope Pius XI, *Radio Message to Lourdes for the Solemn Closing of the Redemption Jubilee*, 28 April 1935 in *OR*, 29–30 April 1935, p. 1.

86   Pope Pius XI, *Papal Allocution to Pilgrims from Vicenza*, 30 November 1933 in *OR*, 1 December 1933. In his encyclical letter *Miserentissimus Redemptor* in *AAS* 20 (1928), p. 178, Pope Pius XI had also used the title of Reparatrix for Our Lady, very similar in content to Coredemptrix: 'May the kindly Virgin Mother of God be present and smile on these our prayers and undertakings, who, since she brought forth Jesus the Redeemer, fed Him, offered Him as a victim at the cross, by her hidden union with Christ, and an altogether singular grace from Him, was likewise the Reparatrix, and is devoutly called that.'

87   Pope Pius XII, Encyclical Letter *Mystici Corporis* (1943), 110.

88   Pope Pius XII, *Radio Broadcast to Pilgrims at Fatima* (13 May 1946) in *AAS* 38 (1946), p. 266.

89   Pope Pius XII, Encyclical Letter *Ad Caeli Reginam* (1954), 39.

90   Cf. *Ibid.*, 38. See also S. Irenaeus, *Adversus haereses* V, 19, 1 in *PG* 7, 1175 and Pope Pius XI, Letter *Auspicatus profecto* in *AAS* 25 (1933), p. 80.

91   Vatican II, *Lumen Gentium*, 58. The same conciliar document had also pointed out earlier (54) that the Council did not have it in mind to give a complete doctrine on Mary, nor does it wish to decide those questions which the work of theologians has not yet fully clarified. Those opinions therefore may be lawfully retained which are propounded in Catholic schools concerning Our Lady, who occupies a place in the Church which is the highest after Christ and yet very close to us.

92   Vatican II, *Lumen Gentium*, 61.

93   Pope John Paul II, Encyclical Letter *Redemptoris Mater* (1987), 18–19.

94   Pope John Paul II, *Discourse at the Marian shrine in Guayaquil, Ecuador* (31 January 1985), in *IG* 8/1 (1985), pp. 318–319. See Vatican II, *Lumen Gentium*, 58. The other four occasions were:
1) In his greetings to the sick after the general audience of 8 September 1982 the Pope said: 'Mary, though conceived and born without the taint of sin, participated in a marvellous way in the sufferings of her divine Son, in order to be Coredemptrix of humanity' (*IG* 5/3 (1982), p. 404).

2) In 4 November 1984, the Feast of his patron saint, Charles Borromeo, in his Angelus address in Arona: 'To Our Lady – the Coredemptrix – St Charles turned with singularly revealing accents' (*IG* 7/2 (1984), p. 1151).

3) On 31 March 1985, in the Angelus message on Palm Sunday and World Youth Day: 'Mary accompanied her divine Son in the most discreet concealment pondering everything in the depths of her heart. On Calvary, at the foot of the Cross, in the vastness and in the depth of her maternal sacrifice, she had John, the youngest Apostle, beside her ... May Mary our Protectress, the Coredemptrix, to whom we offer our prayer with great outpouring, make our desire generously correspond to the desire of the Redeemer.' (*IG* 7/1 (1985), pp. 889–890).

4) In commemorating the sixth centenary of the canonization of St Bridget of Sweden on 6 October 1991: 'Bridget looked to Mary as her model and support in the various moments of her life. She spoke energetically about the divine privilege of Mary's Immaculate Conception. She contemplated her astonishing mission as Mother of the Saviour. She invoked her as the Immaculate Conception, Our Lady of Sorrows, and Coredemptrix, exalting Mary's singular role in the history of salvation and the life of the Christian people.' (*IG* 14/2 (1991), p. 756).

95 *CCC* 618. Cf. Lk 2:35.

96 H. U. von Balthasar, *Theo-Drama. Theological Dramatic Theory, IV. The Action* (San Francisco: Ignatius Press 1994), p. 356.

97 *Ibid.*, p. 358.

98 R. Laurentin, *Le titre de corédemptrice* (Rome: Marianum, 1951), pp. 27ff.

99 See B. Gherardini, 'The Coredemption of Mary : Doctrine of the Church' in AA.VV., *Mary at the Foot of the Cross: Acts of International Symposium on Marian Coredemption 2001*, vol. 2 (Libertyville, IL: Academy of the Immaculate, 2002), pp. 37–48. Gherardini points out that up till now there has not been a solemn dogmatic or *ex cathedra* definition of the Coredemption. Hence it is not at present in the narrow sense a truth of Faith. The Coredemption is a part of the Church doctrine because it is indirectly and derivatively ascribable to the 'sacred deposit'. Consequently, the theological note *de fide* is not to be given it: the doctrinal assertion *proxima fidei* (close to faith) is appropriate for this doctrine. This means it belongs to Revelation, and even if not explicit, it is beyond doubt. The term *proxima fidei* best synthesizes all the intrinsic and extrinsic considerations involved in study of the Coredemption: in particular its connection with Revelation and its presence, even if not in a formal manner, within the ecclesiastical Magisterium.

CHAPTER 8

ASSUMED INTO HEAVEN

She, the Lily of Eden, who had always dwelt out of the sight of man, fittingly did she die in the garden's shade, and amid the sweet flowers in which she had lived. Her departure made no noise in the world ... They sought for her relics, but they found them not ... Her tomb could not be pointed out, or if it was found it was open.

John Henry Newman, *Sermon for the Assumption*, 1849

In the Old Testament, there were some mysterious departures from this life. God granted a special privilege of not dying to Enoch and Elijah. The first case concerns Enoch, referred to in the book of Genesis: 'Enoch walked with God, then was no more, because God took him' (Gn 5:24). The letter to the Hebrews furnishes more information: 'It was because of his faith that Enoch was taken up and did not experience death: he was no more, because God took him; because before his assumption he was acknowledged to have pleased God' (Heb 11:5). Significantly the word *assumption* is adopted.[1] Similarly, the passing of Elijah was extraordinary, since he did not die: 'Now as they [Elijah and Elisha] walked on, talking as they went, a chariot of fire appeared and horses of fire coming between the two of them; and Elijah went up to heaven in the whirlwind' (2 K 2:11; Cf. Si 48:9).

In the New Testament, the fate of the last generation who are present at the time of Christ's appearing in glory is sometimes considered to involve a kind of assumption.

In two passages in the Pauline Letters, the Apostle points out that 'we are not all going to die, but we shall all be changed' (1 Co 15:51) and he affirms that 'those who have died in Christ will be the first to rise and then those of us who are still alive will be taken up in the clouds, together with them to meet the Lord in the air' (1 Th 4:16–17). The opinion that the last generation upon the face of the earth will not die is supported by Greek Fathers including St Gregory of Nyssa and St John Chrysostom and Latin Fathers including Tertullian and St Jerome. The Creed follows the Scriptures by indicating that those who are alive at the Second Coming will not die, for it affirms that Christ will come to judge the *living* and the dead. However, this assumption of a last generation of believers is to be carefully distinguished from the notion of the 'Rapture', current in some Protestant and Pentecostal thought.[2]

The close of Mary's earthly Life

Where Mary passed the last years of her life on earth is a matter for conjecture, although various traditions propose Ephesus or near Jerusalem as possibilities. Some apocryphal works dating from the second to the fourth century are all favourable to the Jerusalem tradition. The letter of Dionysius the Pseudo-Areopagite to the Bishop Titus (363), as well as the *Joannis liber de Dormitione Mariae* (third to fourth century), locate her tomb at Gethsemane. Historically these works have some value despite being apocryphal, since they echo a belief from earlier centuries. The indication of a tomb of the Virgin in the valley of Josaphat dates from about the fifth century, and this tomb became the object of pilgrimage and devotion.[3] St John Damascene bears witness to a tradition that Our Lady passed from this world from Jerusalem: 'Sion is the mother of churches in the whole world, who offered a resting-place to the Mother of God after her Son's

Resurrection from the dead. In it, lastly, the Blessed Virgin was stretched on a small bed.'[4] He indicated Gethsemane as the place of her Assumption: 'Then they reached the most sacred Gethsemane, and once more there were embraces and prayers and panegyrics, hymns and tears, poured forth by sorrowful and loving hearts. They mingled a flood of weeping and sweating. And thus the immaculate body was laid in the tomb. Then it was assumed after three days to the heavenly mansions.'[5] Within this tradition, then, there are various opinions as to whether Mary's tomb was in the Garden of Olives or in the Valley of Josaphat. A pointer towards placing the tomb of Mary in Gethsemane is the basilica erected above the sacred spot, about the end of the fourth or the beginning of the fifth century. The present church was built in the same place in which the old edifice had stood.[6]

Another tradition posits the place of Mary's transition as being in Ephesus. There is no mention made in the Acts of the Council of Ephesus (431) of that city being the one chosen by God for Mary's last days. Only after that Council was there any firm indication placing her tomb in that city. Since St John had lived in Ephesus and had been buried there,[7] it has been inferred that as he took Our Lady into his care after the death of the Lord, she could have lived there after Christ's Ascension, and then passed from this life in that town. Benedict XIV states that Mary followed St John to Ephesus and died there. He intended also to remove from the Breviary those lessons which mention Mary's death in Jerusalem, but died before carrying out his intention.[8] Various private revelations indicate Ephesus as the place of Mary's passage from this life.[9]

The question then arises concerning the nature of her passing, and concretely whether she died or not. This issue examines whether she experienced the separation of the soul from the body. The dogma of the Assumption of the Mother of God leaves open the question of whether or not she died. A minority of theologians hold that she did not in fact suffer death. In the late fourth century, we find the earliest known, non-Apocryphal mention of the close of Mary's life, in the writings of St Epiphanius (315–403), Bishop of Constantia, on the island of Cyprus: 'Whether she died or was buried we do not know ... Say she died a natural death. In that case she fell asleep in glory, and departed in purity, and received the crown of her virginity. Or say she was slain with the sword according to Simeon's prophecy. Then her glory is with the martyrs, and she through whom the divine light shone upon the world is in the place of bliss with her sacred body. Or say she left this world without dying, for God can do what He wills. Then she was simply transferred to eternal glory.'[10] St Epiphanius genuinely may have not known, or else he was being careful not to play into the hands of certain contemporary heretics, the Antidicomarianites and the Collyridians. The former group denied the perpetual virginity of Mary; the latter, erring in the opposite direction, maintained that divine worship should be given to her. To claim that Our Lady died was to give possible fuel to the former heresy (for it was to suggest that the body of Mary was subject to the corruption of the tomb, and thus minimize her prerogatives); to assert that she did not die was to encourage the latter.[11] Around the same time, Timothy of Jerusalem, affirmed that Mary did not die: 'Wherefore the Virgin is immortal up to now, because He who dwelt in her, assumed her to the heavenly regions.'[12]

St Isidore of Seville (d. 636) appears to be the first to cast some doubt upon the fact of Mary's death: 'Nowhere does one read of her death. Although, as some say, her sepulchre may be found in the valley of Josaphat.'[13] Tusaredo, a Bishop in the Asturias province of Spain in the eighth century, wrote: 'Of the glorious Mary, no history teaches that she suffered martyrdom or any other kind of death.'[14] In the early ninth century, Theodore Abou-Kurra likened the death of Mary to the sleep of Adam in the Garden when God formed Eve from one of his ribs.[15] This, obviously, was not a true death.

Most of the Fathers, however, reflecting on Mary's

destiny and on her relationship with her divine Son, proposed that since Christ died, it would be difficult to maintain the contrary for his Mother. St Augustine (354–430), who was not clear concerning the absence of original sin in Our Lady, stated baldly: 'Mary, as a daughter of Adam died as a consequence of sin; Adam died because of sin, and the flesh of the Lord, born of Mary, died to destroy sin.'[16] The Syriac Father, St Jacob of Sarug (d. 521), wrote that when the time came for Mary 'to walk the way of all generations', that is the way of death, 'the group of the Twelve Apostles' gathered to bury 'the virginal body of the Blessed One.'[17] St Modestus of Jerusalem (d. 634), after a lengthy discussion of 'the most blessed dormition of the most glorious Mother of God', ends his eulogy by exalting the miraculous intervention of Christ who 'raised her from the tomb', to take her up with him in glory.[18] St John Damascene (d. 704) asks the basic question: 'For how could she, who brought life to all, be under the dominion of death? But she obeys the law of her own Son, and inherits this chastisement as a daughter of the first Adam, since her Son, who is the life, did not refuse it. As the Mother of the living God, she goes through death to Him.'[19] St Andrew of Crete (d. 720) also followed the line of those who affirmed, with very little argumentation, that Mary died because her Son died.[20]

Many Fathers attest the pious tradition that at least some of the Apostles were present at Our Lady's passing from this world. In the East, St John Damascene wrote: 'When the Ark of God [Mary], departing from Mount Sion for the heavenly country, was borne on the shoulders of the Apostles, it was placed on the way in the tomb. First it was taken through the city, as a bride dazzling with spiritual radiance, and then carried to the sacred place of Gethsemane, angels overshadowing it with their wings, going before, accompanying, and following it, together with the whole assembly of the Church.'[21] In the West, St Gregory of Tours (d. 593) wrote:

When finally the Blessed Virgin had fulfilled the course of this life, and was now to be called out of this world, all the Apostles were gathered together from each region to her house ... and behold the Lord Jesus came with His angels and, receiving her soul, entrusted it to the Archangel Michael and departed. At the break of day the Apostles lifted the body with the couch and laid it in the sepulchre, and they guarded it awaiting the coming of the Lord. And behold the Lord again stood by them, and commanded that the holy body be taken up and borne on a cloud into Paradise, where now, reunited with (her) soul and rejoicing with the elect, it enjoys the good things of eternity which shall never come to an end.[22]

Many of the great Scholastics taught that Mary died, because they were unable to see how she remained free from original sin. St Thomas, since he could not see how Our Lady was conceived without original sin, maintained that she suffered the consequences, and in particular death.[23] In particular, St Bonaventure wrote: 'If the Blessed Virgin was free from original sin, she was also exempt from the necessity of dying; therefore, either her death was an injustice or she died for the salvation of the human race. But the former supposition is blasphemous, implying that God is not just; and the latter, too, is a blasphemy against Christ for it implies that His Redemption is insufficient. Both are therefore erroneous and impossible. Therefore Our Blessed Lady was subject to original sin.'[24] Most interestingly this passage connects the question of Mary's death also with the role which she played in the Redemption. Even those authors who accepted the doctrine of the Immaculate Conception did not always deduce that Mary would have remained without death. Even Blessed John Duns Scotus, who was clear on the Immaculate Conception, did not hold that Mary would have been exempted from death. For Scotus, the sentence of death is so general, that neither Christ nor Mary are exceptions. The resurrection of the body is for him a victory over death, like that of Christ and His Mother.[25]

St Alphonsus Liguori (1696–1787) held a nuanced position on Mary's death, pointing out that in one sense she
should not have died, but in fact did die in order to be like
her Son:

> Death being the punishment of sin, it would seem that the
> Divine Mother all holy, and exempt as she was from its
> slightest stain should also have been exempt from death,
> and from encountering the misfortunes to which the chil-
> dren of Adam, infected by the poison of sin, are subject.
> But God was pleased that Mary should in all things resem-
> ble Jesus; and as the Son died, it was becoming that the
> Mother should also die; because, moreover, He wished to
> give the just an example of the precious death prepared for
> them, He willed that even the most Blessed Virgin should
> die, but by a sweet and happy death.[26]

In the seventeenth century, there was renewed interest in
the question of Mary's death. An Italian theologian
Beverini proposed that Mary did not die.[27] After 1854,
once Pope Blessed Pius IX had defined the Immaculate
Conception the question of whether or not Our Blessed
Lady died gradually became a subject of wide theological
discussion. The impetus for further research out of which
arose the present state of dispute was given by the writings of Dominic Arnaldi (d.1895) of Genoa who proposed
that Our Blessed Lady's complete freedom from sin
demanded her immunity from the penalty of death.[28]
Later in the twentieth century, the clearest proponents of
the thesis that Mary did not die were Roschini and
Gallus.[29] Others like Bonnefoy were clear proponents of
Mary's death: 'the death of the Most Holy Virgin may be
considered as historically proved and explicitly revealed:
as such (explicitly revealed) it may be the subject of a
dogmatic definition: there is no reason why it should not
be.'[30]

Pope John Paul II has come closest to addressing the
issue, and he inclined in favour of Mary's participation in
death: 'The fact that the Church proclaims Mary free from

original sin by a unique divine privilege does not lead to the conclusion that she also received physical immortality. The Mother is not superior to the Son who underwent death, giving it a new meaning and changing it into a means of salvation.'[31] The Pope went on to ask: 'Could Mary of Nazareth have experienced the drama of death in her own flesh?' His response is that reflecting on Mary's destiny and her relationship with her divine Son, 'it seems legitimate to answer in the affirmative: since Christ died, it would be difficult to maintain the contrary for his Mother ... Involved in Christ's redemptive work and associated in his saving sacrifice, Mary was able to share in his suffering and death for the sake of humanity's Redemption.'[32] Clearly the Pope did not wish to close the question, but indicated the theological weight in favour of the position that Mary participated somehow in death's mystery.

There are then two basic reasons in favour of the position that Our Blessed Mother actually died. First, that of conformity to Christ. The condition of the Mother should not be better than that of her divine Son. As the Mother of the passible and mortal Redeemer from whom He took His mortal flesh, Mary, too, had to be passible and mortal. This argument seems *post factum*, proposing to explain the fact of Mary's death once that death had been taken for granted. The Second Council of Orange is quite explicit in its teaching that those who hold that the penalty of death is transmitted to the body without the transmission of sin or the death of the soul to all the children of Adam, do an injustice to God.[33] Hence, where there is no sin there can be no mandatory death of the body in a child of Adam. A second reason favouring Mary's death would involve voluntary acceptance on her part. Some theologians locate this within the framework of Mary's role of Coredemptrix of the human race. They would maintain that Mary died, though she had a right to immortality. She, like her Son, freely accepted death in order that she might coredeem the human race together with Him. Yet the objection can be put that Mary should then have died on Calvary with Christ.

Contrary to the proposition that Mary died, one could say that it seems strange that she should have enjoyed any lesser privilege than Elijah or Enoch from the Old Testament, who seemingly did not die. Moreover, it could be argued that she enjoyed the first fruits of Christ's Resurrection and Ascension, in such a way that she did not die. Furthermore, one may apply to her the words of Jesus to His disciples: 'For the Father loves the Son and shows Him everything He himself does, and He will show Him even greater things than these, works that will aston-ish you. Thus, as the Father raises the dead and gives them life, so the Son gives life to anyone He chooses' (Jn 5:20–21).

Since all theologians are agreed, at least after the defini-tion of the doctrine of the Immaculate Conception, that Mary cannot have died as a penalty for sin, the issue remains as to what was the cause of death. It is clear that she cannot have simply died of illness, a consequence of original sin. Neither would she have died of old age, as this is also connected with original sin. Also, a minority thesis, based on a misinterpretation of the prophecy of Simeon (Lk 2:35), that she suffered martyrdom, has long since been rejected, among others by St Ambrose: 'Neither the letter [of Scripture] nor history, teach us that Mary departed this life after having been assassinated; whereby not the soul but the body was pierced by a material sword.'[34] That leaves various other opinions. One is that she voluntarily gave up her privilege of immortality, in order to be more like her Son. Another line is that she died of sorrow in the aftermath of having seen her Son cruci-fied.[35] Perhaps the soundest approach would be to say, along with St Francis de Sales, that Mary's death was due to a transport of love.[36] He pointed out that as Christ's Mother lived her Son's life, she also died her Son's death: 'The virgin-mother, having collected in her spirit all the most beloved mysteries of the life and death of her Son by a most lively and continual memory of them, and withal, ever receiving directly the most ardent inspirations which her child, the sun of justice, has cast upon human beings in the highest noon of His charity; and besides, making on her part also, a perpetual movement of contemplation, at length the sacred fire of this divine love consumed her entirely as a holocaust of sweetness, so that she died thereof, the soul being wholly ravished and transported into the arms of the dilection of her Son.'[37] The saint also explained that this death was not violent, but rather her 'death was more sweet than could be imagined, her Son sweetly drawing her after the odour of His perfumes, and she most lovingly flowing out after their sacred sweetness even into the bosom of her Son's goodness.'[38]

Finally, it should be remarked that however one conceives of the end of Mary's life, namely whether Mary died or not, she was not subject to the *law of death*, which is the corruption of the body in the grave. If she died, then she was assumed into heaven before her sacred body saw corruption. For, so long as the bodies of the just remain in the dust of the earth, they are under the dominion of death, and they sigh for the ultimate redemption of their bodies.

The Assumption of Our Blessed Lady

The fact that nothing is found explicitly in the New Testament about Our Lady's Assumption is not surprising, since it is possible that much of it may have been composed before the event. This is clearly a matter of conjecture, especially if many of the Apostles were present at her Dormition, as many Fathers propose. No isolated text of the New Testament explicitly affirms the doctrine of the Assumption. However, the Church does not read the Word of God as segmented texts of Scripture alone, but in its fullness in relation to the whole deposit of Revelation as it is also expressed in Tradition.[39] The

Church's Tradition shows that Mary's Assumption was at least implicitly revealed. It is false to maintain, along with the rationalists, that the later tradition of the Church expressing belief in the Assumption is an outgrowth of the Apocrypha.[40] A concrete indication of belief in the Assumption of Mary, is found in the fact that the Church has never looked for the bodily relics of the Blessed Virgin nor proposed them for veneration.[41] It is probable that the revelation made to the Apostles, or to one of them, was even explicit, since otherwise it is difficult to explain the universal tradition of Mary's Assumption in the East and the West from the seventh century at the latest, which is also expressed in the liturgical celebration of the Feast.[42] Nevertheless, 'the liturgy of the Church does not engender the Catholic faith, but rather springs from it, in such a way that the practices of the sacred worship proceed from the faith as the fruit comes from the tree.'[43]

The feast of the Assumption began its life in the East as did many of the older Marian feasts. At first, Mary was implicitly honoured in her Assumption by a celebration known as *The Memory of Mary*, the keeping of which began in the East around the fourth century. Honour was given to Mary's Assumption here because the Church intended to celebrate the 'birthday' of Mary, or her entrance into heaven. Later, *The Memory of Mary* liturgy was changed and became the feast of the *Dormitio*, or the 'Falling to Sleep' of the Blessed Mother. The feast of the *Dormitio* or *Koimesis* celebrated as its object the death, resurrection, and Assumption of the Blessed Mother, and was widely established in the East by the end of the fourth century.

The fact that the feast was even kept by the Churches separated from the Catholic Church is an indication of how early the tradition flourished. The Nestorian Churches separated very early from the Catholic Church (after the Council of Ephesus in 431) and introduced the feast later, under the title of the death or *transitus* of Mary. As regards the *transitus*, normally it was held that Mary remained incorrupt after her death, and that her body awaited the resurrection. The monophysite Churches marked the 15 August with a special celebration dating from the Patristic period. These rejected the Council of Chalcedon in 451, and include the Coptic Church in Egypt today, with a related church in Ethiopia, and the so-called Jacobite Church of Syria, with most of its adherents in South India. However, their theology is far from uniform. While some taught the death and resurrection of Mary, others held that her body remained incorrupt somewhere, awaiting her resurrection from the dead. The Coptic Church normally followed the doctrine of Theodosius, the monophysite Patriarch of Alexandria (d. 567), and celebrated a double feast, the death of Mary on 16 January, and her glorious resurrection on 9 August, 216 days later. Now, since the monks of Gaul adopted many customs from the Egyptian monks this feast is found celebrated in January in sixth century Gaul. The Gallican Liturgy has it on the 18 January, under the title: *Depositio, Assumptio, or Festivitas S. Mariae.*[44] This custom was kept up in the Gallican Church until the introduction of the Roman rite.

In the Greek Church, it seems, some kept this feast in January, with the monks of Egypt; others in August, with those of Palestine. Uniformity was brought about by the Emperor Maurice (582–602), who ordered that the feast be set for the whole Byzantine Empire on 15 August.[45] It is important to note that the Emperor did not establish the feast but merely fixed the date of an already well-established event. The earliest witness to the existence of the feast in the West seems to be the Gospel Lectionary of Würzburg (c. 650) in which the feast for 15 August is found to be *Natale Sanctae Mariae.*[46] Then Pope Sergius I (687–701) decreed that on the feast of the Dormition (as well as on the Annunciation and the Nativity of our Blessed Mother) there should be a procession from the church of St Adrian to the church of St Mary Major. Most likely it was this same Pope who introduced the feast of the Dormition into the Roman calendar. Pope Sergius was a Syrian by birth and so was well acquainted with the celebration from his homeland. After Pope Sergius introduced the feast into Rome, it spread rapidly throughout western Europe. The name of the feast was changed from the *Dormition* to the *Assumption of St Mary* in the eighth century, probably at the behest of Pope Hadrian I.

There are early glimpses within Patristic tradition that Mary's body is incorruptible. St Hippolytus (172–235) associated the Ark of the Covenant of the Book of Revelation (Rv 11:19) with Mary's incorruptible flesh from which Christ's flesh was taken: 'Now the Lord was without sin, being in His human nature from incorruptible wood, that is, from the Virgin, and being sheathed inwardly as it were with the pure gold of the Word and by the Spirit outwardly.'[47] The earliest clear mention of the doctrine of the Assumption dates from the second half of the sixth century, in a homily preached by Bishop Theoteknos of Livias, in Palestine.[48] Theoteknos spoke as though the doctrine were commonplace, and he affirmed several times that Mary's body was raised to the heavens with her soul.[49] The homily describes how Christ, having ascended into heaven, gathered all the saints round the immaculate and pure Virgin. Mary, because of her exalted position, was to receive more than all the other saints: 'She found what Eve lost. She found what Adam had forfeited through his disobedience.'[50] Theoteknos recalled the special privileges traditionally accorded to Enoch and Elijah of escaping the normal deathly end of human life, and declared that Mary's end must be more privileged than theirs: 'How much more then, will He glorify in body and soul the one who has been His mother according to the flesh! In truth He has glorified her, and He will glorify her still.'[51] Theoteknos propounded the sound principle that the Son cannot forsake His Mother, and the Mother in her Mystery cannot be separated from her Son. Significantly, Theoteknos makes much of the link between Mary's being *Theotokos* (God-bearer) and her bodily Assumption:

For it was fitting that the holy one who begot Him should
see her Son upon a high throne, raised above all, and
should see every knee bend before Him of those above the
earth and of those upon the earth, and every tongue
confess Him that will judge the living and the dead ... It
was fitting ... that her all-holy body, her God-bearing
body, godlike, undefiled, shining with the divine light and
full of glory, should be carried by the apostles in company
of the angels, and, after being placed for a short while in
the earth, should be raised up to heaven in glory with her
soul so loved by God.[52]

Another very rich theological argument was the
Trinitarian perspective furnished by Theoteknos: 'For,
she, the holy one, pleased God the Father. She, the Virgin,
pleased the subsistent Word born of the Father from all
eternity. She, the Virgin, pleased the life-giving Spirit, the
enlightener of all, who fashions all the citizens of
heaven.'[53]

The chief patristic witnesses to the doctrine of the
Assumption are to be found in the seventh and eight
centuries, when theological reflection on this theme
became ripe. However, it is clear that before then there
was much written on this subject by figures like Gregory
of Tours whom we have cited above.[54] The aspect of the
incorruptibility of Mary's body was stressed by St
Modestus of Jerusalem (d. 634): 'As the most glorious
Mother of Christ, our Saviour and our God and the giver
of life and immortality, has been endowed with life by
Him, she has received an eternal incorruptibility of the
body together with Him Who has raised her up from the
tomb and has taken her up to Himself in a way known
only to Him.'[55]

St Germanus of Constantinople (d. 733) argued from the
great dignity of the divine maternity and the holiness of
her virginal body, to the fact of the Assumption of Mary:
'You are she who, as it is written, appears in beauty, and
your virginal body is all holy, all chaste, entirely the
dwelling place of God, so that it is henceforth completely

exempt from all dissolution into dust. Though still human, it is changed into the heavenly life of incorruptibility, truly living and glorious, undamaged and sharing in perfect life.'[56] St Andrew of Crete (d. 740) dedicated three beautiful homilies to the Dormition of Our Lady, which are rich in doctrine and devotion. For him the Dormition is a consequence of the Redemptive Incarnation, in which the physical nature of the mystery is highlighted:

> For look, all of you who hear my words, look at what is now before our eyes: the Queen of the nations – I mean the Church of the faithful – today leads the solemn procession for the Queen of our race, who today is received royally into the Kingdom of Heaven by God, the King who rules over all. The Church brings in tribute today her most beautiful and festive possessions. She who turned dust into heaven today strips the dust away, lays aside the veil of this world of change and gives back to the earth what belongs to it.[57]

St John Damascene (d. 749) linked and compared the bodily Assumption of the Blessed Virgin with her other prerogatives and privileges:

> It was fitting that she, who had kept her virginity intact in childbirth, should keep her own body free from all corruption even after death. It was fitting that she, who had carried the Creator as a child at her breast, should dwell in the divine tabernacles. It was fitting that the spouse, whom the Father had taken to Himself, should live in the divine mansions. It was fitting that she, who had seen her Son upon the cross and who had thereby received into her heart the sword of sorrow which she had escaped in the act of giving birth to Him, should look upon Him as He sits with the Father. It was fitting that God's Mother should possess what belongs to her Son, and that she should be honoured by every creature as the Mother and the Handmaid of God.[58]

During the Middle Ages, many saints and doctors further

developed the doctrine concerning Mary's glorious Assumption. St Anthony of Padua reflected, like early writers on the Ark of the Covenant as the prefiguration of the mystery of Mary, mentioned in Psalm 132: 'Go up, Lord, to the place of your rest, you and the ark of your strength.' He illustrated that just as Jesus Christ has risen from the death over which He triumphed and has ascended to the right hand of the Father, so likewise the ark of His sanctification 'has risen up, since on this day the Virgin Mother has been taken up to her heavenly dwelling.'[59] St Albert the Great confirmed a long-standing tradition of belief in the mystery of Mary's Assumption: 'From these proofs and authorities and from many others, it is manifest that the most blessed Mother of God has been assumed above the choirs of angels. And this we believe in every way to be true.'[60] St Thomas Aquinas never developed the theology of the Assumption in detail, but always held that Mary's body had been assumed into heaven along with her soul.[61] St Bonaventure is part of the same chorus of belief. He considered it as entirely certain that, as God had preserved the most holy Virgin Mary from the violation of her virginal purity and integrity in conceiving and in childbirth, He would never have permitted her body to have dissolved into dust and ashes.[62] Further he argued, in a modern key, that Mary's blessedness would not have been complete unless she had been assumed as a person: 'The soul is not a person, but the soul, joined to the body, is a person. It is manifest that she is there in soul and in body. Otherwise she would not possess her complete beatitude.'[63]

By the end of the Middle Ages, belief in Mary's Assumption into heaven was well established theologically and expressed in the devotional life and culture of Christendom. Even among figures of the Reformation, the Assumption remained in some cases an object of devotion. For Martin Luther, Mary's Assumption was an understood fact, as his homily of 1522 indicates, in spite of the fact that Mary's Assumption is not expressly reported in

Sacred Scripture: 'There can be no doubt that the Virgin Mary is in heaven. How it happened we do not know. And since the Holy Spirit has told us nothing about it, we can make of it no article of faith ... It is enough to know that she lives in Christ.'[64] For the Protestant reformer, M. Butzer (1545), there was no reason to doubt about the Assumption of the Virgin into heavenly glory. 'Indeed, no Christian doubts that the most worthy Mother of the Lord lives with her beloved Son in heavenly joy.'[65] H. Bullinger (1590), also a Protestant reformer, sought for a theological foundation for the Assumption in Scripture. He showed that the Old Testament tells of Elias, taken to heaven bodily to teach us about our immortality, and – because of our immortal soul – to respectfully honour the bodies of the saints. Against this backdrop he stated, 'Because of this, we believe that the pure immaculate chamber of the God-bearer, the Virgin Mary, is a temple of the Holy Spirit, that is her holy body, borne by angels into heaven.'[66]

Later, in the counter-Reformation period, St Robert Bellarmine once again adopted the Ark imagery and stated: 'Who, I ask, could believe that the ark of holiness, the dwelling place of the Word of God, the temple of the Holy Spirit, could be reduced to ruin? My soul is filled with horror at the thought that this virginal flesh which had begotten God, had brought Him into the world, had nourished and carried Him, could have been turned into ashes or given over to be food for worms.'[67] Some later authors proposed an argument from appropriateness for the Assumption. Since a basic commandment of both Old and New Testaments is for children to honour their parents, Jesus Christ must Himself have observed this, in the most perfect way possible. St Francis of Sales therefore asks: 'What son would not bring his mother back to life and would not bring her into paradise after her death if he could?'[68] St Alphonsus Liguori set the same idea in a more Christological light by affirming that Jesus did not wish to have the body of Mary corrupted after death, since it would have redounded to His own dishonour to have her virginal flesh, from which He Himself had assumed flesh, reduced to dust.[69]

The development of the doctrine of the Assumption of Mary, involved various elements which can be summarized in this way. A common Patristic theme is that the doctrine of the Second Eve implies assumption as the final and complete victory of the woman. Next, Mary's predestination is always associated with her Son. Further, Mary's Immaculate Conception and sinlessness imply exemption from corruption in the grave, and so lead to her immediate resurrection and glory. Another theme is that the perpetual virginity of Our Lady, as fleshly incorruption, involved exemption from physical corruption after death. A further argument is that the filial piety of the divine Son implied that He would grant her the favour of the Assumption, if it were fitting. Mary at her death was more exalted in dignity than other creatures will ever be. If, then, other Christians are destined to be bodily with Christ in heaven, this must have applied to Mary immediately after her death. Finally, the woman of the Apocalypse is already seen in her glory, after being taken by eagle's wings.[70]

One of the aspects of divine revelation which impressed itself on Newman's mind was its consistency, the fact that all of its truths hang together. By means of the principle of the analogy of faith, what is taught now fits into what has already been received, a principle which, he affirms, is exemplified in many different ways in the structure and the history of doctrine. This principle he applies particularly to Marian doctrines, especially to the Assumption of Our Lady into heaven.[71] This truth is in harmony with the substance of the doctrine of the Incarnation, and without it, Newman points out, Catholic doctrine would be incomplete. It is a truth which he says is received on the basis of centuries of belief, but even from a rational point of view the very fittingness of it recommends it strongly. Mary's Assumption into heaven is, for Newman, in perfect harmony with the other truths of Revelation. His starting point is the doctrine of the divine maternity:

> As soon as we apprehend by faith the great fundamental truth that Mary is the Mother of God, other wonderful truths follow in its train; and one of these is that she was exempt from the ordinary lot of mortals, which is not only to die, but to become earth to earth, ashes to ashes, dust to dust. Die she must, and die she did, as her Divine Son died, for He was man; but various reasons have approved themselves to holy writers, why, although her body was for a while separated from her soul, and consigned to the tomb, yet it did not remain there, but was speedily united to her soul again, and raised by our Lord to a new and eternal life of heavenly glory ... And the most obvious reason for so concluding is this – that other servants of God have been raised from the grave by the power of God, and it is not to be supposed that our Lord would have granted any such privilege to anyone else without also granting it to His own Mother ... Therefore we confidently say that our Lord, having preserved her from sin and the consequences of sin by His Passion, lost no time in pouring out the full merits of that Passion upon her body as well as her soul.[72]

The definition of the dogma of the Assumption was prepared for and preceded by a period of discussion which included a consideration of how the dogma was founded in the Scriptures and in Tradition. In May 1946, with the Encyclical *Deiparae Virginis Mariae*, Pius XII called for a broad consultation, inquiring among the Bishops and, through them, among the clergy and the People of God as to the possibility and opportuneness of defining the bodily Assumption of Mary as a dogma of faith. The result was extremely positive: only six answers out of 1,181 showed any reservations about the revealed character of this truth. The Church propounded that this truth was based in Scripture, and was visibly expressed in Tradition.[73] After many requests, Pope Pius XII solemnly defined the dogma in 1950:

After we have poured forth prayers of supplication again
and again to God, and have invoked the light of the Spirit
of Truth, for the glory of Almighty God who has lavished
his special affection upon the Virgin Mary, for the honour
of her Son, the immortal King of the Ages and the Victor
over sin and death, for the increase of the glory of that
same august Mother, and for the joy and exultation of the
entire Church; by the authority of our Lord Jesus Christ, of
the Blessed Apostles Peter and Paul, and by our own
authority, we pronounce, declare, and define it to be a
divinely revealed dogma: that the Immaculate Mother of
God, the ever Virgin Mary, having completed the course of
her earthly life, was assumed body and soul into heavenly
glory.[74]

Pope Pius XII defined a dogma which had been believed
by the Church for well over a thousand years. The definition took place in 1950, and this was of great historical
significance. In took place in the middle of a century when
the sacredness of the human body was denied theoreti-
cally and practically at many levels. In the first half of the
twentieth century it was denied politically in the totalitar-
ian systems of Marxism and Nazism which denied the
sacredness of the body in theory and in the slaughter of
millions in the gulags and concentration camps. In the
second half of the twentieth century, the assault on the
sacredness of the human body was taken a step further
through the massacre of untold millions through abortion
and euthanasia, and also through sacrilegious experi-
ments carried out on embryos to say nothing of genetic
engineering and attempts to clone the human being. All of
this is counterbalanced by the Church's affirmation that
Our Lady was assumed *body* and soul to the glory of
heaven. The Church, which believes in the resurrection of
the body, believes that this same body has been created in
the image and likeness of God, and is called to a supernatural destiny in Christ.

The Assumption can also be understood in light of the
mystery of the Church, as the Second Vatican Council

elucidated. In the most Blessed Virgin Mary, the Church has already reached that perfection whereby she exists without spot or wrinkle (cf. Ep 5:27), however, the faithful still strive to conquer sin and increase in holiness. 'In the meantime the Mother of Jesus in the glory which she possesses in body and soul in heaven is the image and beginning of the Church as it is to be perfected in the world to come. Likewise she shines forth on earth, until the day of the Lord shall come (cf. 2 Pet. 3:10), a sign of certain hope and comfort to the pilgrim People of God.'[75] For Our Blessed Lady there is no 'intermediate eschatology', namely there is no 'period' of waiting between death and the General Judgement for the body and soul to be reunited, and this sets her apart from us: 'In teaching her doctrine about man's destiny after death, the Church excludes any explanation that would deprive the assumption of the Virgin Mary of its unique meaning, namely the fact that the bodily glorification of the Virgin is an anticipation of the glorification that is the destiny of all the other elect.'[76]

Recent theology has outlined further consequences of the Assumption. One line of enquiry stresses that Adam and Eve lay at the natural origin of humanity, and at the origins of sin and its transmission. On the other hand, Christ and His Mother Mary stand at the origin of the regeneration of humanity. Therefore the eschatological destiny of humanity is revealed in the association of Christ and His Mother Mary. Thus, the Assumption of Mary shows that God's plan is now realized not only in Christ the bridegroom, but also in the bride, signified by the Church, recapitulated in Mary.[77] Thus the Assumption is an exaltation of woman, in contrast to all ancient and modern paganism. If the power of sin has served to oppress women, the Assumption shows how God has empowered a woman for the spread of holiness. The Assumption is a triumph for the nobility of maternity and also of virginity. The Assumption is also an indication of the glory which awaits the body of the Christian, who in this life has been the home of the Body of Christ in the Eucharist. Finally, the Assumption indicates the glorification of the poor and their liberation from oppression, in the fulfilment of the words of the Magnificat: 'The Almighty has done great things for me: Holy is His Name.' The Assumption of Mary is 'the glorious culmination of the mystery of God's preference for what is poor, small, and unprotected in this world, so as to make God's presence and glory shine there.' It offers 'hope and promise for the poor of all times and for those who stand in solidarity with them; it is hope and promise that they will share in the final victory of the incarnate God.'[78] Mary assumed into heaven is also connected with the unity of the Church. Far from being an ecumenical problem, the definition of Mary's Assumption marked a great period of growth for efforts favouring Christian unity. Mary assumed into heaven indicates that only by lifting up one's gaze and one's heart heavenward can one retrieve the lost brotherhood in Christ.[79]

The Queenship of Mary

The mystery of the Assumption of the noble Daughter of Sion is closely linked with the mystery of her eternal glory. The Mother of God is glorified as 'Queen of the Universe.' She, who at the Annunciation called herself the 'handmaid of the Lord', remained throughout her earthly life faithful to what this name expresses. She confirmed that she was a true 'disciple' of Christ, who strongly emphasized that his mission was one of service: the Son of Man came not to be served but to serve, and to give his life as a ransom for many' (Mt 20:28). Mary became the first of those who, serving Christ also in others, with humility and patience lead their brothers and sisters to that King to serve Whom is to reign, and she fully obtained that 'state of royal freedom' proper to Christ's disciples.[80]

The doctrine of Our Lady's Queenship is by no means

new. In the Annunciation episode, the angel Gabriel's greeting ran 'He shall be great, and shall be called the Son of the Most High: and the Lord God shall give unto Him the throne of His father David: And He shall reign over the house of Jacob for ever; and of His kingdom there shall be no end' (Lk 1:32–33). Our Lady's Queenship is thus seen as an association with Christ's Kingship.[81] Then, at the Visitation, Elizabeth used the words 'Mother of my Lord' (Lk 1:43). The word Lord (*Dominus* in Latin and *Kyrios* in Greek) in this passage, as in the New Testament generally, connotes divinity and royalty, according to many modern scholars, and so Elizabeth greets Mary as Mother of God, Mother of the King.[82] Already a fragment of a homily, attributed to Origen, contains this comment on the words Elizabeth spoke at the Visitation 'It is I who should have come to visit you, because you are blessed above all women, you are the Mother of my Lord, you are my Lady.'[83] The text passes spontaneously from the expression 'the Mother of my Lord' to the title, 'my Lady.'

Another line of understanding was also developed, stemming from the Annunciation account and other scriptural testimonies to the Kingship of Christ. This idea is in continuity with the Old Testament figure of the Queen Mother.[84] Mary is described as Mother of the King, by St Ephraem for example (d. 373), and by his contemporary St Gregory Nazianzen, who speaks of the 'Mother of the King of the entire universe.'[85] Then an easy transition occurs from the expression 'Mother of the King' to 'Queen', and it appears for the first time, as far as surviving evidence goes, in the fourth century, again in the writings of St Ephraem: 'Imperial maiden and mistress, Queen, sovereign lady, take me under thy protection, guard me lest Satan, the author of destruction, rise up against me, lest the accursed enemy triumph over me.'[86] Starting from the fifth century, almost in the same period in which the Council of Ephesus proclaims her 'Mother of God', the title of Queen begins to be attributed to Mary. In this way, Mary is raised above all other creatures, exalting her role and importance in the life of every person and of the whole world. The expression 'Lady', meaning sovereign, was later to become Queen, for example in St John Damascene: 'When she became Mother of the Creator, she truly became Queen of all creatures.'[87]

With the dogma of the divine maternity of Mary, her perfect sanctity also emerged in clearer light, resulting in a fuller understanding within the Church of Mary's pre-eminence and dignity. In the sixth and seventh centuries, explicit belief in the Assumption was universal, and Mary, in body and in soul, was envisaged as resplendent with the glory of the risen Saviour. By the end of the patristic period the doctrine of the Queenship is clearly established: a Queenship especially of excellence and grace, but also a Queenship of power, of intercession, protection, and patronage. This Queenship was later to find artistic expression all over Europe in paintings and sculpture depicting the crowning of Mary by her Son. These ideas are greatly developed in the Middle Ages. One of the greatest proponents was Eadmer, the disciple of St Anselm: 'just as ... God, by making all through His power, is Father and Lord of all, so the blessed Mary, by repairing all through her merits, is Mother and Queen of all; for God is the Lord of all things, because by His command He establishes each of them in its own nature, and Mary is the Queen of all things, because she restores each to its original dignity through the grace which she merited.'[88]

Gradually, the concept of the mediation of graces assumed great prominence. Mary is Queen principally through her influence over her Son and the guidance of her children towards salvation. The *Salve Regina* and other antiphons expressed these ideas, and Mary is invoked as Queen of Mercy, whose prayers are all-powerful. Pope Pius XII, in his Encyclical *Ad coeli Reginam*, indicated as the basis for Mary's Queenship in addition to her motherhood, her co-operation in the work of the Redemption. The Pope recalls that Mary, Queen of Heaven and Sovereign of the world, was first the sorrowing Mother

near the Cross of our Lord Jesus Christ.[89] It then established an analogy between Mary and Christ, which helps
us understand the significance of the Blessed Virgin's
royal status. Christ is King not only because He is Son of
God, but also because He is the Redeemer; Mary is Queen
not only because she is Mother of God, but also because,
associated as the new Eve with the new Adam, she co-
operated in the work of the redemption of the human
race.[90]

Mary, the handmaid of the Lord, has a share in the
Kingdom of her Son. This arises from the fact that she co-
operated in Christ's obedience even at the cost of death.
He was therefore raised up by the Father (cf. Ph 2:8–9) and
entered into the glory of his kingdom. To Him all things
are made subject until He subjects Himself and all created
things to the Father, that God may be all in all (cf. 1 Co
15:27–28). The glory of Mary's royal service does not cease
with her exaltation: assumed into heaven, she continues
her saving service, expressed in her maternal mediation
'until the eternal fulfilment of all the elect.'[91] Thus, she
who here on earth loyally preserved her union with her
Son unto the Cross, continues to remain united with Him,
while all things are subjected to Him, until He subjects
Himself to the Father who put all things in subjection
under Him (cf. 1 Co 15:28). In her Assumption into
heaven, Mary is as it were clothed by the whole reality of
the Communion of Saints, and her very union with the Son
in glory is wholly oriented towards the definitive fullness
of the Kingdom, when 'God will be all in all' (1 Co 15:28).
In the next chapter we will see how Mary realizes this as
Mother of the Church.

Notes

1   The expression used in Greek is μετατίθημι which carries the sense
    of being transposed or carried over.
2   See C. E. Olson, *Will Catholics Be Left Behind?* (San Francisco:

Ignatius Press, 2003), which is a thorough critique of the popular Fundamentalist notion of the 'Rapture' – the belief that Christians will be removed from earth prior to a time of Tribulation and the Second Coming.

3   This tradition can be seen for example in the Venerable Bede, *Liber de locis sacris* 2, 5 in *CSEL* 39, 309f.

4   St John Damascene, *Homily 2 on the Dormition of the Blessed Virgin*, 4 in *PG* 96, 730. St Gregory of Tours, St Sophronius, Patriarch of Jerusalem, St Germanus, Patriarch of Constantinople, St Andrew, Bishop of Crete, and the Venerable Bede indicate this same tradition, common to East and West.

5   St John Damascene, *Homily 2 on the Dormition of the Blessed Virgin*, 14 in *PG* 96, 739.

6   See E.-P. Le Camus, *Notre voyage aux pays bibliques*, (Paris: 1894), I, p. 253.

7   See Eusebius, *Historia Ecclesiastica*, III, 31; V, 24, in *PG* 20, 280; 493.

8   Cf. D. Arnaldi, *Super transitu Beatae Mariae Virginis Deiparae expertis omni labe culpae originalis dubia proposita* (Genoa: Montaldum, 1879), I, c. I.

9   According to the meditations of Ven. Catherine Emmerich (d. 1824), compiled and published in 1852, the Blessed Virgin died and was buried a few miles south of Ephesus. In Panaghia Kapoli, on a hill about nine or ten miles distant from Ephesus, the remains of a house were discovered, in which Mary is supposed to have lived, according to the indications given by Ven. Catherine Emmerich in her life of the Blessed Virgin.

10   St Epiphanius, *Adversus Octaginta Haereses* Book 3, Tome 2, Heresy 78, 11 and 24 in *PG* 42, 715–716 and 738.

11   See G. M. Roschini, 'Did Our Lady Die?' in *The Irish Ecclesiastical Record*, 80 (1953), pp. 75–76.

12   Timothy of Jerusalem, *Homily on Simeon* in *PG* 86, 246–247.

13   St Isidore of Seville, *De ortu et obitu Patrum*, 67 in *PL* 83, 150.

14   Tusaredo, *Epistola ad Ascaricum*, II in *PL* 99, 1239–1240.

15   Theodore Abou-Kurra, *Opuscula*, op. 37 in *PG* 97, 1594.

16   St Augustine, *Enarratio in Psalmo 34*, 3 in *PL* 41, 501: 'Maria ex Adam mortua propter peccatum, Adam mortuus propter peccatum, et caro Domini ex Maria mortua est propter delenda peccata.' See chapter 4, pp. 77, 81, 90 above for Augustine's ideas on Mary's sinlessness.

17   St Jacob of Sarug, *Discourse on the burial of the Holy Mother of God*, 87–99 in *EM* 1493–1494. See also C. Vona, *Lateranum* 19 (1953), p. 188.

18   St Modestus of Jerusalem, *Encomium in dormitionem Deiparae semperque Virginis Mariae*, nn. 7 and 14 in *PG* 86 *bis*, 3293; 3311.

19   St John Damascene, *Homily 2 on the Dormition of the Blessed Virgin*, 2 in *PG* 96, 726. See also Idem, *Homily 1 on the Dormition of the Blessed*

Virgin, 10 in PG 96, 714, where St John Damascene asks: 'Why is it that she who in giving birth surpassed all the limits of nature should now bend to its laws, and her immaculate body be subjected to death?' And he answers: 'To be clothed in immortality, it is of course necessary that the mortal part be shed, since even the master of nature did not refuse the experience of death. Indeed, He died according to the flesh and by dying destroyed death; on corruption He bestowed incorruption and made death the source of resurrection.'

[20] St Andrew of Crete, *Oratio 12 in dormitione SS. Deiparae* in PG 97, 1051–1054.

[21] St John Damascene, *Homily 2 on the Dormition of the Blessed Virgin*, 12 in PG 96, 738.

[22] St Gregory of Tours, *De gloria beatorum martyrum*, 4 in PL 71, 708.

[23] See St Thomas Aquinas, *Summa Theologiae* III, q. 14, a. 3.

[24] St Bonaventure, *Commentarius in III Librum Sententiarum Petri Lombardi*, distinction 3, question 2, in *S. Bonaventurae Opera Omnia* (Collegio San Bonaventura: Quaracchi, 1888), Volume III, p. 66.

[25] See Bl John Duns Scotus, *Fragmenta*, in K. Balić (ed.) *Theologiae Marianae elementa* (Sibenik: Kacik, 1933), p. 172.

[26] St Alphonsus Liguori, 'Discourse VII. Of the Assumption of the Blessed Virgin Mary' in *The Glories of Mary* (Rockford, Illinois: Tan, 1977), p. 371.

[27] B. Beverini, *De corporali morte Deiparae* (Roma: Academia Mariana, 1950). This work was republished in 1950, under the editorship of K. Balić.

[28] D. Arnaldi, *Super transitu Beatae Mariae Virginis Deiparae expertis omni labe culpae originalis dubia proposita* (Genoa: Montaldum, 1879).

[29] G. M. Roschini, 'Il problema della morte di Maria SS. dopo la Costituzione Dogmatica Munificentissimus Deus' in *Marianum* 13 (1951), pp. 148–163; T. Gallus, *La Vergine Immortale* (Roma: 1949).

[30] J. F. Bonnefoy, 'Définibilité de l'Assomption' in *Congrès Marial du Puy-en-Velay* (Paris: 1950), p. 241; cf. Idem, 'La Bulle Dogmatique *Munificentissimus Deus* (1 Nov. 1950)' in *Ephemerides Mariologicae* 1 (1951), pp. 104–114.

[31] Pope John Paul II, *Discourse at General Audience* (25 June 1997), 3.

[32] *Ibid.*, 2 and 3.

[33] See Second Council of Orange, canon 2 in DS 372.

[34] St Ambrose, *Expositio Evangelii secundum Lucam*, Book 2, chapter 2, 61 in PL 15, 1574: 'Nec littera, nec historia docet ex hac vita Mariam corporalis necis passione migrasse; non enim anima, sed corpus materiali gladio transverberatur.'

[35] This line was taken by St Peter Damian, *De celebrandis vigiliis*, 1 in PL 145, 801.

36 This was the line of Pope John Paul II, *Discourse at General Audience* (25 June 1997), 4.

37 St Francis de Sales, *Treatise on the Love of God*, book 7, chapter 13.

38 St Francis de Sales, *Treatise on the Love of God*, book 7, chapter 14. He added (13. 24) that 'love at the cross gave her the supreme sorrows of death. So it was right that finally death should give her the sovereign pleasure of love.'

39 See Vatican II, *Dei Verbum*, 9: 'For Sacred Scripture is the word of God inasmuch as it is consigned to writing under the inspiration of the divine Spirit, while sacred tradition takes the word of God entrusted by Christ the Lord and the Holy Spirit to the Apostles, and hands it on to their successors in its full purity, so that led by the light of the Spirit of truth, they may in proclaiming it preserve this word of God faithfully, explain it, and make it more widely known. Consequently it is not from Sacred Scripture alone that the Church draws her certainty about everything which has been revealed. Therefore both sacred tradition and Sacred Scripture are to be accepted and venerated with the same sense of loyalty and reverence.' See also Council of Trent, session IV, *Decree on Scriptural Canons* in DS 1501.

40 E. Renan, *L'Eglise Chrétienne*, in *Histoire des origines du Christianisme*, Vol. 6 (Paris: 1879) p. 513; C. Tischendorf, *Apocalypses Apocryphae* (Leipzig: 1866), p. 34.

41 See St Bernardine of Siena, *In Assumptione B. Mariae Virginis*, Sermo 11.

42 See R. Garrigou-Lagrange, *The Mother of the Savour and Our Interior Life* (Dublin: Golden Eagle Books, 1948), pp. 164–165.

43 Pope Pius XII, Apostolic Constitution *Munificentissimus Deus*, 20.

44 See J. Mabillon, *Notes on the Gallican Liturgy* in *PL* 72, 180.

45 Nicephorus Callistus, *Historia Ecclesiastica*, 18, 18, in *PG* 147, 292.

46 Cf. C. Lee, 'The Feast of the Assumption of the Blessed Virgin Mary', in *The Irish Ecclesiastical Record*, 54 (1939), p. 177.

47 St Hippolytus, *Sermonum Fragmentum* quoted by Theodoret, *Dialogue I* in *EM* 118. See also Ps 132:8: 'Go up, Lord, to the place of your rest, you and the ark of your strength.' See also chapter 4, p. 77 above where a similar citation from Hippolytus has been given in relation to the holiness of Mary.

48 Theoteknos, Bishop of Livias, *Encomium in Assumptionem Beatae Mariae Virginis* in A. Wenger, *L'Assomption de la Très Sainte Vierge dans la tradition byzantine du VIe au Xe siècle* (Paris: Institut Français d'Etudes Byzantines, 1955), pp. 272–291.

49 Theoteknos, *Encomium*, 9, 10, 15, 36.

50 *Ibid.*, 25

51 *Ibid.*, 17. See also, as a New Testament example of how people shared in Christ's Resurrection, Mt 27:52–53, which describes how after Christ's death, the tombs opened and the bodies of many holy

people rose from the dead, and these, after His Resurrection, came out of the tombs, entered the holy city and appeared to a number of people. Mary's privilege must clearly be greater than this.

[52]   *Ibid.*, 8–9.

[53]   *Ibid.*, 12.

[54]   See the current chapter, pp. 212–213 above.

[55]   St Modestus of Jerusalem, *Encomium in dormitionem Sanctissimae Dominae nostrae Deiparae semperque Virginis Mariae*, 14 in *PG* 86–II, 3306.

[56]   St Germanus of Constantinople, *In Sanctae Dei Genitricis dormitionem sermo I* in *PG* 98, 346.

[57]   St Andrew of Crete, *Oratio 2 in Beatae Mariae Virginis Dormitionem*, in *PG* 97, 1081.

[58]   St John Damascene, *Encomium in dormitionem Dei Genitricis semperque Virginis Mariae*, homily 2, n. 14 in *PG* 96, 741.

[59]   St Anthony of Padua, *Sermones Dominicales et in Solemnitatibus, In Assumptione S. Mariae Virginis Sermo.*

[60]   St Albert the Great, *Mariale*, q. 132.

[61]   St Thomas Aquinas, *Summa Theologiae*, I–II, q. 27, a. 1; q. 83, a. 5; *Expositio Salutationis Angelicae; In Symbolum Apostolorum Expositio*, a.5; *In IV Sententiarum*, d. 12, q. 1, a. 3; d. 43, q. 1, a. 3.

[62]   See St Bonaventure, *De Nativitate B. Mariae Virginis*, Sermo V.

[63]   St Bonaventure, *De Assumptione B. Mariae Virginis*, Sermo I.

[64]   See citation from M. Luther, Sermon of 15 August 1522, in R. Bäumer and L. Scheffczyk, (eds.), *Marienlexikon*, vol. 3 (St Ottilien: EOS Verlag: 1991), p. 200.

[65]   See citation from M. Butzer in R. Bäumer and L. Scheffczyk, (eds.), *Marienlexikon*, Volume 3 (St Ottilien: EOS Verlag: 1991), p. 200.

[66]   See citation from H. Bullinger in R. Bäumer and L. Scheffczyk, (eds.), *Marienlexikon*, Volume 3 (St Ottilien: EOS Verlag: 1991), p. 200.

[67]   St Robert Bellarmine, *De Assumption B. Mariae Virginis* in *Conciones Habitae Lovanii* (Coloniae Agrippinae: apud Ioannem Crithium, 1615), n. 40.

[68]   *Oeuvres de St Francois De Sales*, sermon for the Feast of the Assumption.

[69]   See St Alphonsus Liguori, 'Discourse I. On Mary's Immaculate Conception' in *The Glories of Mary*, p. 266.

[70]   See Rv 12:14 and also chapter 3 p. 66 above, where it was stated that the figure of the woman in the book of Revelation 'is symbolic, but in a polyvalent sense, referring to both Mariological and ecclesiological realities.'

[71]   J. H. Newman, *Discourses Addressed to Mixed Congregations* (London: 1886), pp. 360–376.

[72]   J. H. Newman, *Meditations and Devotions of the late Cardinal Newman* (Longman, Green and Co., 1893), pp. 89–91.

73 Pope Pius XII, *Munificentissimus Deus*, 41.

74 *Ibid.*, 44.

75 Vatican II, *Lumen Gentium*, 68

76 Congregation for the Doctrine of the Faith, Letter on certain questions regarding Eschatology *Recentiores episcoporum Synodi* (17 May 1979), 6.

77 See G. Gozzelino, *Vocazione e destino dell'uomo in Cristo* (Leumann: Elle Di Ci, 1985), pp. 151–152.

78 I. Gebara and M. C. Bingemer, *Mary, Mother of God, Mother of the Poor*, vol. 7 of *Liberation and Theology* (Tunbridge Wells: Burns and Oates, 1989), pp. 120–121.

79 See R. Spiazzi, 'Nell'Assunzione di Maria la primizia della reintegrazione universale' in *Sacra Dottrina* 39 (1994), pp. 99–101.

80 See Pope John Paul II, *Redemptoris Mater*, 41. See also Vatican II, *Lumen Gentium*, 36, 55, 59.

81 See E. J. Smith, 'The Scriptural Basis for Mary's Queenship' in *Marian Studies* 4 (1953), pp. 109–115.

82 See L. Cerfaux, 'Le Titre *Kyrios* et la dignité royale de Jesus' in *Revue des Sciences Philosophiques et Théologiques* 11 (1922), pp. 40–71; 12 (1923), pp. 125–153.

83 Origen, *Fragmenta Originis ex Macarii Chrysocephali Orationibus in Lucam* in EM 149: 'Oportebat me ad te venire: tu enim super omnes mulieres benedicta: tu Mater Domini mei: tu mea Domina.'

84 This concept was discussed in chapter 2, pp. 32–33 above.

85 St Gregory Nazianzen, *Poemata Dogmatica*, 18, 58 in *PG* 37, 485.

86 St Ephraem, *Oratio ad Santissimam Dei Matrem* in EM 346. He also refers to Mary as the universal Queen. See Idem, *Sermo de sanctissimae Dei Genetricis Virginis Mariae laudibus* in EM 350. The expression is 'Regina omnium'.

87 St John Damascene, *De fide orthodoxa*, 4, 14 in *PG* 94, 1157.

88 Eadmer, *De excellentia Virginis Mariae*, c. 11 in *PL* 159, 508.

89 See Pope Pius XII, Encyclical Letter *Ad caeli Reginam*, 36.

90 *Ibid.*, p. 38.

91 Vatican II, *Lumen Gentium*, 62.

CHAPTER 9

MOTHER OF THE CHURCH

The mystery of Mary and the mystery of the Church are one, so much so that one can be defined through the other.
A. Müller, *Ecclesia-Maria.*
Die Einheit Marias und der Kirche

Mary, Member of the Church

The Mother of God enjoyed a key position in the life of the primitive Church as portrayed in the Acts of the Apostles,. Mary was present from the beginning of the primitive community (cf. Ac 1:14), while she shared with the disciples and some women believers the prayerful expectation of the Holy Spirit, who was to descend on them. After Pentecost, the Blessed Virgin continued to live in fraternal communion with the Church and took part in the prayers, in listening to the Apostles' teaching, and in the 'breaking of bread', or the Eucharistic celebration (cf. Ac 2:42). She who had lived in close union with Jesus in the house of Nazareth, now lives in the Church in intimate communion with her Son, present in the Eucharist.

As a member of the first community, Mary the Mother of Jesus was surely respected and venerated by all. All the early Christians understood the pre-eminence of Mary who brought forth the Son of God, the one universal Saviour. 'Furthermore, the virginal character of her Motherhood allows her to witness to the extraordinary contribution to the Church's good offered by the one who, giving up human fruitfulness through docility to the Holy Spirit, puts herself completely at the service of God's kingdom.'[1] The Holy Spirit reveals the Theotokos and she is the one, who in a unique way is the revelation of the Holy Spirit in the Church.[2] In the life of the Mother of God one can distinguish two descents of the Holy Spirit. The first occurred, when by the power of the Holy Spirit, she received the Son of God into her womb in the Incarnation, and the second took place during the descent of the Holy Spirit upon her and the Apostles at Pentecost. The former had the objective function of Mary's divine maternity, the latter was personal: a realization in her person of the degree of holiness that corresponded to her unique function within the Church. The words of the crucified Christ on Golgotha: 'Woman, behold your Son' (Jn 19:26), with which her role as the universal mother of believers was begun, unfolded new and limitless horizons for her Motherhood. The gift of the Holy Spirit, received at Pentecost through the exercise of this mission, induced her to offer the help of her motherly heart to all who are on their way towards the total fulfilment of God's kingdom. Mary is constituted a pre-eminent and as a wholly unique member of the Church.[3] Mary occupies a place in the Church which is highest after Christ and yet at the same time is also closest to us.[4]

Mary's particular membership of the Church was first highlighted by St Augustine. He places Mary before the Church as member of the body of Christ: 'Mary is part of the Church, a holy member, a quite exceptional member, the supremely wonderful member, but still a member of the whole body.'[5] Then, St Chromatius of Aquileia observed with keen discernment: 'The Church was united ... in the Upper Room with Mary the Mother of Jesus and with His brethren. The Church therefore cannot be referred to as such unless it includes Mary the Mother of our Lord, together with His brethren.'[6] As theological reflection deepened, Mary was envisaged as a model member, in a Trinitarian perspective. For by her complete adherence to the Father's will, to His Son's redemptive work, and to every prompting of the Holy Spirit, the Virgin Mary is the Church's model of faith and charity. Thus she is the 'exemplary realization' or type of the Church.[7]

Mary, Type of the Church

Just as various Old Testament images were a type of Mary, Mother of God, so also is Mary a living type of the Church.[8] The plan of salvation which orders the prefigurations of the Old Testament to fulfilment in the New Covenant likewise determines that Mary would live in a perfect way what was later to be fulfilled in the Church. St Paul uses the word 'type', to give tangible form to a spiritual reality. He regards the crossing of the Red Sea by the People of Israel as a 'type', or image, of Christian Baptism, and in the manna and in the water which gushed from the rock, a 'type' or image of the Eucharistic food and drink (cf. 1 Co 10:1–11). Mary is a type of the Church, since in her we see the visible figure of the Church's spiritual reality, and in her spotless Motherhood, the announcement of the Church's virginal motherhood. In Mary, the spiritual reality proclaimed is completely fulfilled.

Among the Fathers, St Ambrose proclaimed this truth explicitly: 'Yes, she [Mary] is betrothed, but she is a virgin because she is a type of the Church which is immaculate but a bride: a virgin, she conceived us by the Spirit; a virgin, she gave birth to us without pain.'[9] Augustine develops this theme further in that he places Mary before the Church as her ideal image: 'Therefore Mary alone both in Spirit and in flesh is a mother and a virgin: both the mother of Christ, and a virgin of Christ; but the Church, in the Saints who shall possess the kingdom of God, in the Spirit indeed is altogether the mother of Christ, altogether a virgin of Christ.'[10]

In the Middle Ages, some theologians deepened the concept, specifying what constitutes this typological relationship. For instance, Blessed Isaac of Stella, a disciple of St Bernard, indicated that in the maternal dimension both Mary and the Church, as mothers and virgins, conceive through the power of the Holy Spirit. Mary has given birth in body to her Head; the Church gives to this Head her body. 'The one and the other are mothers of Christ: but neither of the two begets Him entirely without the other. Properly for that reason ... that which is said in general of the virgin mother Church is understood especially of the virgin Mother Mary; and that which is said in a special way of the virgin Mother Mary must be attributed in general to the virgin mother Church; and all that is said about one of the two can be understood without distinction of one from the other.'[11]

Various later theologians including Scheeben, further elaborated this idea: 'Mary is ... the prototype of the Church, as the idea of the Church is originally realised in her person and in the most perfect manner. Since she herself belongs to the Church and at the same time forms the head-member as root and heart, the idea of the Church as a supernatural principle assisting Christ also obtains its full, concrete and living figure.'[12] Theological reflection leads us to consider that Mary is type of the Church, but with certain limitations to this concept. First, while Mary is a single person, the Church is a communion of persons. Thus, the attribution of maternity to a individual and to a group of people, can only be applied in an analogous way. Second, Mary is a 'type of the Church in the order of faith, charity and perfect union with Christ' as the Vatican Council put it, echoing St Ambrose.[13] Now the Church is not only a community of salvation, but also a hierarchical institution of salvation, endowed with a ministerial priesthood and with sacraments. With regard to this latter aspect, Mary cannot be seen as a type of the Church, since she is not the prototype of the hierarchical element. Catholic realism rejects the existentialist idealism of

Bultmann who accepted a typology of Mary, but interpreted it in a purely symbolic sense. For him, the Blessed
Virgin was not actually present on Calvary, and John
merely gave her a place there in order to represent and
typify the Old Testament.[14]

Otto Semmelroth presented Mary in relation to the
Church, by proposing her as archetype (*Urbild*). For
Semmelroth, the basic relationship of Mary to the Church
in terms of type, has a threefold significance. First, a
personification or representation of a spiritual entity
through some sort of image. Second 'the similarity
between Mary and the Church is the consequence of a
very real, inner connection. The features that make the
archetype similar to the image have somehow grown from
the archetype into the image.'[15] Third, Semmelroth insists,
in a realist key, that Mary's relation to the Church and her
members is factual and ontological, and only as a consequence can she be a moral example, as a result of this
relationship.[16] Semmelroth's basic Mariological principle
is that Mary is archetype: 'Because Mary was to be the
type of the Church, she was given existence as the virginal
Mother of God. There is no other Marian mystery which,
as the intentional principle, could precede and give root to
the position that Mary holds as type of the Church ... all
other Marian mysteries draw their inner meaning and
connection from this basic mystery.'[17] He also indicates
that in her divine Motherhood, 'Mary was given the most
perfect opportunity to prefigure the Church in a coredemptive way.'[18] Semmelroth concludes that Mary, like
the Church whose archetype she is, also mediates all
graces. Mary does so first, when as Coredemptrix, she
received the fruits of Christ's salvation and assumed them
for herself and the Church. Second, through her 'intercession' she enables these fruits to flow into the Church.
Third, she mediates by exemplifying that man must co-
operate with his own redemption in the way Mary
co-operated with the redemption of the entire Church.[19]

Balthasar considered various archetypes in the nature of

the Church. Among these were the Apostolic and the Marian principles. Within this archetypal view, Balthasar considers the Marian 'fiat' as the foundational form of the apostolic archetypes, as indeed of all the members of the Church. Mary's self-surrendering 'Yes' preceded and made possible the Incarnation of Christ the Head and thus the formation of the communion within His mystical Body, constituted by the abiding in His love (cf. Jn 15).[20] While few are called to carry the Petrine office, every Catholic is called to pronounce Mary's faith-filled 'fiat', the mould in which the Church is formed. Therefore, 'the Petrine universality is subject to the formative influence of the Marian, but not vice versa.'[21]

Pope John Paul II drew on Balthasar's thought when he also remarked that the Virgin Mary is the archetype of the Church because of her divine maternity. The Church, like Mary, should be and desires to be mother and virgin. The Church lives by this authentic Marian dimension, which is just as fundamental for the Church, if not more so, than the Petrine dimension, to which the Marian dimension is profoundly united. This link between the two dimensions of the Church, the Marian and the Petrine, is therefore close, profound and complementary, although the first one (the Marian) precedes the second (the Petrine) both in the plan of God and in time; it is also higher and pre-eminent, and richer both in its personal and communitarian implications. Mary also precedes all of us, as she precedes the entire Church in which we live.[22] For the Church, which often feels the weight of history and the siege of evil, the Mother of Christ is the luminous emblem of humanity redeemed and enveloped in saving grace.[23]

Mary, Mother of the Church

As He was dying on the Cross, Jesus entrusted His Mother to St John, with the words: 'Woman, this is your son.' He also entrusted St John to Mary: 'This is your mother.' From that hour the disciple took Mary into his home (cf. Jn 19:26–27). The parallel between the expressions 'this is your son' and 'this is your mother' highlights the fact that here beyond the historical fact of John's care for Our Lady, there are the outlines of a spiritual motherhood of Mary within the Church.[24]

Although the title 'Mother of the Church' was only relatively recently attributed to Mary, it expresses the Blessed Virgin's maternal relationship with the Church as shown in several New Testament texts. Since the Annunciation, Mary was called to give her consent to the coming of the messianic kingdom, which would take place with the formation of the Church. When, at Cana, Mary asked her divine Son to exercise His messianic power, she made a fundamental contribution to implanting the faith in the first community of disciples, and she co-operated in initiating God's kingdom, which has its 'seed' and 'beginning' in the Church. On Calvary, Mary united herself to the sacrifice of her Son and made her own maternal contribution to the work of salvation, which took the form of labour pains, the birth of the new humanity. In addressing the words 'Woman, behold your son' to Mary, Jesus Crucified proclaims her motherhood not only in relation to the Apostle John but also to every disciple. John himself, by saying that Jesus had to die 'to gather into one the children of God who are scattered abroad' (Jn 11:52), indicates the Church's birth as the fruit of the redemptive sacrifice with which Mary is maternally associated. Finally, St Luke mentions the presence of Jesus' Mother in the first community of Jerusalem (Acts 1:14). In this way he stresses Mary's maternal role in the new-born Church, comparing it to her role in the Redeemer's birth. The maternal dimension thus becomes a fundamental element of Mary's relationship with the new People of the redeemed.

Following Sacred Scripture, Patristic teaching recognized Mary's Motherhood in the work of Christ and therefore in that of the Church, although in terms which are implicit. According to St Irenaeus, Mary 'became a cause of salvation for the whole human race.'[25] St Ambrose developed a similar idea: 'A Virgin has begotten the salvation of the world, a Virgin has given life to all things.'[26] the Mother of the Saviour is, as St Augustine teaches, 'surely the mother of His members.'[27] Some other Fathers, like Severianus of Gabala even call Mary 'Mother of salvation.'[28] The Middle Ages saw further development in this regard, for instance when St Anselm addressed Mary in this way: 'You are the mother of justification and of the justified, the Mother of reconciliation and of the reconciled, the mother of salvation and of the saved',[29] while other authors attributed to her the titles 'Mother of grace' and 'Mother of life'. Rupert of Deutz indicated how the Mother of Jesus became our mother on Calvary: 'In the passion of her only Son, the Blessed Virgin brought forth (*peperit*) salvation to us all; from that time on, she is obviously, to all of us, our mother.'[30]

The first statement in which a Pope described the filial sentiments of the Church, which recognizes Mary as her most beloved mother, and indirectly proclaimed her Mother of the Church, occurred in 1748 with Pope Benedict XIV.[31] This expression was found in the teaching of Pope Leo XIII, in which it is affirmed that Mary is 'in all truth mother of the Church.'[32] The title was later used many times in the teachings of John XXIII and Paul VI. In particular, it was Pope Paul VI who solemnly proclaimed Mary to be Mother of the Church at the close of the Third Session of the Second Vatican Council on 22 November 1964:

> For the Church is not constituted just by her hierarchical order, her sacred liturgy, her sacraments, her institutional structure. Her inner vitality and peculiar nature, the main source of her effectiveness in sanctifying men, is to be found in her mystical union with Christ. We cannot conceive of this union apart from she who is the Mother of the Incarnate Word, and whom Christ so intimately associated with Himself in bringing about our salvation ... And so, for the glory of the Blessed Virgin and our own conso-

lation, We declare Mary Most Holy to be the Mother of the Church, that is of the whole Christian people, both the faithful and the bishops, who call her a most loving Mother. We decree that from now on the whole of the Christian people should use this sweetest of names to pay more honour to the Mother of God and to pour out their prayers to her.[33]

Pope Paul VI repeated his faith in Mary Mother of the Church in his solemn profession of faith in 1968: 'and we believe that the Blessed Mother of God, the New Eve, Mother of the Church, continues in heaven her maternal role with regard to Christ's members, co-operating with the birth and growth of divine life in the souls of the redeemed.'[34] Pope John Paul II has also often used the title. As Mother of the Church, Mary 'continually brings to birth children for the mystical Body of her Son. She does so through her intercession, imploring upon them the inexhaustible outpouring of the Spirit. Mary is the perfect icon of the motherhood of the Church.'[35] Mary, our Mother, is an icon of the Church, the symbol and anticipation of humanity transfigured by grace, the model and the unfailing hope for all those who direct their steps towards the heavenly Jerusalem. In this sense, she is also the Mother through whom the unity of Christians will come about.

Our Lady's central role with regard to the Church on earth is one of intercession, as many theologians down the centuries have expressed. For example, St Fulgentius of Ruspe declared, 'Mary is the window of heaven, since through her God shone the Light of the ages. Mary is the ladder of heaven; for by Mary God descended from Heaven into the world, that by her men might ascend from earth to Heaven.'[36] Newman perceived this same truth in a profound way. He recognized that this office of Mary is represented in iconography by her up-lifted hands:

I consider it impossible then, for those who believe the Church to be one vast body in heaven and on earth, in which every holy creature of God has his place, and of which prayer is the life, when once they recognise the sanctity and dignity of the Blessed Virgin, not to perceive immediately, that her office above is one of perpetual intercession for the faithful militant, and that our very relation to her must be that of clients to a patron, and that, in the eternal enmity which exists between the woman and the serpent, while the serpent's strength is that of being the Tempter, the weapon of the Second Eve and Mother of God is prayer ... As then these ideas of her sanctity and greatness gradually penetrated the mind of Christendom, so did that of her intercessory power follow close upon them and with them.[37]

It is also right to consider the Virgin Mary as Mother of the Faithful Departed. In fact, with regard to the supernatural life of every man, Mary's role is comparable to that of a mother with regard to her children during their earthly life. After death, Mary never abandons her children, especially those who are not very far from joining God. Mary contributes, then, to their 'purification' by making them capable of being welcomed into the heavenly City. She does this all the more willingly when we ask her trustfully. By standing at the foot of the Cross, and uniting herself with the sacrifice of her Son, Mary acquired the capacity to intercede for all people whose mother she had become. Standing permanently near the heart of the glorified Christ, she desires to see the souls still in Purgatory introduced as soon as possible into intimacy with God: 'The Blessed Virgin Mary has the power of delivering souls from purgatory by her prayers, and by applying her merits for them. This is especially true for souls that were devoted to her on earth.'[38] The intercessory power of Our Lady for the souls in purgatory has also been expressed in poetic form by Frederick Faber:

> O turn to Jesus, Mother! Turn,
> And call Him by His tenderest names;
> Pray for the Holy Souls that burn
> This hour amid the cleansing flames.

Ah! They have fought a gallant fight:
In death's cold arms they persevered;
And, after life's uncheery night,
The harbour of their rest is neared.

In pains beyond all earthly pains,
Favourites of Jesus! There they lie
Letting the fire wear out their stains
And worshipping God's purity.

Spouses of Christ they are, for He
Was wedded to them by His Blood;
And angels o'er their destiny
In wondering adoration brood.

They are the children of thy tears;
Then hasten, Mother! To their aid;
In pity think each hour appears
An age while glory is delayed.

O Mary, let thy Son no more
His lingering Spouses thus expect;
God's children to their God restore,
And to the Spirit His elect.

Pray then, as thou hast ever prayed;
Angels and Souls, all look to thee;
God waits thy prayers, for He hath made
Those prayers His law of charity.[39]

Our Lady's crucial role as the Mother of the Church on earth, the Mother of the saints and the Mother of the Faithful Departed reminds us of her vital capacity as the Mother of the *entire* Mystical Body. Again, we observe God's goodness and order in providing for His People, regardless of their stage in the oftentimes perilous journey to the New Jerusalem. He has given to us and to the saints and to the Holy Souls the best of mothers who consoles us in our weaknesses and challenges us to persevere in our true and sole goal: the real and lasting imitation of Jesus the Lord.

Mary is the eschatological icon of the Church. In her we contemplate what the Church already is on her own 'pilgrimage of faith,' and what she will be in the homeland at the end of her journey. There, in the glory of the Most Holy and Undivided Trinity, in the communion of all the saints, the Church is awaited by the one she venerates as Mother of her Lord and as her own mother. In the meantime the Mother of Jesus, in the glory which she possesses in body and soul in heaven, is the image and beginning of the Church as it is to be perfected in the world to come. Likewise she shines forth on earth until the day of the Lord shall come, a sign of certain hope and comfort to the pilgrim People of God.[40]

Mary and the Eucharist

Within the Church, Our Lady enjoys a particular place in relation to the Eucharist. Recent reflection has enlarged upon this aspect. Mary's relation to the Eucharist flows from two fundamental aspects. The first is the continuity of the mystery of the Incarnation, exactly as John presents it in his Gospel: an indissoluble connection between the Word made flesh (see Jn 1:14) and the Flesh that He gives for the life of the world (see Jn 6:51ff.). In the measure that the mystery of the Incarnation is connected to the Virgin Mary, of whom the Word takes flesh, we can say that Mary is necessarily linked with the Eucharist. St Augustine remarked: 'Of the flesh of Mary, He took flesh, in this flesh the Lord walked here, and He has given us this same flesh to eat for our salvation; and no one eats that flesh without having first adored it . . . as we do not sin adoring it, but sin if we do not adore it.'[41] The second fundamental aspect is that the Eucharist is the memorial of the death of Christ, and in that moment of Calvary, John recalls Mary's presence at the foot of the Cross. It is a presence in which the Virgin is associated with the offering of Christ to His Father, and in the offering of herself to the Father. The

Virgin Mary is essentially present in this mystery, of which the Eucharist is the sacramental connection. Therefore, both as a result of her participation in the Incarnation and because of her sharing in the sacrifice of the Cross, Mary is linked with the Eucharist in a special manner.

Moreover, there are numerous expressions of the Fathers of the Church that tie the mystery of the Incarnation closely to that of the Eucharist. Peter Chrysologus said that Christ is 'the Bread sown in the Virgin, leavened in the Flesh, kneaded in His Passion, baked in the oven of the Sepulchre, placed in the Churches, and set upon the Altars, which daily supplies Heavenly Food to the faithful.'[42] St Epiphanius also adopts a Eucharistic imagery for Mary: 'You are, O Mary, the field that was not ploughed. You conceived the Word as a grain of wheat and germinated the shoot. You are the spiritual furrow that holds the fire and the bread of life, the holy Mother of the Saviour who gave birth to the Word of the Father, the Word who was made incarnate from you.'[43] The relation between the Eucharist and the Virgin Mary is an integral part of Tradition, and this is expressed liturgically. For example in the Ethiopian liturgy, this prayer is recited: 'O Virgin, source of the fruit that is eaten and drunk. The Bread that comes from you is life and salvation, to those who eat it with faith. The Chalice that comes from you is wisdom and life, to those who drink it in faith.'[44]

Papal Tradition has further developed the theme. Pope Pope VI recalled the intimate link between Our Lady and the Eucharist. 'To perpetuate down the centuries the Sacrifice of the Cross, the divine Saviour instituted the Eucharistic Sacrifice, the memorial of His death and resurrection, and entrusted it to His spouse the Church, which, especially on Sundays, calls the faithful together to celebrate the Passover of the Lord until He comes again. This the Church does in union with the saints in heaven and in particular with the Blessed Virgin, whose burning charity and unshakeable faith she imitates.'[45] Pope John Paul II has developed in greater detail how Our Blessed Lady participates in the Eucharistic celebration in a special way:

> Her motherhood is particularly noted and experienced by
> the Christian people at the Sacred Banquet – the liturgical
> celebration of the Mystery of the Redemption – at which
> Christ, His true Body born of the Virgin Mary, becomes
> present. The piety of the Christian people has always very
> rightly sensed a profound link between devotion to the
> Blessed Virgin and worship of the Eucharist: this is a fact
> that can be seen in the liturgy of both the West and the
> East, in the traditions of the Religious Families, in the
> modern movements of spirituality, including those for
> youth, and in the pastoral practice of the Marian Shrines.
> Mary guides the faithful to the Eucharist.[46]

Indeed, it may be said that Mary is an integral part of this
profound relationship between the Church and the
Eucharist. The Church and the Eucharist are inseparably
united, and the same can be said of Mary and the
Eucharist. This is one reason why, since ancient times, the
commemoration of Mary has always been part of the
Eucharistic celebrations of the Churches of East and West.

At first sight, the Gospels are silent on this subject. The
account of the institution of the Eucharist on the night of
Holy Thursday makes no explicit mention of Mary. Yet
she was present among the Apostles who prayed 'with
one accord' (cf. Acts 1:14) in the first community which
gathered after the Ascension in expectation of Pentecost.
Certainly Mary must have been present at the Eucharistic
celebrations of the first generation of Christians, who were
devoted to 'the breaking of bread' (Acts 2:42). However, in
addition to her sharing in the Eucharistic banquet, an indirect picture of Mary's relationship with the Eucharist can
be had, beginning with her interior disposition. Mary is a
'woman of the Eucharist' in her whole life. The Church,
which looks to Mary as a model, is also called to imitate
her in her relationship with this most holy mystery.[47]

Mary lived her Eucharistic faith even before the institution of the Eucharist, by the very fact that she offered her

virginal womb for the Incarnation of God's Word. The Eucharist, while commemorating the Passion and Resurrection, is also in continuity with the Incarnation. At the Annunciation, Mary conceived the Son of God in the physical reality of His Body and Blood, thus anticipating within herself what to some degree happens sacramentally in every believer who receives, under the signs of bread and wine, the Lord's Body and Blood. As a result, there is a profound analogy between the 'fiat' which Mary uttered in reply to the angel, and the 'Amen' which every believer says when receiving the Body of the Lord. Mary was asked to believe that the One whom she conceived 'through the Holy Spirit' was 'the Son of God' (Lk 1:30–35). In continuity with the Virgin's faith, in the Eucharistic mystery we are asked to believe that the same Jesus Christ, Son of God and Son of Mary, becomes present in His full humanity and divinity under the signs of bread and wine. Mary also anticipated, in the mystery of the Incarnation, the Church's Eucharistic faith. When, at the Visitation, she bore in her womb the Word made flesh, she became in some way a 'tabernacle', the first 'tabernacle' in history in which the Son of God, still invisible to our human gaze, allowed himself to be adored by Elizabeth, radiating His light as it were through the eyes and the voice of Mary. Also 'is not the enraptured gaze of Mary as she contemplated the face of the new-born Christ and cradled Him in her arms, that unparalleled model of love which should inspire us every time we receive Eucharistic communion?'[48]

There is a profound parallel between the prefiguration of the Eucharist at Cana in Galilee when Mary was present and the Institution of the Eucharist at the Last Supper. The words of Christ at the Last Supper: 'Do this in memory of me!', resemble the invitation of Mary's to obey Him without hesitation: 'Do whatever he tells you' (Jn 2:5). With the same maternal concern which she showed at the wedding feast of Cana, Mary seems to say to us: 'Do not waver; trust in the words of my Son. If He was able to change water into wine, He can also turn bread and wine into His body and blood, and through this mystery bestow on believers the living memorial of his Passover, thus becoming the Bread of Life.'[49]

Mary, throughout her life at Christ's side and not only on Calvary, made her own the sacrificial dimension of the Eucharist. In her daily preparation for Calvary, Mary experienced a kind of 'anticipated Eucharist' one might say a 'spiritual communion' of desire and of oblation, which would culminate in her union with her Son in his Passion, and then find expression after Easter by her partaking in the Eucharist which the Apostles celebrated as the memorial of that Passion:

> What must Mary have felt as she heard from the mouth of Peter, John, James and the other Apostles the words spoken at the Last Supper: 'This is my body which is given for you' (Lk 22:19)? The body given up for us and made present under sacramental signs was the same body which she had conceived in her womb! For Mary, receiving the Eucharist must have somehow meant welcoming once more into her womb that heart which had beat in unison with hers and reliving what she had experienced at the foot of the Cross.[50]

In the Eucharist the Church is completely united to Christ and His sacrifice, and makes her own the spirit of Mary. In this sense Mary's Magnificat can be read in a Eucharistic key. The Eucharist, like the Canticle of Mary, is first and foremost praise and thanksgiving. When Mary exclaims: 'My soul magnifies the Lord and my spirit rejoices in God my Saviour', she already bears Jesus in her womb. She praises God 'through' Jesus, but she also praises Him 'in' Jesus and 'with' Jesus. This is itself the true 'Eucharistic attitude'. At the same time Mary recalls the wonders worked by God in salvation history in fulfilment of the promise once made to the fathers (cf. Lk 1:55), and proclaims the wonder that surpasses them all, the redemptive Incarnation. Lastly, the Magnificat reflects the eschatological tension of the Eucharist. Every time the Son of God comes again to us in the 'poverty' of the sacramental signs of bread and wine, the seeds of that new history wherein the mighty are 'put down from their thrones' and 'those of low degree are exalted' (cf. Lk 1:52), take root in the world. Mary sings of the 'new heavens' and the 'new earth' which find in the Eucharist their anticipation and in some sense their program and plan. The Magnificat expresses Mary's spirituality, and there is nothing greater than this spirituality for helping us to experience the mystery of the Eucharist. The Eucharist has been given to us so that our life, like that of Mary, may become completely a Magnificat.[51]

Mary, Mediatrix of All Graces

Earlier, it was seen how Mary co-operated as Coredemptrix in the *objective Redemption* or the once-for-all acquisition by the sacrifice of Calvary of the claim to all grace and forgiveness.[52] Here we will consider how Our Lady co-operates as Mediatrix in the *subjective Redemption* or distribution of that grace and forgiveness throughout all ages after Calvary. What Mary began on earth in association with the saving mission of Jesus, she continues still, in union with the risen Christ.[53]

First, Mary's maternal mediation does not obscure the unique and perfect mediation of Christ. On this point some have objected interpreting the words of St Paul: 'There is only one God, and there is only one mediator between God and humanity, himself a human being, Christ Jesus, who offered himself as a ransom for all' (1 Tm 2:5–6). This passage of Scripture does not exclude a participation of others in Christ's role as Mediator. St Thomas Aquinas explained this many centuries ago, and before the rise of Protestantism: 'Christ alone is the perfect mediator between God and man ... but there is nothing to prevent others in a certain way from being called mediators between God and man in so far as they, by preparing or serving, co-operate in uniting men to God.'[54] This formulation opens the possibility for others in a certain way to be called mediators, co-operating with the perfect mediation of Jesus Christ. Mary's mediation starts and focuses on the central truth of her divine Motherhood, for through her Christ came into the world. Christ, the source of grace and truth came through Mary into this world, and then through her also redeemed fallen humanity: 'The first moment of submission to the one mediation between God and man – the mediation of Jesus Christ – is the Virgin of Nazareth's acceptance of motherhood ... Mary's Motherhood, completely pervaded by her spousal attitude as handmaid of the Lord, constitutes the first and fundamental dimension of that mediation which the Church confesses and proclaims in her regard and continually commends to the hearts of the faithful.'[55]

The mediation of Mary continued in Mary's whole life of discipleship and co-operation with her Son up till her Co-redemptive active on Calvary. Thereafter she is the Mediatrix of the victory that Calvary achieved. Mary's role as Mediatrix was implicit in the early Patristic understanding of the Mary as the New Eve. One of the earliest examples is that of St Irenaeus, who pointed out that just as Eve disobeyed God, Mary was drawn to obey Him: 'Just as the human race was bound to death by a virgin, so it was released by a Virgin.'[56] St Jerome stated that 'Death came through Eve, life through Mary.'[57] The first who seems to have used the title of Mediatrix explicitly seems to have been St Ephraem (d. 373), who addressed Our Lady thus: 'After the Mediator, you are Mediatrix of the whole world.'[58] At the Council of Ephesus (AD 431), St Cyril of Alexandria highlighted Mary's function as Mediatrix 'through whom' the works of salvation are accomplished, in one of the greatest Marian sermons of the Christian East:

Hail then, from us, O holy mystical Trinity, who has gathered us all together in this Church of Mary, the Mother of

God. Hail from us Mary, Mother of God, majestic treasure
of the whole world, the lamp unquenchable, the crown of
virginity, the sceptre of orthodoxy, the indestructible
temple, the dwelling of the Illimitable, Mother and Virgin
... Hail, you who contained Him, who cannot be
contained, in your holy virginal womb; you through whom
the Holy Trinity is glorified and adored throughout the
whole world; through whom heaven rejoices, through
whom angels and archangels are glad; through whom
devils are put to flight; ... through whom the fallen creature is taken up into heaven; through whom all creation,
held fast by the madness of idolatry, has come to the
knowledge of the truth; through whom holy baptism has
come to believers, and the oil of gladness; through whom
churches are erected throughout the world; through whom
the nations are brought to repentance.[59]

Another Father of the Council of Ephesus, Antipater of
Bostra, addressed Mary as the Mediatrix who intercedes
for the human family: 'Hail, you who acceptably intercede
as a Mediatrix for mankind.'[60]

From the same century comes the testimony of
Severianus of Gabala (d. 408), who wrote of Mary's mediatory intercession: 'We also have Mary, the Holy Virgin and
Mother of God, interceding on our behalf. For if any ordinary woman has gained the victory, how much more the
Mother of Christ confounds the enemies of truth.'[61]
Another contemporary, Basil of Seleucia (d. 459), came up
with a similar, yet more explicit, expression: 'Hail full of
grace, who mediates between God and man that the divid-
ing-wall of enmity be taken away and the things on earth be
made at one with the things in heaven.'[62] Basil thus arrives
at the point of suggesting a certain parallelism between the
mediation of Our Lady and that of Christ. Basil's text is
reminiscent of the passage from the Letter to the Ephesians
(Ep 2: 14–18), where St Paul speaks of Christ breaking down
the wall and giving us access in one Spirit to the Father, and
the text of Colossians (Col 1: 20), where he affirms that the
Father reconciled all things to Himself through Christ.

In the eighth century the term Mediatrix was clearly attributed to Our Lady, in the works of St Andrew of Crete (d. 720): 'Hail Mediatrix (*mesitis*) of the law and of grace, the seal of the Old and the New Testament.'[63] St Germanus of Constantinople addressed Our Lady in this form: ' No one obtains salvation except through you, O most holy One! ... To no one is mercy granted except through you!'[64] St John Damascene (d. 794) was most eloquent describing Mary's mediatory power: 'She opened to us the unspeakable abyss of God's love for us. Through her the old enmity against the Creator is destroyed. Through her our reconciliation with Him is strengthened, peace and grace are given to us, men are the companions of angels, and we, who were in dishonour, are made the children of God. From her we have plucked the fruit of life. From her we have received the seed of immortality. She is the channel of all good things.'[65]

During the Scholastic period, understanding of Mary's mediation grew and developed fruitfully. One of the first to express this reality was St Peter Damian, who offered the principle of Mary's mediation as an action that begins with Christ and should be imitated by humanity: 'As the Son of God has designed to descend to us through you [Mary], so we also must come to Him through you.'[66] From this follows that in Mary's hands are the mercies of God.[67] St Anselm (d. 1109), expressed in his well-known prayers his belief in her maternal care for humankind and in her power as Mother of God, stressing her mediation as unfailing and all-powerful intercession:

> For as everyone, O most blessed, who is turned away from you and disregarded by you must perish, so it is impossible that anyone who turns towards you and is regarded by you should be lost ... For if you, Lady, are His Mother, are not your other sons His brothers? ... Hence with what assurance should we hope and with what consolation can we fear whose salvation or damnation depends on the decision of our good Brother and our loving Mother ... Let our good Mother pray and beseech for us, let her demand and petition what is for our good.[68]

Peter Abelard (d. 1142), not renowned for pious sentimentalism or devotional excesses, was most clear about explicitly ascribing mediation to Mary: 'She is our Mediatrix with her Son, as the Son Himself is (our) Mediator with the Father. The Son could not but listen to His Mother asking on our behalf. Nor could He, who so greatly commends the honour of parents, offend her by any refusal.'[69]

St Bernard (d. 1153) who strongly differed with Abelard on some other issues, developed even more clearly the doctrine of Mary's mediation. Certain of his phrases became classical stepping stones for this truth, including 'God has willed that we should have nothing that would not pass through the hands of Mary.'[70] This teaching is further confirmed and defined in passages such as the following: 'This is the will of Him who wished us to have everything through Mary ... God has placed in Mary the plenitude of every good, in order to have us understand that if there is any trace of hope in us, any trace of grace, any trace of salvation, it flows from her'.[71] Bernard often used the image of the aqueduct (see Si 24:41), as an illustration of Mary's role: 'That stream from heaven flows down through the aqueduct, not indeed representing the fullness of the source (not indeed bringing us the fullness of the source), but rather carrying the trickling flow of grace into our parched hearts, to some in greater abundance and to others in less. The aqueduct indeed is full, so that others may receive of that fullness, but not the fullness itself.'[72] Bernard, of course, adopted the expression Mediatrix explicitly as well: 'Our Lady, our Mediatrix and our advocate, reconcile us to your Son, commend us to your Son, represent us to your Son.'[73]

The pneumatological aspect of Mary's mediation was elucidated by Theophanes of Nicaea (d. 1381) who recognized the sublime union of the Holy Spirit and the Mother of Jesus in the distribution of the graces of redemption: 'She receives wholly the hidden grace of the Spirit and amply distributes it and shares it with others, thus manifesting it. ... The Mother [Mary] ... is the dispenser and distributor of all the wondrous uncreated gifts of the divine Spirit, which makes us Christ's brothers and coheirs, not only because she is granting the gifts of her natural Son to His brothers in grace, but because she is bestowing them on these as her own true sons, though not by ties of nature but of grace.'[74]

St Bernardine of Siena (d. 1444) marked a turning point in the understanding of Our Lady's universal mediation. He elaborated how every grace that is granted to this world comes to us in three stages. It is handed down in order from God to Christ, from Christ to the Virgin Mary , and from the Virgin Mary to us. Mary has received a certain jurisdiction over all graces. Thus, St Bernardine arrived at the celebrated expression: 'No grace comes from heaven to earth but what passes through Mary's hand.'[75] Francis Suárez (d. 1619), who was the first to create a scientific Mariology, enumerated the various ways in which Our Lady has co-operated in salvation. As she collaborated by her merits on earth, she now co-operates by her most efficacious intercession in heaven. He pointed out that the Blessed Virgin Mary ought to be invoked before all the other saints, also because her prayer is more universal. For whatever other saints obtain by their prayers, they obtain in some manner through the Blessed Virgin, because, as St Bernard said, she is the Mediatrix with the Mediator, and she is like the neck by which life passes from the head to the body.[76]

St Louis Marie Grignon de Montfort (d. 1716) in his classic work, *True Devotion to Mary*, made an outstanding contribution to the understanding of Our Lady's part in this context: 'God the Son has communicated to His Mother all that He acquired by His life and His death, His infinite merits and His admirable virtues; and He has made Her the treasurer of all that His Father gave Him for His inheritance. It is by her that He applies His merits to His members, and that He communicates His virtues and distributes His graces. She is His mystic channel; she is His aqueduct, through which He makes his mercies flow gently and abundantly ... The Holy Spirit gives no gift to men which does not pass through her virginal hands.'[77] St Alphonsus Liguori (d. 1787), Marian Doctor of the Church succinctly sums up the universal character of the distribution of all graces by Mary: 'God, who gave us Jesus Christ, wills that all graces that have been, that are, and will be dispensed to men to the end of the world through the merits of Jesus Christ, should be dispensed by the hands and through the intercession of Mary.'[78]

More recently, many authors have affirmed that Mary is universal Mediatrix, and among these Scheeben: 'Not only Mary's whole position as Mediatrix, but also her preceding mediatorial functions are entirely designed for a universal mediation of grace, and condition the communication of all grace without exception. For all Mary's functions as Mediatrix form mutually one organic whole, in which the later ones are based on the preceding and make their influence felt.'[79] Scheeben anchors this mediation in a pneumatological perspective: 'The distinguishing mark of her person as bride of Christ is conceived fully in her capacity of bearer and temple of the Holy Spirit. Likewise, the foundation for this special power and dignity of her activity must be traced to this capacity of her person ... Mary is the organ of the Holy Spirit, who works in her in the same way that Christ's humanity is the instrument of the Logos.'[80] The sanctifying activity of the Mediatrix must rightly be traced to her mission as the human instrument of the Holy Spirit in their one, unified mission of sanctification given by the Father. This understanding and model of Mary as the human instrument of the Holy Spirit in the distribution of graces, comparable to the humanity of Christ as human instrument of the Word, is a monumental breakthrough in understanding the mysterious distribution of graces by the Spirit and the Mediatrix.

The Papal Magisterium has had much to say on the subject of Mary's mediation over the past hundred years or so. In 1883, Pope Leo XIII declared: 'We judge nothing more powerful and better for this purpose than by religion and devotion to deserve well of the great Mother of God, the Virgin Mary, who is the treasurer [*sequestra*] of our peace with God, and the Mediatrix [*administra*] of graces.'[81] Later, in 1891, he clarified this further, indicating that nothing at all of that very great treasury of all grace which the Lord brought us is imparted to us except through Mary, since God so wills, so that just as no one can come to the Father except through the Son, so in general, no one can come to Christ except through His Mother.[82] The Pope also illustrated the relation between Mary's part in the Redemption and her part in the distribution of its fruits: 'She who had been the minister [*administra*] of the mystery of human redemption, was equally the minister [*administra*] of the grace to be given from it for all time, practically immeasurable power being given to her.'[83] Pope Benedict XV granted to all bishops who petitioned for it, permission to celebrate the Liturgical Office and Mass of Mary, Mediatrix of All Graces.[84]

Pope Pius XII affirmed the same dynamic of Marian mediation: 'Having been associated, as Mother and Minister, with the King of martyrs in the ineffable work of human Redemption, she is always associated, with a practically measureless power, in the distribution of the graces that derive from the Redemption ... And her kingdom is as vast as that of her Son and God, since nothing is excluded from her dominion.'[85] Pope Pius XII showed how this mediation is inserted into the whole economy of God's salvation: 'When the little maid of Nazareth uttered her fiat to the message of the angel, she became not only the Mother of God in the physical order of nature, but also in the supernatural order of grace she became the Mother of all, who through the Holy Spirit would be made one under the Headship her divine Son. The Mother of the Head would be the Mother of the members. The Mother of the Vine would be the Mother of the branches.'[86] Pope

John XXIII also expressed the Church's faith in Mary's universal mediation: 'For the faithful can do nothing more fruitful and salutary than to win for themselves the most powerful patronage of the Immaculate Virgin, so that by this most sweet Mother, there may be opened to them all the treasures of the divine Redemption, and so they may have life, and have it more abundantly. Did not the Lord will that we have everything through Mary?'[87]

The Second Vatican Council illustrated how Mary is our Mother in the order of grace and this motherhood in the economy of grace lasts without interruption, from the consent which she gave in faith at the Annunciation, and which she unhesitatingly bore with under the Cross, even to the perpetual consummation of all the elect. Mary continues to win the gifts of eternal salvation for us. By her motherly love, she takes care of the brothers of her Son who are still in pilgrimage and in dangers and difficulties, until they be led through to the happy fatherland. 'For this reason, the Blessed Virgin Mary is invoked in the Church under the titles of Advocate, Auxiliatrix, Adiutrix, and Mediatrix. This however is to be so understood that it takes nothing away, or adds nothing to the dignity and efficacy of Christ the one Mediator.'[88] Vatican II added that Mary's function as mother of men in no way obscures or diminishes this unique mediation of Christ, but rather shows its power. Therefore, far from being an obstacle to the exercise of Christ's unique mediation, Mary instead highlights its fruitfulness and efficacy. 'The Blessed Virgin's salutary influence on men originates not in any inner necessity but in the disposition of God. It flows forth from the superabundance of the merits of Christ, rests on His mediation, depends entirely on it and draws all its power from it.'[89] Pope John Paul II has several times affirmed Mary's universal mediation, and explained what it involves in precise theological terms: 'Thus there is a mediation: Mary places herself between her Son and mankind in the reality of its wants, needs and sufferings. She puts herself "in the middle," that is to say, she acts as a Mediatrix not as an outsider, but in her position as mother. She knows that, as such, she can point out to her Son the needs of mankind and in fact, she "has the right" to do so. Her mediation is thus in the nature of intercession: Mary "intercedes" for mankind.'[90]

In conclusion, it may be said that Mary's mediation is based Scripturally at Cana and on Calvary, which reveal not only the power of Mary's intercession with her Son but her complete conformity with Him in mind and will. However for Mary like for Christ, Calvary was not the end of the story, but the beginning. It marks the dawn of a new role which is already outlined in the position which she held in the infant Church. The argument runs like this: Mary was associated in a unique way with her Son in the first phase of redemption which culminates in the sacrifice of Calvary. The gifts of God are given and not taken back. As Mary co-operated in the acquisition of grace, so she co-operates in the distribution of grace. She is, in fact, the universal Mediatrix of Graces. She merited in equity (*de congruo*) what Christ merited in justice (*de condigno*). Merit implies a certain title to that which is merited. As, therefore, Christ by reason of His condign merit has an absolute right to the distribution of the graces of redemption, so Mary has a title in equity to the distribution of those graces which, with Him and under Him, she purchased.[91]

As regards the dogmatic status of the doctrine of Our Lady's universal mediation of grace, the Magisterium, particularly in the last hundred years, has without interruption taught it in authentic public documents addressed to the whole Church. The majority of theologians, at the very least, say that it is a doctrine which may be held. The doctrine of Our Lady's Mediation of all Graces is implicitly contained in the deposit of Revelation, whereby this activity of Mary is the prolongation and outcome of her co-operation with Christ on earth, and of her spiritual motherhood of men. It is in harmony with all of Tradition. For these reasons it seems legitimate to claim that the doctrine has been formally and implicitly revealed and consequently that this doctrine might, at some point, be defined by the infallible Magisterium as a dogma of Catholic Faith.[92]

Mary is also Mediatrix for the angels, as Oriental theology has often pointed out. Mary, being nearest to God, is the only one worthy of receiving all of the grace of the Holy Spirit. St Gregory Palamas (AD 1350) also pointed out the importance of the Theotokos after her departure from this world. She stands at the right hand of God the Father together with Christ. Mary's participation in the history of salvation did not end with the mystery of the Incarnation, but continues to the final fulfilment of God's plan.[93] St Gregory Palamas considered not only the significant role of Mary during her earthly life, but also after her Dormition. Dwelling close to God, the Theotokos intercedes for those who remain on earth:

> You are a vessel containing every grace, the fullness of all things good and beautiful, the tablet and living icon of every good and all uprightness, since you alone have been deemed worthy to receive the fullness of every gift of the Spirit. You alone bore in your womb Him in Whom are found the treasures of all these gifts and became a wondrous tabernacle for Him; hence you departed by way of death to immortality and were translated from earth to Heaven, as is proper, so that you might be with Him eternally in an abode above the heavens. From thence you always care diligently for your inheritance and by your unsleeping intercessions with Him, you show mercy to all. To the degree that she is closer to God than all those who have drawn close to Him, by so much has the Theotokos been deemed worthy of greater audience. I do not speak of men alone, but also of the angelic hierarchies themselves.[94]

Mary's mediation enjoys a special dimension during the end times, in an eschatological perspective. This begins in the mystery of the Assumption, according to which Mary is 'united by a close and indissoluble bond' to Christ. If as Virgin and Mother, Mary was singularly united with Him

in His first coming, so through her continued collaboration with Him she will also be united with Him in
expectation of the second. 'Redeemed in an especially
sublime manner by reason of the merits of her Son,'[95] she
also has that specifically maternal role of Mediatrix of
mercy at His final coming, when all those who belong to
Christ 'shall be made alive,' when 'the last enemy to be
destroyed is death' (1 Co 15:26).'[96] In this phase too Mary's
maternal mediation does not cease to be subordinate to
Him who is the one Mediator, until the final realization of
'the fullness of time,' that is to say until 'all things are
united in Christ' (cf. Ep 1:10).

One may also consider the figure of the woman in the
Book of Revelation, which is symbolic, but in a polyvalent
sense, referring to both Mariological and ecclesiological
realities.[97] The Marian interpretation is not opposed to the
ecclesial meaning of the text, since Mary is a 'figure of the
Church.'[98] The dragon, who evokes Satan and evil, rises
against Mary and the Church, as already indicated in the
symbolism of the Old Testament; red is the sign of war,
slaughter, spilt blood; the 'seven heads' crowned indicate
a tremendous power, while the 'ten horns' recall the evil
strength of the beast described by the prophet Daniel (Dn
7:7), also the image of the power of the Lost One that rages
in history.[99] In this way, good and evil confront one
another. Mary, her Son, and the Church represent the
apparent weakness and littleness of love, truth and justice.
Against them is unleashed the monstrous devastating
energy of violence, falsehood and injustice.

However, the Woman remains in this shelter of the
desert, as the Apocalypse underlines (see Rv 12:6, 14) only
for a limited period. The time of anguish, of persecution,
of trial is not, therefore, indefinite: in the end there will be
deliverance and it will be the hour of glory. Contem-
plating this mystery from a Marian perspective, it can be
affirmed: 'Mary, next to her Son, is the most perfect icon of
the liberty and deliverance of humanity and the cosmos. It
is to her that the Church, of which she is mother and

model, must look to understand the meaning of her mission in its fullness.'[100] Mary is thus the icon of the pilgrim Church in the desert of history, but outstretched to the glorious end of the heavenly Jerusalem where she will shine as the Bride of the Lamb, Christ the Lord. Mary's mediation in these end times is, like the Eastern Church indicates, as the *Odighitria*, she who 'shows the Way,' namely Christ, only Mediator to lead us fully to the Father.

The ultimate end of human events will take place when 'God may be all in all' (1 Co 15:28) and, as the Apocalypse announces, 'there was no longer any sea' (Rv 21:1), namely the sign of destructive chaos and of evil has been finally eliminated. The Church will present herself to Christ as a 'Bride adorned for her Husband' (Rv 21 :2). That will be the moment of intimacy and flawless love. However, already now, by looking at the Virgin taken up to heaven, the Church has a foretaste of the joy that will be given to her in fullness at the end of time. In the pilgrimage of faith through history, Mary accompanies the Church like the 'model of the ecclesial communion in faith, charity and union with Christ. Eternally present in the mystery of Christ, she is, in the midst of the Apostles, in the heart itself of the Church being born and of the Church of all times. In fact, the Church was congregated in the upper room of the cenacle with Mary, who was Jesus' mother, and with his brothers. Therefore, one cannot speak of the Church if Mary, the Mother of the Lord, is not present with his brothers.'[101] Mary is the Icon shining at the centre of the Church as a perfect reflection of Christ and is a sign raised among the people, as a 'city placed at the top of a mountain' and 'an oil lamp on a pedestal, to give light to all.'[102]

Notes

[1]   Pope John Paul II, *Discourse at General Audience* (30 July 1997), 4.
[2]   Cf. A. Schmemann, 'Mary and the Holy Spirit' in *The Virgin Mary. The Celebration of Faith. Sermons*, Volume 3 (Crestwood, NY: 1995), p. 72.

3 See Vatican II, *Lumen Gentium*, 53.

4 See Paul VI, *Allocution to the Council* (4 Dec 1963) in *AAS* 56 (1964), p. 37. See also Vatican II, *Lumen Gentium*, 54.

5 St Augustine, *Sermo 25*, 7 in *PL* 46, 938: 'Maria portio est ecclesia, sanctum membrum, excellens membrum, supereminens membrum, sed tamen totius corporis membrum.'

6 St Chromatius of Aquileia, *Sermo 30*, 1 in *SC* 164, p. 134.

7 See *CCC* 994, and also Vatican II, *Lumen Gentium*, 53, 63.

8 See chapter 2, pp. 25–27 above for an explanation of the theological expression 'type'.

9 St Ambrose, *Expositio Evangelii secundum Lucam*, II, 7 in *CCL* 14, 33, 102–106.

10 St Augustine, *De sancta virginitate*, 6 in *PL* 40, 399.

11 Blessed Isaac of Stella, *Sermo 51*, 7–8 in *SC* 339, pp. 202–205. He also said that both Mary and the Church are the Mother of Christ, but 'neither brings forth the whole Body independently of the other.'

12 M. J. Scheeben, *Mariology*, trans. by T. L. M. J. Geukers, Volume 1 (St Louis: B. Herder Book Co., 1954), p. 217.

13 Vatican II, *Lumen Gentium*, 53. See also St Ambrose, *In Ev. sec. Luc.*, II, 7 in *CCL* 14, 33, 102–106.

14 See R. K. Bultmann, *Evangelium des Johannes* (Göttingen: Vandenhoeck & Ruprecht, 1953), p. 521.

15 O. Semmelroth, *Mary, Archetype of the Church*, translated by M. von Eroes and J. Devlin (New York: Sheed and Ward, 1963), p. 30.

16 *Ibid.*, pp. 28–32. See also pp. 157–158, where Semmelroth states: 'Mary, the archetype, represents also the ideal type, the model and moral example against whom the Church as a whole and all her members can examine their own attitude toward their redemption and fullness of grace as they work out their own lives … The Church living in her individual members needs Mary for her growth toward what she is and toward her hidden potential. Mary causes the essence of the Church to shine before individual human beings to appeal to their own moral efforts.'

17 *Ibid.*, p. 52.

18 *Ibid.*, p. 117.

19 See *Ibid.*, p. 102–103.

20 See H. U. von Balthasar, *The Office of Peter and the Structure of the Church*, translated by A. Emery (San Francisco: Ignatius Press, 1986), p. 208: 'The Marian fiat, unequalled in its perfection, is the all-inclusive, protective and directive form of all ecclesial life. It is the interior form of communio, insofar as this is an unlimited mutual acceptance, far more than a human "getting along together" or fraternization. The space and time limitations of the human condition remain external to this (ideally) unlimited receptivity.'

21 *Ibid.*, pp. 206–207.

22 See Pope John Paul II, *Address to the Roman Curia* (22 December 1987). See also his Apostolic Letter *Mulieris Dignitatem* (1988) note 55, where the Pope remarked, citing from the same *Address to the Roman Curia*: 'This Marian profile is also – even perhaps more so – fundamental and characteristic for the Church as is the apostolic and Petrine profile to which it is profoundly united ... The Marian dimension of the Church is antecedent to that of the Petrine, without being in any way divided from it or being less complementary. Mary Immaculate precedes all others, including obviously Peter himself and the Apostles. This is so, not only because Peter and the Apostles, being born of the human race under the burden of sin, form part of the Church which is "holy from out of sinners", but also because their triple function has no other purpose except to form the Church in line with the ideal of sanctity already programmed and prefigured in Mary. A contemporary theologian has rightly stated that Mary is "Queen of the Apostles without any pretensions to apostolic powers: she has other and greater powers" (H. U. von Balthasar, *Neue Klarstellungen*).' See also *CCC* 773.

23 See Pope John Paul II, *Discourse at General Audience* (14 March 2001), 3.

24 See chapter 3, pp. 65–67 above.

25 St Irenaeus, *Adversus Haereses* 3, 22, 4 in *PG* 7, 959.

26 St Ambrose, *Epistola 63*, 33 in *PL* 16, 1198.

27 St Augustine, *De sancta Virginitate*, 6 in *PL* 40, 399: 'The Mother of the Head, in bearing Him corporally became spiritually the Mother of all members of this Divine Head.'

28 Severianus of Gabala, *Oratio 6 in mundi creationem*, 10 in *PG* 54, 4.

29 St Anselm, *Oratio 52*, 8 in *PL* 158, 957. See also *Oratio 47*, in *PL* 158, 945 where Anselm states: 'What could ever be deemed more suitable than for you to be the mother of those whose father and brother Christ deigned to become?'

30 Rupert of Deutz, *In Evangelium Sancti Johannis* in *PL* 169,790.

31 See *Bullarium Romanum*, series 2, t. 2, n. 61, p. 428.

32 Pope Leo XIII, Encyclical Letter *Adjutricem populi christiani*, (1895).

33 Pope Paul VI, *Discourse at the Close of the Third Session of the Second Vatican Ecumenical Council* (22nd November 1964).

34 Pope Paul VI, *Credo of the People of God*, 15.

35 Pope John Paul II, Encyclical Letter *Rosarium Virginis Mariae* (2002), 15.

36 St Fulgentius of Ruspe (attr.), *Sermo 36. De laudibus Mariae ex partu Salvatoris* in *PL* 65, 899: 'Facta est Maria fenestra coeli, quia per ipsam Deus verum fudit saeculis lumen; facta est Maria scala coelestis, quia per ipsam Deus descendit ad terras, ut per ipsam homines ascendere mereantur ad coelos.'

37 J. H. Newman, *The Mother of God* edited with an Introduction and Notes by S. L. Jaki (Pinckney, MI: Real View Books, 2003), p. 64.

38 St Bernardine of Siena, *Sermo 3, De glorioso nomine Virginis Mariae,* art. 2, cap. 3, in Bernardinus Senensis, *Sermones pro festivitatibus Sanctissimae et Immaculatae Virginis Mariae* (Venetiis: 1745), IV, 80, col. 2. In the same sermon, St Bernardine affirms: 'In the prison of Purgatory, Mary has a certain dominion and plentitude of power not only to relieve the suffering souls, but even to deliver them from their pains.'

39 F. Faber, 'The Queen of Purgatory'.

40 See *CCC* 972 and also Vatican II, *Lumen Gentium,* 68–69, and 2 Pt 3:10.

41 St Augustine, *Commentary on Psalm 98,* 9 in *PL* 37, 1264.

42 St Peter Chrysologus, *Sermon 67* in *PL* 52, 392.

43 St Epiphanius (attr.), *De Laudibus Virginis* in *PG* 43, 492. See also another passage from the same homily in *PG* 43, 496: 'The Virgin is the spiritual furrow who has brought the world as spiritual nourishment the burning fire and burning bread of life of which Christ, the Saviour of the world, said: 'Take and eat! This is my body broken for you and for the forgiveness of sins'. The table of the Virgin is rich and full of goodness.'

44 Abba Heriacus, *Anaphora Mariae Virginis Filiae Dei* in A. Hänggi, *Prex eucharistica; textus e variis liturgiis antiquioribus selecti* (Fribourg: Éditions Universitaires, 1968), p. 165.

45 Pope Paul VI, Apostolic Exhortation *Marialis Cultus* (1974), 20.

46 Pope John Paul II, Encyclical Letter *Redemptoris Mater,* 44

47 See Pope John Paul II, Encyclical Letter *Ecclesia De Eucharistia* (2003), 53.

48 *Ibid.,* 55.

49 *Ibid.,* 54.

50 *Ibid.,* 56.

51 *Ibid.,* 58.

52 See chapter 7, pp. 187–201 above.

53 See National Conference of US Bishops, *Behold Your Mother* (1973), 69.

54 St Thomas Aquinas, *Summa Theologiae,* III, q. 26, a. 1.

55 Pope John Paul II, *Redemptoris Mater,* 38.

56 St Irenaeus, *Adversus haereses,* Book 3, chapter 22 in *PG* 7, 958.

57 St Jerome, *Epistola 22,* 21 in *PL* 22, 408.

58 St Ephraem, *Oratio ad Deiparam* in *EM* 341.

59 St Cyril of Alexandria, *Homilia IV in Deiparam* in *PG* 77, 991–993.

60 Antipater of Bostra, *In S. Joannem Baptistam,* 9 in *PG* 85, 1771.

61 Severianus of Gabala, *Homilia de Legislatore* in *PG* 56, 409. The Greek expression for 'interceding' is *mesiteuousan,* which signifies mediating.

[62] Basil of Seleucia, *Oratio 39* in *PG* 85, 444. The Greek expression for 'mediates' is *mesiteuousa*.

[63] St Andrew of Crete, *In Nativitate Mariae Oratio 4* in *PG* 97, 866.

[64] St Germanus of Constantinople, *Homilia in Sanctae Mariae zonam* in *PG* 98, 379–380.

[65] St John Damascene, *Homily on the Dormition 2*, 16 in *PG* 96, 743–744. In n. 17, he puts these words on Mary's lips: 'Now angels surround me, and divine grace abounds in me. I am the physician of the sick. I am a perpetual source of health, and the terror of demons. I am a city of refuge for fugitives. Approach with faith and you will receive a sea of graces.' See *PG* 96, 745–746.

[66] St Peter Damian, *Sermo 46* in *PL* 144, 761.

[67] See St Peter Damian, *Sermo 44 in Nativitatem Beatae Mariae Virginis* in *PL* 144, 740.

[68] St Anselm, *Oratio 7 ad Sanctam Mariam*; cf. *Oratio 5* and *6*.

[69] Peter Abelard, *Sermo 26 in Assumptione Beatae Mariae* in *PL* 178, 544.

[70] St Bernard, *In Vigilia Nativitatis Domini Sermo 3* in *PL* 183, 100.

[71] Idem., *In Nativitate Beatae Mariae Virginis Sermo* in *PL* 183, 441.

[72] Idem., *Sermo De Aquaeductu* in *PL* 183, 440.

[73] Idem., *De Adventu Domini Sermo 2* in *PL* 183, 43.

[74] Theophanes of Nicaea, *Sermo in Sanctissimam Deiparam*.

[75] St Bernardine of Siena, *Sermo 5 de Nativitate Beatae Mariae Virginis*, cap. 8.

[76] See F. Suárez, *De Mysteriis Vitae Christi* in *Opera Omnia* (Paris: 1877), Volume 19, disp. 23, art. 4, sect. 3, n. 5.

[77] St Louis Grignon de Montfort, *True Devotion to the Blessed Virgin Mary*, nn. 24–25.

[78] St Alphonsus de Liguori, *The Glories of Mary* (Rockford, Illinois: Tan, 1977), p. 136.

[79] M. J. Scheeben, *Mariology*, tr. T. Geukers, (St Louis: Herder, 1946), Volume II, p. 265.

[80] *Ibid.*, p. 185.

[81] Pope Leo XIII, Encyclical Letter *Supremi Apostolatus officio* (1883) in *ASS* 16 (1883), p. 1113.

[82] Pope Leo XIII, Encyclical Letter *Octobri mense adventante* (1891) in *ASS* 24 (1891), p. 196.

[83] Pope Leo XIII, Encyclical Letter *Adiutricem populi* (1895) in *ASS* 28 (1895) p. 130. See also Pope St Pius X, Encyclical *Ad diem illum*, (1904) in *ASS* 36 (1904) pp. 453–454.

[84] Sacred Congregation of Rites, *Rescript* (12 January 1921). Based on the Mass and Office of Our Lady, Mediatrix of all Graces of 1921, the Congregation for Divine Worship approved a Mass of the Blessed Virgin Mary, Mother and Mediatrix of Grace in 1971. See *Collection of Masses of the Blessed Virgin Mary*, Volume 1, *Sacramentary*, (New York: Catholic Book Company, 1992).

85 Pius XII, Radiomessage to Fatima, *Bendito seia* (13 May 1946) in *AAS* 38 (1946) p. 266.

86 Pope Pius XII, *Message to the Marian Congress of Ottawa* (19 July 1947) in AAS 39 (1947), p. 271.

87 Pope John XXIII, *Epistle to Cardinal Agaganian*, Legate to Marian Congress in Saigon (31 Jan 1959) in *AAS* 51 (1959), p. 88.

88 Vatican II, *Lumen Gentium*, 62.

89 *Ibid.*, 60.

90 Pope John Paul II, *Redemptoris Mater*, 21.

91 For further development on *de condigno* and *de congruo* merit, see chapter 7, p. 196 and note 81 on pp. 205–206.

92 See M. O'Grady, 'Mary's Mediation of Graces' in K. McNamara, *Mother of the Redeemer* (Dublin: Gill, 1959), pp. 181–183. The distinction between truth and certitude needs to be taken into account. The former has to do with what is objective, what is independent of the mind, the reality of a proposition in itself; the latter has to do with the state of mind confronted with the proposition. Somewhat the same distinction holds with regard to the teaching of the Church in the different stages of its evolution. The objective truth of a proposition and its relation to revealed doctrine is one thing. It is to be distinguished from the clarity and the certitude with which it is held throughout the Church at this or that particular period of history. Witness the doctrine of the Immaculate Conception. That doctrine from the beginning was part of the divinely revealed truth. However, in the fourteenth century, for example, since the infallible Magisterium had not intervened on its behalf, it was a pious opinion that could be and was, in fact, freely disputed. Such was its juridical status at that time.

93 '[The Theotokos] is not merely a companion but she also stands at God's right hand, for where Christ sat in the heavens, that is, at the 'right hand of majesty' (Heb. 1:3), there too she also takes her stand, having ascended now from earth into the heavens. Not merely does she love and is loved in return more then every other, according to the very laws of nature, but she is truly His Throne, and wherever the King sits, there His Throne is set also.' St Gregory Palamas, *A Homily on the Dormition of Our Supremely Pure Lady Theotokos and Ever-Virgin Mary* (Homily 37) in *PG* 151, 469–470.

94 St Gregory Palamas, *A Homily on the Dormition of Our Supremely Pure Lady Theotokos and Ever-Virgin Mary* (Homily 37) in *PG* 151, 469–470.

95 Vatican II, *Lumen Gentium*, 53.

96 See Pope John Paul II, *Redemptoris Mater*, 41. On this particular aspect of Mary's mediation as implorer of clemency from the Son as Judge, see Saint Bernard, *In Dominica infra octava Assumptionis*

Sermo, 1–2 in S. Bernardi Opera, V, 1968, 262f; Pope Leo XIII, Encyclical Letter *Octobri Mense* (22 September 1891).

[97] See chapter 3, p. 66 above.

[98] Vatican II, *Lumen Gentium*, 63.

[99] See Pope John Paul II, *Discourse at General Audience* (14 March 2001), 1.

[100] Congregation for the Doctrine of the Faith, *Libertatis conscientia* (1986), 97; see also Pope John Paul II, *Redemptoris Mater*, 37.

[101] Congregation for the Doctrine of the Faith, *Communionis notio* (1992) 19; see also Chromatius of Aquileia, *Sermon* 30, 1 in *SC* 164, p. 134.

[102] See Pope John Paul II, *Discourse at General Audience* (14 March 2001), 5; see also Mt 5:14–15. See also Congregation for the Doctrine of the Faith, *Letter to the bishops of the Catholic Church on the collaboration of men and women in the Church and in the world* (31 May 2004), 15, where it is proposed that the figure of Mary constitutes the fundamental reference in the Church. Mary is like 'a mirror placed before the Church, in which the Church is invited to recognize her own identity as well as the dispositions of the heart, the attitudes and the actions which God expects from her.'

SELECT BIBLIOGRAPHY

AA.VV., *Mary at the Foot of the Cross: Acts of International Symposium on Marian Coredemption 2001*, Volume 2. Libertyville, IL: Academy of the Immaculate, 2002.

AA.VV., *Maria e L'Eucaristia*. Rome: Centro di Cultura «Madre della Chiesa», 2000.

BEINERT W. (ed.), *Il culto di Maria oggi*. Rome Edizioni Paoline, 1978.

BLANCY, A., and JOURJON, M., *Mary in the Plan of God and in the Communion of Saints*. New York: Paulist Press, 1999.

BOUYER, L., *The Seat of Wisdom*. New York: Pantheon Books, 1962.

BOYCE, P (ed.), *Mary. The Virgin Mary in the Life and Writings of John Henry Newman*. Leominster/Grand Rapids, MI: Gracewing/Eerdmans, 2001.

CALKINS, A. B., *Totus tuus: John Paul II's program of Marian consecration and entrustment*. Libertyville, IL: Academy of the Immaculate, 1992.

CAROL, J. B., *Fundamentals of Mariology*. New York: Benziger Brothers, 1956.

CAROL, J. B., *Mariology*, Volume 1. Milwaukee: The Bruce Publishing Company, 1955.

CAROL, J. B., *Mariology*, Volume 2. Milwaukee: The Bruce Publishing Company, 1955.

DALEY, B. E., *On the Dormition of Mary: Early Patristic Homilies*. Crestwood, New York: St Vladimir's Seminary Press, 1998.

DE FIORES, S., *Maria nella teologia contemporanea*. Rome: Centro di Cultura Mariana, 1991.

DE FIORES, S., *Maria nel mistero di Cristo e della Chiesa*. Rome: Centro Mariano Monfortano, 1968.

DE FIORES, S., and MEO, S., *Nuovo dizionario di Mariologia*. Rome: Paoline, 1985

DE FREITAS FERREIRA, J., *Conceição Virginal de Jesus*. Rome: Università Gregoriana Editrice, 1980.

DE LA POTTERIE, I., *Maria nel mistero dell'alleanza, Studi biblici e giudaistici* vol. 6. Genoa: Marietti, 1992.

DEISS, L., *Mary, daughter of Sion*. Collegeville: The Liturgical Press, 1972.

ESQUERDA BIFET, J. M., *Mariology for a Missionary Church*. Rome: Pontificia Università Urbaniana, 1994.

FOLEY, D. A., *Marian Apparitions, the Bible, and the Modern World*. Leominster: Gracewing, 2002.

FOLEY, R., *Mary and the Eucharist*. Newtonsville, OH: Hope of Saint Monica, 1997.

GALOT, J., *La fede di Maria e la nostra, Problemi d'oggi*, Volume 11. Assisi: Cittadella Editrice, 1973.

GAMBERO, L., *Mary and the Fathers of the Church: the Blessed Virgin Mary in Patristic Thought*, tr. T. Buffer. San Francisco: Ignatius Press, 1999.

GAMBERO, L., *Maria nel pensiero dei teologi latini medievali*. Cinisello Balsamo, Milan: San Paolo, 2000.

GONZÁLEZ, C. I., *Mariologia. Maria, madre e discepola*. Casale Monferrato (AL): Piemme, 1988.

HAHN, S., *Hail, Holy Queen: The Mother of God in the Word of God*. New York: Doubleday, 2001.

JAKI, S. L., *Fifteen Mysteries*. Pinckney, MI: Real-View-Books, 2001.

JAKI, S. L., *The Virgin Birth and the Birth of Science*. Front Royal, VA: Christendom Press, 1990.

LAURENTIN, R., *Les évangiles de l'enfance du Christ*. Paris: DDB, 1982.

LAURENTIN, R., *The Eucharist and Mary, Marian Library Studies*, Volume 106. Dayton: University of Dayton, 1964.

LAURENTIN, R., *A Short Treatise on the Virgin Mary.* Washington, New Jersey: AMI Press, 1991.

MACQUARRIE, J., *Mary for All Christians.* London: Collins, 1990.

MANELLI, S., *All Generations Shall Call Me Blessed.* New Bedford, Massachusetts: Academy of the Immaculate, 1995.

McHUGH, J., *The Mother of Jesus in the New Testament.* London: Darton, Longman & Todd, 1975.

McLOUGHLIN, W., and PINNOCK, J., *Mary is for Everyone.* Leominster: Gracewing, 1997.

McLOUGHLIN, W., and PINNOCK, J., *Mary for Earth and Heaven. Essays on Mary and Ecumenism.* Leominster: Gracewing, 2002.

McNAMARA, K. (ed.), *Mother of the Redeemer. Aspects of Doctrine and Devotion.* Dublin: Gill and Son Ltd., 1959.

MEWS, C. J., *Listen Daughter.* New York, NY: Palgrave, 2001.

MIGUEL, A., *O segredo que conduz o Papa. A Experiência de Fátima no Pontificado de Joãn Paolo II.* Cascais: Principia, 2000.

MIRAVALLE, M. I., *The dogma and the triumph.* Santa Barbara, CA: Queenship Pub. Co., 1998.

MIRAVALLE, M. I., *Introduction to Mary heart of Marian doctrine and devotion.* Santa Barbara, CA: Queenship Publishing Company, 1993.

MIRAVALLE, M. I. (ed.), *Mary Co-Redemptrix: Doctrinal Issues Today.* Goleta, CA: Queenship Publishing Company, 2002.

NICOLAS, J. H., *La virginité de Marie.* Fribourg: Editions Universitaires, 1962.

POZO, C., *María en la Escritura y en la fe de la Iglesia, Biblioteca de autores cristianos* Volume 18. Madrid: Biblioteca de Autores Cristianos, 1981[2].

POZO, C., *María en la obra de la salvación, Biblioteca de autores cristianos* Volume 360. Madrid: La Editorial Católica, 1974.

RAHNER, H., *Our Lady and the Church,* tr. S. Bullough. London: Darton, Longman & Todd, 1961.

RATZINGER, J., *Daughter Zion: meditations on the Church's Marian belief*, tr. J. M. McDermott. San Francisco: Ignatius Press, 1983.

SCHEEBEN, M. J., *Mariology*, St. Louis, MO: Herder, 1946–1947. 2 Volumes.

SCHEFFCZYK, L., *Die Mariengestalt im Gefüge der Theologie: Mariologische Beiträge, Mariologische Studien* Volume 12. Regensburg: Pustet, 2000.

SCHEFFCZYK, L., *Maria, crocevia della fede cattolica*, tr. M. Hauke. Pregassona (Lugano): Eupress, 2002.

SEMMELROTH, O., *Mary, Archetype of the Church*, translated by M. von Eroes and J. Devlin. New York: Sheed and Ward, 1963.

SHOEMAKER, S. J., *Ancient Traditions of the Virgin Mary's Dormition and Assumption*. Oxford: Oxford University PRESS, 2003.

SMITH, G. D., *Mary's Part in our Redemption*. London: Burns and Oates, 1954.

VANDRY, F., *The Queenship of Mary*, Marian Library Series Volume 107. Dayton: University of Dayton, 1964.

VOLLERT, C. O., *A Theology of Mary*. New York: Herder and Herder, 1965.

INDEX